COGNITIVE CONTROL ALONG THE LANGUAGE CONTINUUM

This book provides a comprehensive review of the interactions between language and cognitive control in children. Broadening its scope beyond specific dimensions of language and cognition, it provides an extensive review of the dynamic changes in cognitive control along the entire language continuum. It integrates behavioral and neurophysiological findings from different disciplines, such as bilingualism, cognitive psychology, and communication disorders. A better understanding of the relationship between cognitive control and language in various speakers allows us to develop more sensitive experimental paradigms, as well as more efficient assessment and intervention methods. This title is part of the Flip it Open Programme and may also be available open access. Check our website Cambridge Core for details.

KLARA MARTON is a professor at Brooklyn College and the Graduate Center of the City University of New York and at ELTE Eotvos Lorand University, Budapest. A neuropsychologist with a doctorate in psychology and in speech-hearing sciences, she has received funding from the National Institutes of Health and the European Union, and a fellowship for excellence from the American Speech-Language-Hearing Association.

COGNITIVE CONTROL ALONG THE LANGUAGE CONTINUUM

KLARA MARTON

*Brooklyn College and the Graduate Center
of the City University of New York*

ELTE Eotvos Lorand University

Shaftesbury Road, Cambridge CB2 8EA, United Kingdom

One Liberty Plaza, 20th Floor, New York, NY 10006, USA

477 Williamstown Road, Port Melbourne, VIC 3207, Australia

314–321, 3rd Floor, Plot 3, Splendor Forum, Jasola District Centre, New Delhi – 110025, India

103 Penang Road, #05–06/07, Visioncrest Commercial, Singapore 238467

Cambridge University Press is part of Cambridge University Press & Assessment, a department of the University of Cambridge.

We share the University's mission to contribute to society through the pursuit of education, learning and research at the highest international levels of excellence.

www.cambridge.org
Information on this title: www.cambridge.org/9781108834193

DOI: 10.1017/9781108992299

© Klara Marton 2024

This publication is in copyright. Subject to statutory exception and to the provisions of relevant collective licensing agreements, no reproduction of any part may take place without the written permission of Cambridge University Press & Assessment.

First published 2024

A catalogue record for this publication is available from the British Library

A Cataloging-in-Publication data record for this book is available from the Library of Congress

ISBN 978-1-108-83419-3 Hardback

Cambridge University Press & Assessment has no responsibility for the persistence or accuracy of URLs for external or third-party internet websites referred to in this publication and does not guarantee that any content on such websites is, or will remain, accurate or appropriate.

Contents

List of Figures		*page* vii
Acknowledgments		viii
Introduction		1
1	**The Language Continuum**	**5**
	1.1 Language Ability versus Proficiency: Conceptual Foundation	5
	1.2 The Language Ability Continuum	7
	1.3 Language Characteristics of Children with DLD: A Cross-Linguistic Perspective	10
	1.4 Language Proficiency	13
	1.5 Similarities in Language Development in Typically Developing Monolingual Children and Bilingual First Language (L1) Speakers	17
	1.6 Similarities in Language Development in Monolingual and Bilingual Children with DLD	19
	1.7 Conclusions	21
2	**Cognitive Control**	**22**
	2.1 Conceptual Foundation	22
	2.2 Current Cognitive Control Frameworks	29
	2.3 Behavioral Paradigms Used to Assess Cognitive Control	33
	2.4 Conclusions	39
3	**Methodological Issues**	**40**
	3.1 Identifying the Appropriate Conceptual Framework	40
	3.2 Matching Conceptual Frameworks and Research Designs	41
	3.3 Data Analysis	49
	3.4 Bridging the Gap between Scientific Research and Clinical and Educational Approaches	52
	3.5 Conclusions	53
4	**The Effect of Age on First Language Acquisition, Second Language Learning, and Cognitive Control Development**	**54**
	4.1 Age and Language Ability	54
	4.2 Age and Language Proficiency	59

vi *Contents*

4.3	Age and Cognitive Control Development	61
4.4	Conclusions	71

5 Associations between Language Ability, Language Proficiency, and Cognitive Control — 72

5.1	Conceptual Background, Terminology, and Measures	72
5.2	The Relationship between Language Proficiency, Exposure, and Language Use	74
5.3	Language Proficiency and Cognitive Control	75
5.4	Language Ability and Cognitive Control	78
5.5	Conclusions	86

6 The Impact of Language Input on Cognitive Control — 87

6.1	Language Input, Intake, and Exposure in Monolingual and Bilingual Children	87
6.2	The Relationship between Language Input and Cognitive Control	90
6.3	Delayed or Reduced Language Input and Cognitive Control	92
6.4	Conclusions	104

7 Cognitive Control and Social Context of Language Use — 105

7.1	Social Context: Conceptual Foundations	105
7.2	Social Context, Emotions, and Cognitive Control	108
7.3	Cultural Background and Cognitive Control	109
7.4	Social Context and Cognitive Control in Children with Different Language Skills	111
7.5	Conclusions	116

8 Processing Speed and Cognitive Control — 117

8.1	Behavioral and Neural Correlates of Processing Speed	117
8.2	Processing Speed and Cognitive Control	118
8.3	Age-Related Changes in Processing Speed during Childhood and Adolescence	121
8.4	Language Status and Processing Speed	124
8.5	Conclusions	132

9 Cognitive Training and Language — 133

9.1	Conceptual Foundations	133
9.2	Training to Improve Cognitive Control	141
9.3	Training Effects in Children with Different Language Skills	145
9.4	Conclusions	151

10 Conclusions — 153

10.1	Current Issues	153
10.2	Future Research	158

References — 162

Index — 214

Figures

1.1	Language dimensions	*page* 6
2.1	Working memory updating paradigms	37
2.2	Switching paradigms	38
3.1	Methodological issues and suggestions	48
4.1	Age-related changes in cognitive control	67
4.2	Interactions among language acquisition and proficiency, cognitive control, and environmental factors in bilingual speakers	70
5.1	Conflict paradigm: Verbal categorization task	77
6.1	Individual and global components influencing language intake	88
6.2	Interactions between input and intake	103
7.1	Levels of social context	106
8.1	Language proficiency and processing speed: Path analysis	130
9.1	Training designs	136
9.2	Cognitive control tasks and target functions in training	151

vii

Acknowledgments

Many colleagues and students have influenced my thinking about the relationship between cognitive control and language; and I am grateful for all of their ideas.

Special thanks go to the current and former students of the Cognition and Language Laboratory at the Graduate School and University Center of the City University of New York (CUNY). Their intellectual curiosity is a great motivator for me.

I was only able to complete this book because I received a sabbatical fellowship from Brooklyn College, CUNY. I thank my colleagues in the Department of Communication Arts, Sciences, and Disorders for taking over multiple tasks from me, so I could focus on my writing.

A research grant from the Hungarian Academy of Sciences (MTA-ELTE: Language-Learning Disorders, Research Program for Public Education Development) encouraged me to think about the educational implications of my main arguments.

I also received a Tow Faculty Research and Creativity Grant from Brooklyn College that supported the editing work of this book. I am particularly grateful to Elizabeth Caplan and Thorfun Gehebe for their time and attention to details while editing the text and the figures.

I received continuous support from Stephen Acerra, Psychology and Neuroscience Editor, Cambridge University Press. Thank you for your patience and encouragement!

Finally, I thank my family for their support. They believed in me, even when I experienced some self-doubt.

Introduction

The aim of this book is to provide a comprehensive review of the dynamic interactions between language and cognition in children, by stressing the role of cognitive control. Cognitive control is a critical contributor to language development and to children's academic performance. Significant progress has been made in the past decades in both the cognitive and neuroscience literature in describing and interpreting the control mechanisms that are needed for language learning and everyday functioning. As a result, scholars in both bilingualism and language impairment disciplines have shown a growing interest in the development of the cognitive control processes. Despite the relatively large number of studies on cognitive control in populations with different language skills, no previous work has provided an exhaustive overview of the associations and dissociations between the control processes and variations in language ability and proficiency. The goal of this book is to integrate information across disciplines and provide a synthesized review of theory and practice in an accessible format for professionals with assorted disciplinary backgrounds.

By describing the behavioral and physiological associations between language and cognitive control and the modulating factors that contribute to their variations in individuals with different language competencies, a trajectory is presented that reflects converging and diverging paths of cognitive and language skills. The emerging picture demonstrates that certain cognitive control functions may be more advanced in individuals with superior language skills, while those very same functions are impaired in people with language disorders. Through the integration of findings from different disciplinary literatures, a pattern appears to reveal that particular cognitive control functions are more closely linked to specific language skills, whereas others show less interaction with language variations. The outcomes provide evidence suggesting that the interaction between cognitive control and language is part of a dynamic system that is highly influenced by variations in culture, social context, and previous experiences.

The findings strongly support the argument that we need to extend our studies to more linguistically and culturally diverse populations, including minority language speakers and emerging bilingual individuals, as well as to people who exhibit language disorders, in hopes of gaining more in-depth knowledge about interactions between human cognition and language. By improving our understanding of the relationship between cognitive control and language across speakers with various competencies, we will be able to develop more sensitive and efficient experimental paradigms as well as assessment and intervention methods that will help us to solve some of the current theoretical debates and certain ongoing clinical problems, such as the misclassification of children. With more efficient clinical tools, we will also be able to raise our awareness of children with developmental language disorder (DLD) and children with low language proficiency, because these populations are still underserved, particularly in minority groups and non-English-speaking families. Although the main focus across chapters is on studies including children and adolescents, there are some references to findings in young adults when relevant questions have not been explored in children.

Chapter 1 defines the basic terms and language-related concepts and clarifies the distinction between the two main language dimensions (i.e., language ability and proficiency). A clear conceptual differentiation between language ability and proficiency is important and has both theoretical and clinical/educational implications, particularly for children who speak minority languages, are emerging bilingual speakers, and/or exhibit DLD. Nevertheless, we also need to examine the interactions between these dimensions and the resulting complex language patterns in children (e.g., multilingual children with a language talent or children with bilingual DLD). Chapter 2 provides a theoretical foundation for discussion of the cognitive control processes. It presents the main concepts and major theoretical accounts, in order to better understand the control mechanisms, the recruitment of control resources, and the selection of task-relevant processes. Chapter 3 imparts the current methodological issues related to participant selection; task sensitivity and impurity; and the identification of target control functions. Additional points to this discussion include the need for a solid conceptual framework and the selection of appropriate analyses.

Following these introductory chapters on the theoretical, conceptual, and methodological foundations of language and cognitive control, the remaining seven chapters focus on particular interactions between specific language and cognitive control components. Chapter 4 reviews the effects of age on language development and cognitive control. Particularly for the early years, the review describes developmental trends and identifies associations and dissociations by examining the interactions among these processes. During a more detailed inspection of these interactions, it further reveals how individual differences in language acquisition are linked to the development of nonlinguistic cognitive skills, neural maturation, and variations in environmental influences.

The complex interactions between cognitive control and language are discussed in more depth along the two main language dimensions in Chapter 5. The links between cognitive control and language ability and the associations between cognitive control and language proficiency are reviewed, first separately, and then in relationship to each other and to the development of academic skills and social interactions. Subsequently, Chapter 6 shows how the quality and quantity of language input affects both children's language ability and their cognitive control development. A nuanced exploration of the distinctions between input and intake as well as between input and exposure points to a complex pattern of interactions between these components and children's communicative skills. The effect of the social context is further analyzed in Chapter 7, by revealing how local (e.g., language register use) and global (e.g., culture, socioeconomic status) changes affect children's cognitive control and language performance, as indicated by neural and behavioral findings. This chapter provides a unique overview of the interactions among language, cognition, and social context by examining how individuals with different language abilities and varying language proficiencies respond to assorted social-communicative demands.

Chapter 8 highlights the close links between cognitive control and processing speed and uncovers how this interaction is influenced by age; task type and complexity; targeted cognitive functions; and children's language skills. The focus in this chapter is on the complex interactions among these variables and on their modulating effects on processing speed. Chapter 9 provides a review of recent cognitive training studies, with a concentration on those training methods that have most widely been associated with language development. The discussion of fundamental training-related questions, such as neuroplasticity, transfer, and individual differences, is proceeded by a more detailed examination of one domain-specific method (i.e., working memory training) and a multi-domain approach (i.e., music training). The final Chapter 10 offers a synthesis of the previously discussed findings. It provides a more holistic picture about the relationship between cognitive control and language by presenting the most critical issues and offering solutions for future research, including a discussion about the way an individual-differences approach may be combined with experimental designs to provide a method within which variability in performance is viewed as key information. Additional focus is placed on the need for interprofessional collaborations among researchers across disciplines, as well as between researchers and practitioners and educators, in order to better serve children with various language skills.

CHAPTER I

The Language Continuum

1.1 Language Ability versus Proficiency: Conceptual Foundation

The language continuum is defined in this book by the dimensions of language ability (from language talent to language disorder) and bilingualism (from monolingual to multilingual); the latter is typically expressed by the level of language proficiency. These two language dimensions and the factors that contribute to their development (e.g., amount of exposure, frequency of use, communicative context) serve as the foundation for analyzing the relationship between language and cognitive control. Unfortunately, "language ability" and "proficiency" are often used interchangeably in the literature, particularly in studies on bilingualism, resulting in many inconsistencies. Within our conceptual framework, language ability refers to a child's language and communication skills measured with standardized language tests that indicate the presence or absence of a language delay or disorder (see Figure 1.1). In contrast, language proficiency is defined as the overtly observable, functional language use across different domains that are specified as contexts of bilingual language use (Birdsong, 2014; Jilka, 2009). In addition to the mixed use of "language ability" and "proficiency," the measures of these constructs are also used inconsistently. Specific tests of language ability, such as expressive and receptive vocabulary measures, have often been used to determine the level of language proficiency in bilingual children and adults without consideration of the fact that these standardized language tests were developed to assess language knowledge and not functional language use and were normed, in most cases, on monolingual participants. Moreover, the relationship among these measures is highly influenced by other factors of the bilingual experience, such as the number of years of active bilingual language use and the percentage of exposure to the second language. Bedore and colleagues (2012) reported that most tests that were developed to determine language

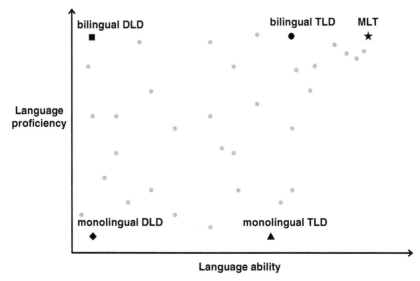

DLD = developmental language disorder; TLD = typical language development; MLT = multilingual language talent

Figure 1.1 Language dimensions

proficiency were not designed to identify children with a language disorder, and that the tests that were developed to measure children's language ability, namely, to determine the presence or absence of a language disorder, do not provide appropriate measures of language proficiency.

The use of incorrect assessment methods has negative consequences for both research and clinical outcomes. For example, English Language Learners (ELL) represent an increasing proportion of school-age children in the United States (2018, 2021, www.pewresearch.org). While the prevalence of language disorder is 7–8 percent in the general child population, almost 50 percent of ELL students were classified as having language problems (Norbury et al., 2016; Tomblin et al., 1997). Such rampant classification errors occur because ELL students and bilingual children with developmental language disorder (DLD) often perform similarly on traditional language tests but for different reasons. ELL students without a language disorder may perform poorly on standardized language tests because of their low language proficiency in English. In contrast, bilingual children with DLD perform poorly on the same tests because of their low language ability resulting from their language disorder. Hence, ELL students are often overdiagnosed, while bilingual children with DLD are often underdiagnosed, as it is assumed that the latter group shows difficulty on standardized language tests because of their low English-language proficiency. Thus, many ELL students receive unnecessary speech-language therapy, while they are deprived of valuable academic opportunities because of their misdiagnoses, whereas bilingual children with DLD might miss precious years of intervention. These classification and diagnostic errors have negative consequences for children's academic careers because intervention for these two groups is vastly different and incorrect placement results in inadequate access to services.

1.2 The Language Ability Continuum

1.2.1 Language Talent

The differentiation between language ability and level of proficiency is no easier at the higher end of the language continuum. Children's language talent (high level of language ability) is often measured by the number of languages they have acquired and by their native-like accent in a second language (Reiterer et al., 2011). Even though several scholars have emphasized a distinction between proficiency and talent (e.g., Jilka, 2009), talent is often still equated with high language proficiency in multiple languages. Using multilingualism as an indicator of language talent, however, may be misleading. Many children become multilingual because they grow up in a country where a number of languages are spoken or have parents and grandparents who come from different language backgrounds, so several languages are spoken within the family. Even children with DLD may speak two to three languages if they come from a multilingual environment. Thus, it is important to distinguish between the two language dimensions (i.e., language ability and multilingual proficiency) when defining language talent. There is no single or universal definition of talent. In the human resources literature, individuals are identified as talented if they have the potential to reach high levels of achievement (Tansley, 2011). Gagne (2000) argued that talent earmarks the superior mastery of abilities and knowledge in a given area of development, such as language. This notion is in line with the talent concept of the second language (L2) acquisition literature, which defines the term in reference to aptitude. Aptitude has been specified as unusual cognitive strengths that an individual demonstrates during language acquisition. Others have emphasized the effort aspect of development, pointing out that talented people excel with ease and achieve their goals without trying hard (Thorne & Pelant, 2007).

These definitions – potential to reach high levels of achievement, superior mastery of abilities, and exceling with ease – can be efficiently applied to language acquisition if we consider both language ability and proficiency, as well as interactions with specific environmental factors.

The idea that talent reflects the potential to achieve high levels of performance can easily be synthesized with the concept of dynamic assessment. Dynamic assessment is a testing and intervention approach that measures children's potential to grow rather than their current knowledge in a given subject area. Although this is an approach that has often been used with children who exhibit low language proficiency and/or ability, including emerging bilingual children and children with a language disorder (Hasson & Joffe, 2007; Peña et al., 2001), it has yet to be used to identify children with language talent. Lidz and Macrine (2001) applied dynamic assessment during the selection of gifted children in a school with a large number of culturally and linguistically diverse students. In previous years, when children were identified as gifted based on their achievements on standardized tests, fewer than 1 percent of the students qualified from this particular school. In contrast, the proportion of students identified in the study by Lidz and Macrine matched the proportion of gifted students across the entire school district (i.e., about 5 percent). By using dynamic assessment, they were able to enroll significantly more culturally and linguistically diverse students in gifted programs than in previous years.

The use of dynamic assessment may contribute to the reconciliation of the debate in the literature on the nature of talent. Currently, there are two distinct views in the L2 literature. Jilka (2009) argues that talent is independent of motivation, practice, and experience. These factors may contribute to the degree of language proficiency but not to the degree of talent. In contrast, other scholars have linked talent to different learning contexts, attitudes, and experiences (Moyer, 2014; Wen & Skehan, 2011). In this book, we take an individual-differences approach when discussing talent. We are particularly interested in those higher-level cognitive skills that contribute to efficient language acquisition along the language ability continuum.

1.2.2 Developmental Language Disorder (DLD)

DLD is a neurodevelopmental disorder. According to the Diagnostic and Statistical Manual of Mental Disorders (DSM-5), children with DLD have persistent difficulties in language use and/or comprehension, and their difficulties may impact their spoken and/or written language, as well as their sign language. The disorder often exists beyond childhood and affects

1.2 The Language Ability Continuum

children's social lives and academic careers. Thus, the language problems are long-standing and cannot be remedied by general educational procedures (McGregor et al., 2020).

In recent years, there has been a shift in terminology from specific language impairment (SLI) to DLD (Bishop et al., 2016, 2017), although there are diverging views on this issue (see Volkers, 2018). The notion that the language impairment in these children is not "specific" has been widely acknowledged in the literature. Our own research on different cognitive control functions also provides support for this idea, because children with DLD exhibit difficulties in a number of cognitive functions even when nonverbal tasks are employed (Marton, 2008, 2009; Marton et al., 2005).[1]

Although all children with a diagnosis of DLD exhibit significant language difficulties, their cognitive-linguistic profiles may differ because of the complexity of the cognitive-linguistic system and the heterogeneity of the population. There are notable variations in both the severity and pervasiveness of these children's language disorder, including differences across language areas (phonology, morphology, syntax, vocabulary, etc.) and modalities (expressive or receptive language, or both). For classification purposes, a number of diagnostic criteria have been proposed in the literature. Some authors suggest defining the language difficulties relative to the child's age or nonverbal intelligence (Peterson & McGrath, 2009), while others suggest considering the extent of the difficulties in language use, comprehension, and functional communication, as well as the developmental trajectory of language, including the age of onset (Reilly et al., 2014). These criteria help researchers and clinicians to distinguish children with DLD from children with other neurodevelopmental disorders, such as autism spectrum disorder. Hearing screening is typically used to exclude children with hearing impairment, and nonverbal IQ is administered to exclude children with intellectual disabilities. Nonetheless, the definition of DLD allows dual diagnoses because children with language impairment may also exhibit attention problems (Finneran et al., 2009); weaknesses in different cognitive control functions (Kapa & Plante, 2015); poor working memory skills (Marton & Schwartz, 2003); difficulties in motor control (Zelaznik & Goffman, 2010); and problems in social cognition (Marton et al., 2005).

The prevalence of DLD is around 6–8 percent in kindergarten children, and it is more frequent (1.3:1) in males than in females (Norbury et al., 2016; Tomblin et al., 1997). However, the percentage of children identified with

---

[1] Although many studies referenced in this book used the term SLI, we use the term DLD in each chapter for consistency with the current view.

DLD varies across studies depending on the age of the participants, the cut-off point used to establish the diagnosis, and the definition adopted (Gilger & Wise, 2004). Despite the high frequency of the occurrence of DLD, there is still low awareness about the disorder in the general public, even among educators (Marton et al., 2005; McGregor et al., 2020). Consequently, a large number of children with DLD are unidentified and/or underserved, particularly those who speak a minority language, come from immigrant families, or belong to underrepresented minority groups (McGregor et al., 2020; Morgan et al., 2017). This is particularly worrisome in light of these children's high risk for academic failure and mental health conditions. Children with DLD are six times more likely to have reading disabilities and spelling problems, four times more likely to exhibit weaknesses in math, and twelve times more likely to encounter difficulties in all three subject areas compared to their peers (Young et al., 2002). Different mental health issues, such as anxiety, depression, and low self-esteem, are also more common among these children (Conti-Ramsden & Botting, 2008; Marton et al., 2005).

Overall, it is important to call attention to this group and raise awareness in the general public about DLD. The number of missed, underdiagnosed, and underserved children needs to be decreased drastically, particularly for children from disadvantaged families. Teachers in general education need more information about the characteristics, signs, and risk factors of language disorders. Interprofessional collaborations need to be supported among teachers, speech-language pathologists, and other therapists who provide services to children with DLD.

1.3 Language Characteristics of Children with DLD: A Cross-Linguistic Perspective

This section provides a brief overview of the major language issues of children with DLD, focusing on an area that causes these children great difficulty: morpho-syntax. Children with DLD exhibit weaknesses in marking verb inflections; in comprehending and producing complex sentence structures; and in detecting grammatical violations (e.g., Leonard et al., 1997; Norbury et al., 2002; van der Lely, 1996). By taking a cross-linguistic perspective rather than focusing on English alone, we can highlight some general problems across languages, while also noting language-specific features. Grammatical morphology has been identified as a problem area in children with DLD across languages, and one of the most highly researched topics within morphology was tense marking. Children with DLD performed

1.3 Language Characteristics of Children with DLD

more poorly on tasks measuring tense marking than their typically developing peers in each language, even though the manifestation of the problem differed across languages (e.g., Dromi et al., 1999; Hansson et al., 2000; Rice & Wexler, 1996). One predictor of the level of accuracy was the frequency of occurrence of the inflection (Lukács et al., 2009). In languages that are rich in inflectional morphology (e.g., Spanish, Italian), children with DLD often substituted one tense marker for another; in other languages, such as English, they produced the infinitives (Leonard, 2014).

A universal pattern was also observed with the omission of auxiliary verbs in obligatory contexts by children with DLD (Grela & Leonard, 2000; Hansson, 1997; Vukovic & Stojanovik, 2011). This was an aspect of language in which children with DLD differed from both their age-matched and their younger, language-matched peers. These findings indicate that this is one of the more severe problems in children with DLD, and this was further evidenced by specific data from French-speaking children. Even though French-speaking children with DLD correctly produced the preposition "*a*" most of the time, they performed very poorly when "*a*" served as the third-person past auxiliary (Pizzioli & Schelstraete, 2008).

Noun morphology has received less attention in the DLD literature than verb morphology; nevertheless, the error data from a number of languages (e.g., Arabic, Hebrew, Hungarian, German, Greek, Serbo-Croatian, Spanish) indicate problems with noun inflections as well (Marton & Yoon, 2014). Children with DLD often use the singular instead of the plural form of the noun or they produce substitution errors of case (e.g., nominative instead of the accusative). The error types across languages differ and reflect an interaction between linguistic complexity and cognitive demands. In a study where we compared the interaction between linguistic complexity and working memory in English- and Hungarian-speaking children, the results revealed that linguistic complexity impacted the accuracy of working memory performance differently across languages. While in English, an increase in syntactic complexity affected verbal working memory performance, in Hungarian, an increase in morphology and not in syntax resulted in decreased accuracy for working memory performance (Marton et al., 2006).

Even though there is no specific language structure that would be impaired in children who speak any certain language yet intact in young speakers of other languages, children with DLD might show salient weaknesses that vary across languages. For example, while English-speaking children experience extreme difficulty with the acquisition of tense and agreement markers, morpho-syntax is no more impaired than some other language areas in French-speaking preschoolers (Thordardottir & Namazi, 2007). Although Spanish-speaking children with DLD make fewer errors with tense marking than their English-speaking peers, they make frequent errors with articles and clitics, adjective-agreement inflections, and number agreement of nouns (Jacobson & Schwartz, 2002, 2005). Cross-linguistic findings show an interesting difference in error patterns with object clitics production. While Italian and French-speaking children with DLD tend to omit object clitics, Spanish-speaking children make substitution errors but do not omit clitics. Paradis and colleagues (2003) suggest that these cross-linguistic variations reflect prosodic differences across languages. The duration difference between stressed and unstressed syllables is smaller in Spanish than in French or Italian. The omission of object clitics in French is a clinical marker for DLD.

Word-order errors also varied across languages. While word order was the most relevant cue in sentence comprehension for English-speaking children, speakers of a verb-second language, such as German or Swedish, paid only an intermediate attention to this linguistic aspect (Clahsen et al., 1997; Hansson & Nettelbladt, 1995). Consequently, German-speaking children with DLD frequently violated the verb-second rule. These differences are also related to the developmental trajectories of these language features. While English-speaking children acquire the word order of their language earlier than specific forms of agreement (e.g., third person singular -s), Japanese-speaking children master word order and grammatical agreement cues simultaneously (Murao et al., 2017). In contrast, Hungarian-speaking children acquire assorted suffixes before the word order cues. An important difference between English and Hungarian is that the latter language has more complex verb marking. Unlike English-speaking children, Hungarian children do not need to rely on word order because subjects and objects are distinguished by their case marking. Hungarian word order is therefore more variable than English, but it is not free of rules. Our study on grammatical sensitivity showed that children with DLD detected a similar amount of agreement violations and word-order violations when the errors occurred in the sentence-initial position but detected more word-order violations than agreement violations in sentence-final positions (Marton & Yoon, 2014). These findings also indicate an interaction between cognitive and linguistic functions, specifically with working memory.

These examples show that children with DLD demonstrate weaknesses in a number of areas across languages, indicating universal problems, even though the manifestation of errors can vary from language to language. In addition to the common patterns, there are some features, such as clitics or gender, that exist only in particular languages, and such forms present difficulties for children with DLD in acquiring their first language (L1). The current findings from cross-linguistic studies in children with DLD demonstrate that the most vulnerable language functions may differ across languages. Furthermore, children with DLD vary in accuracy rates and error types for given linguistic functions across languages, and these error patterns may reflect the structural features of the given language. In the future, it is critical that the linguistic characteristics of children with DLD are studied in more languages, particularly in languages that have received little or no attention in the past and that may offer new perspectives about the nature of DLD because of their unique linguistic features, such as the use of classifiers.

1.4 Language Proficiency

Within our conceptual framework, language proficiency is the functional language use that can be overtly observed and measured across different social contexts and modalities (Birdsong, 2014; Jilka, 2009). Grosjean (1989) differentiates between spoken and written modalities, including speaking and spoken language comprehension and reading and writing. Measuring language proficiency is challenging because most objective measures (e.g., standardized language tests) focus on language abilities rather than proficiency, and the subjective measures (e.g., self-reports, questionnaires) are not very reliable. Bilingual individuals often over- or underestimate their language proficiency (De Bruin, 2019), particularly when parents are filling out the questionnaires for their children. They may only hear their child speaking one language at home, and they may not realize the degree of language development the child has in the other language when it is spoken only outside of the house.

Moreover, the tasks that are used interchangeably to measure language proficiency often show no or low correlations. According to the outcomes of a survey (Hulstijn, 2012), only half of the empirical studies on bilingualism included an objective proficiency measure. Likewise, an analysis by Surrain and Luk (2019) revealed that out of 186 studies, only 29 percent measured proficiency using a subjective questionnaire, only 30 percent applied an objective measure, and only 17 percent included both subjective and objective measures. These findings not only show inconsistencies in the literature but also indicate that a number of studies that include bilingual speakers do not even measure their participants' language proficiency.

One objective measure that is not a test of language abilities is the Diagnostic Language Assessment (DIALANG; Weber, 2007). DIALANG is a free, computer-based online language proficiency task (https://dialangweb.lancaster.ac.uk/) that has been used in the L2 education literature. DIALANG was developed based on the Common European Framework of Reference for Languages (CEFR; Council of Europe, 2001) and includes six levels of proficiency: from A1 to C2, with A1 representing the lowest level and C2 the highest. Currently, this assessment tool is available for fourteen languages (e.g., English, Spanish, German) and measures five language areas: vocabulary, reading, writing, listening, and structures, with a focus on functional language use (Chapelle, 2006).

Just a few studies compared the outcomes from subjective and objective measures, but they all suggested no or minimal correlation among these outcomes (Blumenfeld et al., 2016; Tomoschuk et al., 2019). In a study examining the relationship among different language tasks in mono- and bilingual children with and without language impairment, we also showed no or just minimal correlation among common measures of language proficiency, such as the Language Experience and Proficiency Questionnaire (LEAP-Q; Marian et al., 2007); the Clinical Evaluation of Language Fundamentals; and the Expressive One Word Picture Vocabulary Test (Gazman et al., 2019). These findings suggest that the various tasks that have been used to test language proficiency measure distinct underlying mechanisms. Therefore, they should not be used as alternatives to each other. One reason for this view is that language proficiency is dependent on other aspects of the bilingual experience, such as the frequency of language use, language dominance, or language exposure.

To demonstrate this interaction, we examined college students' language proficiency outcomes in relationship to their language exposure (Gehebe et al., 2023) on different subjective measures, such as the LEAP-Q and the American Council on the Teaching of Foreign Languages (ACTFL) performance indicators for language learners, along with objective measures including the DIALANG. Exposure was measured by the percentage to English (nonnative language) in daily life (i.e., 20–40 percent; 50–70 percent; 80–95 percent). While the proficiency outcomes across tasks and modalities strongly correlated for the participants in the high (80–95 percent) exposure group, there was only a moderate correlation among these measures for the participants in the medium (50–70 percent) exposure group; this is similar to findings by de Bruin and colleagues (2017). The outcomes from the low exposure group (20–40 percent) were less clear and showed only a moderate correlation. These data signal a complex interaction between language proficiency and exposure. Therefore, measures of proficiency must be chosen carefully,

1.4 Language Proficiency

particularly for bilingual speakers with only medium or low daily exposure to the nonnative language.

Considering the complex interactions among components of the bilingual experience, most studies used only one to two aspects of the bilingual experience when determining the selection criteria (De Bruin, 2019; Kaushanskaya & Prior, 2015). As a result, individuals with similarities in one bilingual component (e.g., language proficiency) were grouped together, despite their differences in a number of other aspects (amount of exposure, frequency of language use, bilingual language-switching frequency, etc.). Thus, it is important for future studies to consider the interactions among language proficiency along with other components of the bilingual experience. For example, when children speak one language at home and another language at school and during extracurricular activities after school, then the frequency of use and the amount of exposure to each language need to be taken into account when creating groups of speakers with different proficiency levels. Furthermore, if the children are not balanced bilingual speakers with high language competency in both languages, then language proficiency should be measured using both objective and subjective tasks.

1.4.1 Measuring Language Proficiency in Children with DLD

With the demographic changes in the United States and Europe, a growing number of children exhibit low language proficiency in academic settings. Despite the continuous development of new diagnostic methods, the differentiation between low proficient bilingual students and bilingual children with DLD remains a challenge for researchers, educators, and clinicians. Separating language proficiency from ability in bilingual children with DLD is difficult with objective measures because the same tests are typically used to assess both language ability and proficiency. When objective language measures – standardized tests – are employed to assess language proficiency in bilingual children with DLD, the outcomes can indicate the degree of language impairment instead of the level of bilingual proficiency. To identify language disorder in children from culturally and linguistically diverse groups, Kohnert and colleagues (2006) recommended distinguishing between experience-based measures, such as standardized language tests, and processing-dependent measures that require minimal previous language experience, such as nonword repetition and the competing language processing task. Three groups of eight–fourteen-year-old children participated in their study: monolingual English-speaking children with

DLD; monolingual typically developing children; and English–Spanish bilingual typically developing children. While the processing-dependent tasks clearly separated monolingual children with and without DLD, they did not distinguish clearly these two groups among the bilingual speakers. The results revealed that performance on the processing-dependent tasks was not independent of previous language experience. Even though these tasks were processing-dependent measures and not traditional language tests, they were still verbal tasks.

Another processing-dependent task for identifying bilingual children with DLD is sentence repetition. Although such tasks show high specificity and sensitivity in monolingual children, the findings are mixed with bilingual children (Marinis & Armon-Lotem, 2015). Children's performance is highly influenced by the structural characteristics of the sentences in each language. Given that bilingual children with DLD are at a disadvantage when using experience-based measures, and that the few verbal processing-dependent measures that have been used in the literature revealed inconsistent findings, we developed a series of nonverbal cognitive control tasks to distinguish between bilingual children with language impairment and typically developing bilingual children with low proficiency (i.e., ELL). Although this research is still ongoing, the first results are promising. There appears to be an interaction between bilingualism and language disorder in bilingual children with DLD when performing minimally verbal or nonverbal cognitive control tasks (e.g., N-back with single letters or abstract shapes). In simple task conditions (e.g., small set sizes, no interference), bilingual children with DLD performed similarly to typically developing monolingual children and outperformed their monolingual peers with DLD. With an increase in task complexity, however, bilingual children with DLD performed similarly to monolingual children with DLD and more poorly than monolingual typically developing children. Thus, bilingualism attenuated the negative effects of DLD in simple task conditions, but this cognitive benefit disappeared in the more complex conditions, where all children with DLD performed more poorly, regardless of the number of languages they spoke (Marton et al., 2019). In contrast, ELL students performed similarly to monolingual typically developing children even in the more complex conditions. More research is needed to strengthen these findings, but the data we have so far suggest that nonverbal cognitive control tasks may have the diagnostic power to differentiate between bilingual children with DLD and ELL students.

A further challenge is to determine bilingual children's language ability separately from their language proficiency, particularly in children with

1.5 *Monolingual and Bilingual First Language Speakers*   17

DLD. To overcome the problem that results from using the same tests to measure language proficiency and language disorder in children with DLD, we used a new within-subject approach to assessing language proficiency. First, we determined the expressive vocabulary scores of children in English and in Spanish. Then, we rescaled the scores of the less proficient language as a function of the more proficient language using a ratio of the scores from the stronger and weaker languages. To do this, we applied the following formula: $y = ((L2 - minimum) / (L1 - minimum)) * 100$ (Little, 2013). When using this formula, we worked with children's percentile ranks and not standard scores because the minimum of zero as a vocabulary score would not be meaningful. The same method can be applied to values from Likert scales that have been used in bilingual questionnaires (e.g., LEAP-Q). Although the power of this method has to be further evaluated using larger samples, our preliminary results have been encouraging.

1.5 Similarities in Language Development in Typically Developing Monolingual Children and Bilingual First Language (L1) Speakers

The goal for this section is to identify patterns of language acquisition that characterize children's development, regardless of the number of languages they speak. Therefore, the focus is on monolingual children and bilingual L1 speakers who are exposed to two or more languages from birth. From the bilingual population, we concentrate on bilingual L1 children only because both monolingual children and bilingual L1 speakers acquire language early in life, when the brain is most plastic and before they have had experience with formal instructions. Bilingual L1 speakers differ from successive bilingual children, even from those who acquire their L2 early in life, in learning processes, language experiences, and in the rate of acquisition (De Houwer, 2011; Meisel, 2011). The comparison of language development in monolingual children and bilingual L1 speakers has been criticized in the literature, suggesting that the language competencies of these bilingual L1 children should be evaluated on their own merit to avoid the implications of a deficit view (Genesee, 2019). By identifying and discussing similarities in language development, we believe that both preventing the creation of a deficit view and highlighting common features can be accomplished.

Although there are inconsistencies in the literature, primarily because of the heterogeneity of the bilingual population, there is converging evidence suggesting that the overall course and the rate of bilingual L1 and monolingual language development are remarkably similar (Genesee & Nicoladis, 2007; Kovács & Mehler, 2009). This does not, of course, mean that bilingual L1 speakers' competency is exactly the same in their two languages. Even though bilingual L1 acquisition means that children are exposed to their two languages at the same time, there may be differences in the language context, the amount of exposure, and the frequency of language use (De Houwer, 2009). Thus, the bilingual language experience may affect these children's development of specific vocabulary items or structures, but it has no negative effects on the major milestones of development.

For example, both monolingual and bilingual infants produce their first words around one year of age and reach a fifty-word expressive vocabulary at around eighteen months (Kovács & Mehler, 2009). Other milestones of lexical acquisition are also reached for both languages in a similar manner, as long as the bilingual child receives equal exposure. The variations in vocabulary size in children between eight and thirty months of age have been associated with individual differences in early vocabulary development and not with the number of languages a child speaks (Pearson et al., 1993). Even in monolingual children, there is a wide range in the number of words they actively use at this age. In addition to the similarities in vocabulary size, the distribution of lexical categories (noun, verb, adjective, etc.) is also comparable between monolingual and bilingual children (Genesee & Nicoladis, 2007). Unfortunately, even today, there are only a few bilingual language tests available (e.g., Bilingual Verbal Ability Tests; Muñoz-Sandoval et al., 2005). Therefore, bilingual children's vocabulary has typically been measured in only one language in the past, and then compared to monolingual children's vocabulary (Oller et al., 2007; Umbel et al., 1992). This is not a fair comparison, however, because there are words that bilingual children may know in one language but not in the other, depending on their bilingual experience. When we assess bilingual children's total conceptual vocabularies (i.e., every concept for which they know the word in at least one language), then we find no disadvantage for bilingual children. Their cumulative lexical knowledge may even be larger than that of their monolingual peers (Hoff, 2013).

With regards to grammatical structures, the findings from different language pairs also indicate similar patterns between monolingual children and bilingual L1 speakers. Both groups showed similar developmental trajectories from single-word utterances, to two-word stages, to multiple-word expressions, and finally to complex sentences (De Houwer, 2009). There are, of course, language-specific features that develop at different

1.6 Language in Mono- and Bilingual Children with DLD 19

times in the two languages, but even the morphological and syntactic errors are similar for monolingual children and bilingual L1 speakers. For example, French–English-speaking two–three-year-old bilingual toddlers acquired finite verb forms earlier in French than in English and used subject pronouns in French only with finite verbs, despite the fact that they used subject pronouns in English with both finite and nonfinite verbs (Genesee & Nicoladis, 2007). These performance patterns resembled those of monolingual children acquiring either French or English. The grammatical errors in both monolingual children and bilingual L1 speakers reflect age effects and age-related individual variations rather than the impact of bilingualism (Hudson Kam, 2014). Moreover, grammatical performance in bilingual English-French speaking three-year-old children was highly influenced by their exposure to each language (Thordardottir, 2015). Bilingual children with high language exposure used assorted grammatical forms in their spontaneous speech, equal to their monolingual peers. Thus, children with bilingual L1 exhibit similar individual variations, developmental patterns, age-effects, and error types as monolingual children, as long as their language exposure is also similar.

1.6 Similarities in Language Development in Monolingual and Bilingual Children with DLD

Research in bilingual children with DLD started later than in monolingual children with the main question being whether bilingualism worsens the language difficulties of children with DLD. In other words, is the language profile of bilingual children with DLD affected more strongly by their language impairment or by their bilingualism? One critical question was whether bilingual children with DLD exhibit more severe forms of language impairment than their monolingual peers. Today, we know that the linguistic profiles of monolingual and bilingual children with DLD are similar (Gutiérrez-Clellen et al., 2009; Rothweiler et al., 2012). For example, English-French speaking bilingual children with DLD showed comparable performance to monolingual children with DLD in a number of morphological tasks (Paradis et al., 2003). A slightly different picture emerged when the child's second language was a minority language in their country. Such children showed a disadvantage on linguistic measures (Verhoeven et al., 2011), but only if they were tested in their weaker language. Notably, the performance gap for children with and without DLD who learned a minority language (e.g., Dutch) was no greater than the gap between monolingual children with DLD and their monolingual TD peers (Leonard, 2014). These findings revealed that language performance in bilingual children with DLD is more strongly affected by their language impairment than by bilingualism.

In this section we focus on children's morpho-syntactic skills because this is the most vulnerable area of language in children with DLD who speak multiple languages. The overall findings suggest that the performance patterns of bilingual children with DLD are similar to those of monolingual children with DLD, and this is true for both simultaneous and early successive bilingual children. To examine universal patterns, the following examples include Turkish-German, Frisian-Dutch, French-English, and German-Italian language pairs.

Subject-verb agreement was studied in six-year-old German monolingual and Turkish-German bilingual children with DLD. The similarities in agreement errors in monolingual and bilingual children with DLD suggest that language impairment affects the use of grammar in each language, independently from the order of acquisition, and there is no extra cost of bilingualism (Rothweiler et al., 2012). Likewise, subject-verb agreement errors in an obligatory context have been found in Dutch monolingual and Frisian-Dutch bilingual kindergarten and school-age children with DLD (Spoelman & Bol, 2012). Children's errors were divided into three main categories: omission of the agreement marker; substitutions of a plural by a singular agreement marker; and verb forms not marked for person, number, or tense. There was no difference between the monolingual and bilingual children with DLD in the total number of agreement errors, in the different agreement error types, or in the use of subject-verb agreement in an obligatory context. Furthermore, the two groups did not differ in the production and number of omission errors in intransitive and transitive structures either. Dative case marking was studied in German and German-Italian four–seven-year-old children with DLD. Spontaneous speech samples with 74 utterances containing an obligatory context for a dative case marking were analyzed for each child. Similar to previous results, there was no difference in dative case marking between the speech samples of monolingual and bilingual children with DLD (Scherger, 2018).

Finally, French-English bilingual children were compared to two groups of monolingual children, one speaking English and the other French. All children were around seven years of age and had a diagnosis of DLD. To examine whether bilingual children with DLD experience difficulties with the same morpho-syntactic structures as their monolingual peers, spontaneous speech samples in each language were analyzed targeting tense-bearing and nontense-bearing morphemes (Paradis et al., 2003). There was no difference in accuracy scores across the groups. Thus, bilingual and monolingual children with DLD exhibited difficulties in tense marking to the same extent, and all children's production of nontense morphemes was better than their use of tense markers. These findings suggest that bilingual children with DLD do not have more severe language impairment than their monolingual peers, an outcome further supported by data suggesting that the gap in performance between bilingual children with and without DLD is no greater than the gap between typically developing monolingual children and children with DLD (Leonard, 2014). The results from these different studies also show that bilingual children with DLD do not have additional problems in morpho-syntax compared to their monolingual peers.

1.7 Conclusions

In this book, we systematically differentiate between language ability and levels of language proficiency by defining the two terms, describing the groups that vary along these two language dimensions, and identifying specific measures of ability vs. proficiency. Regrettably, both the bilingualism and language impairment literatures use these terms inconsistently, often even interchangeably. As a result, a much larger proportion of bilingual children are diagnosed with language disorder, particularly among emerging bilingual children (i.e., with low language proficiency), compared to expectations based on the prevalence of DLD in the general population. There is an increasingly large amount of evidence showing that bilingualism does not have a negative effect on children's language development, even if they exhibit a language disorder.

It is important to distinguish clearly between these language dimensions, even if the standardized language tests show some overlapping outcomes for bilingual children with DLD and for emerging bilingual typically developing children. It is critical to prevent misdiagnoses in these language groups because when children are under- or overdiagnosed, they do not receive the appropriate services and placement, so their academic careers are therefore severely hindered. These misdiagnoses may negatively affect children's later career choices and job selections, as well as their motivation and self-esteem, possibly leading to emotional disturbances, such as depression and anxiety, as obstacles to realizing their full potential.

CHAPTER 2

Cognitive Control

2.1 Conceptual Foundation

Given that the main theme of this book is about the relationship between cognitive control and language, specifically about the changes in cognitive control in populations with different language abilities and levels of proficiency, this chapter introduces various theoretical constructs and conceptual models of cognitive control. The description and interpretation of the core constructs are followed by a critical review of particular theoretical models and behavioral paradigms that have been used to measure cognitive control skills in children. This chapter provides the theoretical foundation of cognitive control for subsequent chapters that discuss various aspects of language development and their interactions with cognitive control. More details for consideration of cognitive control abilities across populations with different language skills are presented in Chapters 4–10.

Cognitive control is a comprehensive construct that encompasses all the processes necessary for adapting the cognitive system to achieve goal-directed behavior, even if there are other compelling or habitual acts present and the conditions keep changing (Botvinick et al., 2001; Cohen, 2017). Cognitive control is constantly needed in everyday-life situations that involve switching between activities, thoughts, or languages (Dreisbach, 2012). Depending on the context, people either complete the switch or resist the interference and keep performing the current task while monitoring their own behavior. Adaptive and flexible responses play essential roles in learning situations in general and even more so during language acquisition and language processing (Mazuka et al., 2009). To perform well on cognitive-linguistic tasks, one needs to mobilize complex cognitive control processes, including working memory, inhibition, and attention control. Although the term "cognitive control" is often used interchangeably with "executive functions" in the literature, they are not synonymous. The cognitive control framework (Botvinick et al., 2001; Egner, 2017) has

22

been used in this book because the control processes play critical roles in language-related tasks: in word production (Badre & Wagner, 2007), language comprehension (Van Dyke & Johns, 2012), and bilingual language production (Abutalebi & Green, 2007). Furthermore, the behaviors associated with the cognitive control accounts are clearly defined and closely linked to specific neurobiological structures and processes (Botvinick et al., 2004; Luna et al., 2015; Shenhav et al., 2013). In contrast, "executive functions" is a broad umbrella term that has been used with various meanings and definitions in the literature (Engle, 2002; Miyake et al., 2000; Zelazo & Müller, 2002). Although the terms, executive functions, and cognitive control, reflect differences in scientific approach, theory, and methods, it is important to note that both constructs comprise a number of similar cognitive components, such as switching and inhibitory control.

There are different theoretical accounts defining and describing the mechanisms of cognitive control, and while a number of them complement each other well, they do differ in their focus on specific components or processes of the control system (e.g., Botvinick & Braver, 2015; Botvinick et al., 2001; Cohen, 2017; Shenhav et al., 2013). Most conceptual frameworks of cognitive control seek to answer fundamental questions about the mechanisms that are related to the core features of cognitive control; the recruitment of control resources; the selection of task-relevant processes; and the increase of efficiency during performance.

2.1.1   Critical Issues

2.1.1.1   Capacity Limitations

One of the most widely discussed, yet controversial topics in the literature is the capacity limitation of the control processes. Capacity constraints have been attributed to both functional (computational) and structural limitations, but no agreement has been reached about their nature, source, or extent (Botvinick & Cohen, 2014; Musslick & Cohen, 2021). There is more agreement, however, about the notion that these constraints determine the number of control-demanding tasks that can be carried out simultaneously, therefore these constraints affect all human behaviors that require control-dependent processes. Thus, both lower-level (e.g., perception) and higher-level (e.g., problem-solving) processes are influenced by capacity constraints.

The working memory literature provides a demonstrative example of different theoretical accounts with various explanations for capacity limitations. Although similar attempts can be noticed in the literature on attention control and visual processing, most of those studies also examined the capacity limitations in relation to working memory (Martin et al., 2021; Unsworth et al., 2021). Working memory studies have shown significant advancement in the past few decades, which is reflected by the amount of complex theoretical models and by the number of publications. The changes in working memory accounts over time indicate a gradual shift in conceptualization, moving away from theories that concentrate on the number of memory representations and control-dependent processes to models that focus on the nature and integrity of representations and control processes. The earlier models emphasized either the temporal or the numerical constraints (i.e., number of representations and control-demanding processes).

The first models explaining working memory constraints were the traditional decay theories (e.g., Baddeley, 2003; Baddeley & Hitch, 1974). The key assumptions of these accounts were that memory representations decay over time, unless individuals mobilize specific reactivation processes, such as rehearsal. Baddeley's working memory account is a multicomponent model, and one of the modality-specific units is the phonological loop where verbal material can be stored for a limited amount of time. To maintain the memory items in working memory, verbal rehearsal has to be employed. Thus, the capacity constraints, according to the decay models, are associated with temporal limitations. However, the decay process can be prevented by specific strategy use (i.e., verbal rehearsal).

The concept of numeric constraints was described by the resource theories examining the amount of activation needed to store items in working memory and perform computations during task completion (e.g., Just & Carpenter, 1992; King & Just, 1991). They compared the activation demands of various tasks to the working memory capacity of the participants. Most of these studies employed variations of span tasks (e.g., listening span, reading span). According to the resource theories, if there is a shortage in the storage function of working memory, then information will be forgotten, while a shortage in the activation of the computational functions results in slower processing. The resource theories have been criticized in the literature for not being specific enough in their definitions of activation, capacity, and resources (Cohen, 2017; Hasher et al., 2007).

An integration of the temporal and numeric processes can be seen in the time-based resource-sharing model (Barrouillet & Camos, 2001). This account argued that the maintenance of items in working memory depends on both the number and complexity of the information to be remembered and the passage of time. The model held further that, during task performance, attention must be switched continuously between information processing and reactivation of the decaying memory traces.

2.1 Conceptual Foundation

More recent accounts of working memory capacity attribute the constraints to interference between memory representations and/or control processes. To dispute the accounts of temporal constraints, Lewandowsky and Oberauer conducted a series of experiments with the "serial order in a box" model (e.g., Lewandowsky et al., 2008, 2009; Oberauer & Lewandowsky, 2008). The results indicated that recall efficiency of memory items is highly influenced by the information that must be encoded. The more similar the pieces of information, the higher the chance for interference. In these experiments, recall performance was linked to the uniqueness of items at encoding rather than to the number of elements to be remembered or to the passage of time. A number of language studies also focused on interference effects. Although all of their findings indicated that similarity-based interference plays a critical role in sentence comprehension, it remains unclear whether this interference occurred during encoding or at retrieval (Gordon et al., 2002; Van Dyke & McElree, 2006).

Taken together, our current understanding of capacity constraints is still limited. There is evidence supporting various aspects of the aforementioned theories. Computational studies provide a promising line of research, highlighting more specific interactions and trade-offs between representations and control processes (Musslick & Cohen, 2021). To better understand these dynamic relationships and the nature of the control processes, future studies must continue synthesizing behavioral and neural approaches of cognitive control research.

2.1.1.2 The Continuum of Processes: From Controlled to Automatic Behavior

The applied research literature, such as studies on bilingualism, developmental disorders, and second language learning, tends to categorize the cognitive control skills of people into specific groups. One group shows more advanced skills than others; they make fewer errors; or they perform faster than their peers. These are, of course, simplifications that reflect, in part, the limitations of the tasks that are being used and some constraints in conceptualization. Cognitive control is not a dichotomic system and can only be characterized along a continuum from automatic behaviors that require no or only minimal control to highly controlled behaviors. An important task for the system is to decide whether a behavior can be performed automatically, with some control, or with a high degree of control. A related question is whether a certain behavior consistently requires the same amount of control all the time.

One contributing factor to the degree of control is the context of the behavior. The cognitive control system adapts most efficiently during a goal-directed performance when the voluntary mobilization of the control system is aligned with both the task-goals and the context of the given behavior (Bocanegra & Hommel, 2014). To demonstrate the effect of context, a number of scholars (see later on) have referred to the Stroop task. Any typically developing school-age child or adult would need only minimal cognitive control to name the color of given objects when using their primary language. Color naming would be basically automatic as reflected by fast response times, high accuracy rates, no or minimal monitoring, and minimal effort exertion (Meiran et al., 2015). In contrast, naming the color of the ink in the Stroop test, especially for the incongruent condition of mixed blocks (i.e., only some color-words are printed in matching ink, e.g., "green" in green ink vs. "green" in red ink), would greatly challenge the cognitive system because of the interference between the color of the ink and the meaning of the color-word (MacLeod, 1991). This would be seen by an increase in reaction time and in error rate, as well as in effortful performance. In the Stroop task, one needs to overcome the interference between the color of the ink and the meaning of the color-word, whereas in a simple color naming task, there is no interference. Thus, the same skill, such as color naming, might be automatic in one condition but not in another (Marton & Wellerstein, 2008).

At the neural level, earlier studies linked these differences in context processing to activation changes in the prefrontal cortex (Cohen & Servan-Schreiber, 1992). Later studies, such as the gating model (Braver & Cohen, 1999), added the modulating effect of the dopamine system. This model proposed that goal-directed behavior is supported by the activation of context processing in the prefrontal cortex, which is initiated by the dopamine system. Thus, context maintenance and updating are enabled through interactions between the prefrontal cortex and the dopamine modulatory system. One of the newest models provides a framework for synthesis and expansion of previous accounts by postulating dual mechanisms of control (Braver, 2012). According to this model, there are two operating modes for cognitive control: proactive and retroactive. Goal-relevant information is maintained in an anticipatory manner in the lateral prefrontal cortex through the proactive control mode, whereas reactive control is used to reactivate goals in conditions with interference. An example of reactive control is post-error adjustment (i.e., post-error slowing, post-error increase in accuracy, post-error reduction in interference).

Practice is another major factor contributing to the degree of control. Most cognitive and motor tasks are performed faster and more accurately with practice. This can be observed at both the behavioral and neural levels. The role of the striatum has been proven critical at the subcortical level during these processes. Early learning/practice has been linked to the associative striatum, while neurons in the sensorimotor striatum show activation once automaticity has been developed for a given behavior (Ashby et al., 2010). Moreover, newer findings provide strong evidence that the striatum produces multiple learning signals and contributes to a distributed network, including other brain areas specialized for learning (Shohamy, 2011). At the neural level, the degree of automaticity is closely linked to activation in the prefrontal cortex. An essential role has been attributed to the posterior-to-anterior gradient system for more controlled processes, whereas the more automatic processes are linked to the posterior-confined system with the involvement of posterior regions (Jeon & Friderici, 2015).

Individual differences in cognitive control skills also affect how efficiently children reach automaticity in task performance. The following chapters provide examples from children with advanced cognitive control skills, as well as from children with weaknesses in their control processes. While children with a language talent have shown advanced cognitive control skills and efficient achievement of automaticity (Dörnyei & Skehan, 2003), those with language impairment have shown difficulties in cognitive control and have demonstrated slower, less efficient learning with a need for more practice to reach automaticity (Marton & Scheuer, 2020; Marton et al., 2014). The weaknesses in cognitive control in children with language impairment appear to interfere with these children's ability to achieve automaticity efficiently (Pauls & Archibald, 2016).

Finally, a critical issue, that has received the most attention in sports psychology, concerns the impact of the application of top-down control to behaviors that are typically automatic. The previous examples have demonstrated how the context of a task, the level of familiarity or practice with the task, and the individual's abilities may determine the degree of control that is needed to perform a given task. There are, however, certain instances when applying control to an otherwise automatic behavior may interfere or even impair task performance. In a color-shape selection task, Bocanegra and Hommel (2014) showed that with sufficient contextual information for the cognitive system to mobilize automatic processes during task performance, the application of top-down control impaired the goal-directed behavior. These outcomes are in line with the matched filter hypothesis (Chrysikou et al., 2014), suggesting that the degree of cognitive control needed varies depending on task demands. Research with individuals who stutter further supported this hypothesis. With the use of a dual-task paradigm, Eichorn demonstrated that the speech fluency of individuals who stutter may improve when the degree of cognitive control is reduced and participants are able to rely on more implicit modes of processing (Eichorn & Marton, 2015; Eichorn et al., 2016). These findings support the notion that depending on

28 Cognitive Control

the context, demands of the task, amount of practice, and individual differences, the rule of "less can be more" may provide a more efficient approach for studies focusing on the continuum between automaticity and control.

2.1.1.3 Cognitive Flexibility

During our discussion of the effects of context and practice on the control processes, we have already highlighted the importance of adaptability and flexibility in cognition. Cognitive flexibility is a hallmark of cognitive control, and it refers to an essential set of skills that enable the system to selectively focus on the most relevant information, suppress irrelevant items, shift attention, and adapt itself to new and/or changing conditions. While performing goal-directed behavior, cognitive flexibility is recruited to maintain the task-goals; resist automatic responses that could interfere with current performance; and temporarily store and process information in working memory (Diamond, 2013). Frequent updating is needed to support the cognitive system's adaptation processes during changes in task-goals, contexts, or other demands (Dreisbach & Fröber, 2019). An essential question related to the mechanisms that drive flexibility concerns the nature of the representational code that guides performance (Cohen, 2017). Although there is debate in the cognitive control literature about the features of this code and the acquisition and regulation of control representations, there are clear behavioral indicators when either inappropriate representations are engaged, or the representations have not been updated.

One of the behaviors that signals when the system fails to perform the above processes is perseveration. It takes place when a previously appropriate response is repeated even though the task-goal or context or task demands have changed, rendering the given response no longer appropriate (Sandson & Albert, 1984). Perseveration may be caused by attentional inertia, a weakness in working memory updating, or a combination of these processes along with a problem in inhibitory control. In case of attentional inertia, the activation of the previous task-goal remains too high, which prevents the system from switching to the current goal. Therefore, redirecting attention becomes difficult (Kirkham et al., 2003). Alternatively, if the latent working memory representations of the old rule are stronger than the current ones, then previous memory traces may interfere with current processes (Morton & Munakata, 2002). A third suggestion is that it is not the failure of any single mechanism that is responsible for the perseverative behavior but rather a dysfunctional interaction among the set of cognitive control skills (Diamond, 2016).

A further line of research describes the dynamic nature of the cognitive control system by the competition between stability and flexibility (e.g., Fröber et al., 2018; Hund & Foster, 2008). In general, the repeated presentation of specific items, cues, and contexts (i.e., practice) strengthens the particular representations related to these task elements, while flexibility is required to respond to changes in task conditions. This dynamic interaction between stability and flexibility can be demonstrated by using task-switching paradigms where performance on stay trials is improved by stronger stability, whereas performance on the switch trials requires a great amount of flexibility (see more details under "Behavioral Paradigms"). While stability helps to maintain and shield task-goals from distraction, flexibility aids the system in adapting to changing conditions. Finding a balance between stability and flexibility creates a great challenge for the cognitive control system. Different theoretical accounts provide distinct explanations about the mechanisms that are involved in detecting when control is needed, as some theories focus more on the regulatory processes, while others on the evaluative mechanisms.

2.2 Current Cognitive Control Frameworks

2.2.1 The Conflict Monitoring Hypothesis

The conflict monitoring account suggests that the cognitive demands during task performance are evaluated through a monitoring process (Botvinick et al., 2001). As indicated by the name of the model, it has been proposed that information processing is continuously monitored for conflict between competing representations and processes. Conflict monitoring has been linked to the anterior cingulate cortex (ACC), while the implementation of control for goal-directed behavior has been associated with the prefrontal cortex (e.g., Botvinick et al., 2004; Kerns et al., 2004). Specifically, the ACC detects any conflict between competing representations and then signals the dorsolateral prefrontal cortex to resolve the conflict (Carter & van Veen, 2007).

Conflict may occur at various levels of the control process; however, most attention has been given to conflicts among competing responses. These conflicts are related either to strategies or to automatic behaviors. For instance, an automatic or habitual response may interfere with the current goal-demanded response (e.g., reading the word in the Stroop task might interfere with naming the color of the ink). Another example is failure to withhold a response in a Stop-Signal or Go-NoGo task. The Stop-Signal task measures the ability to suppress a relatively automatic response in the presence of an auditory cue. Participants are typically instructed to press a button to indicate the direction of a visual stimulus on the computer screen (e.g., left-pointing or right-pointing arrow) but to withhold this response upon hearing an auditory beep signal. The Stop-Signal delay can be adjusted. The more frequent the go trials in the task, the more difficult it is to withhold the response when a cue is presented. When three conditions were created (i.e., certain go, uncertain go, stop), preparation time was negatively associated with performance; specifically, greater preparation time resulted in shorter reaction time, signaling more efficient task performance (Chikazoe et al., 2009).

Another indicator of conflict monitoring is the post-error behavior. When an error is made, the cognitive system quickly corrects the behavior or performs specific adjustments (e.g., post-error slowing). These corrections are signaled by error-related negativity (ERN) in electrophysiological studies and by the activation of the ACC in imaging studies (Hajcak et al., 2005; Miltner et al., 2003). Some scholars view errors as conflicts, while others distinguish between conflict monitoring and error detection theories. Nevertheless, a number of studies have shown that the ERN indicates a conflict between an erroneous response and a subsequent correct response (Yeung et al., 2004). Moreover, the amplitude of the ERN was greater for corrected than for uncorrected errors (Rodríguez-Fornells et al., 2002). Another conflict-driven phenomenon is post-error slowing (Botvinick et al., 2001). When participants make an error, they typically slow down, even if no explicit feedback is provided. Several methods have been suggested to calculate post-error slowing; one of the most widely accepted measures is the comparison of pre-error and post-error reaction times (Dutilh et al., 2012). The reaction time difference signals a trade-off between accuracy and speed of processing. While some studies interpreted these changes as an indication that the monitoring system recognized the error and devoted more efficient attention to the response, others viewed this phenomenon as a reflection of a change in the strategic priming of the response (Carter & van Veen, 2007).

In sum, a large number of empirical data from both the behavioral and the neurophysiological literature provide support for the conflict-monitoring theory. Most of the studies, however, focused on adults. In the future, more developmental studies are needed to better understand the age-related changes in ERN and in post-error behaviors (Tamnes et al., 2013; Wiersema et al., 2007).

2.2.2 The Expected Value of Control (EVC)

The expected value of control account provides an integrative and expansive description of the different roles of the ACC, with a specific focus on the dorsolateral anterior cingulate cortex (dACC; Shenhav et al., 2013). This account posits that in addition to conflict/error monitoring, the dACC is also responsible for determining how much allocation of control

2.2 *Current Cognitive Control Frameworks* 31

is needed and the value of returns (Shenhav, 2017). The EVC hypothesis suggests that the dACC combines information about the expected costs and rewards associated with a control-demanding task to determine the final value of control allocation for that particular task. Thus, the allocation of control is part of a decision process. When the system is faced with competing tasks, it is the dACC that determines whether it is worthwhile to allocate control to a given task and how much control should be invested. This decision-making process is the specification of the control signal (Shenhav et al., 2013). When a response conflict, interference, delay, or error is detected, the control signal has to be respecified because those problems indicate that insufficient control has been engaged. The respecification process of the control signal is linked to the effort to maximize the expected reward, such as the feeling of being correct. For instance, in the Stop-Signal task, when the auditory beep is presented with the visual stimuli (e.g., left or right arrows), there is competition between the responses: "respond to the arrow" or "respond to the beep." The system needs to evaluate the outcomes, as well as the costs of control allocation. These processes – "How much control to engage?" and "Which task to choose?" – together determine the EVC.

Musslick et al. (2015) have used the EVC theory in a computational study to evaluate whether the idea can be applied to task-switching paradigms. Their model provided a valuable framework to explain how participants adjust control – balance stability and flexibility – in order to optimize the reward rate. Unlike other task-switching paradigms, the EVC allows the participants to choose which task to perform, how much control to engage, and how long to perform the task. For example, when the reward was increased for one previously avoided task, the model switched, despite the higher difficulty level of the task. When the difficulty level was increased, the model allocated more control processes. However, if the difficulty level kept increasing, the model switched to the easier task.

To apply this idea to everyday situations, Kool and Botvinick (2014) integrated the cognitive control theory with economic models. In daily life, we often have to make decisions about accepting or declining certain tasks/projects. In each case, we have to consider how much cognitive effort the task requires – control allocation – and how much reward it provides. Furthermore, we all live with time constraints. Therefore, we also need to consider whether we benefit more from performing that particular task or from declining the assignment and relaxing into easier, more comfortable habits. Kool and Botvinick (2014) examined different scenarios of decision-making about cognitive labor versus leisure. The overall results revealed that cognitive labor/leisure decisions depend on preferences that simultaneously evaluate income and leisure. When wage reductions occurred, participants tended to work less, and accepted a smaller income, while they were willing to give up leisure and work more when wage increases were promised. Thus, the expected reward played an important role in the decision process about cognitive investment.

2.2.3 The Integrative Model of Cognitive Control Development

The previously discussed models were based on behavioral and neural findings in young adults, as well as on data from computational studies. Although cognitive control skills start developing early in childhood, the maturation process continues through adolescence into adulthood (Geier & Luna, 2009). Originally, developmental studies were focused on individual cognitive control components, such as inhibition, error-monitoring, and working memory (Bjorklund & Harnishfeger, 1990; Conklin et al., 2007; Velanova et al., 2008), whereas follow-up research has taken a more integrated view by studying the interactions among different cognitive control components and the development of underlying brain mechanisms (Gratton et al., 2018; Grayson et al., 2014).

While critical reorganization of functional connectivity happens during brain development, there are several large-scale network features that develop early in childhood and remain stable over time, indicating that functional brain networks are organized similarly across ages (Power et al., 2010). When functional connectivity analysis was combined with wiring distance measures of white-matter fibers, the outcomes revealed that large-scale brain networks develop through the decrease of short-range functional connectivity along with the simultaneous increase of long-range functional connectivity (Supekar et al., 2009). Thus, the control networks involve both segregation (i.e., the attenuation of short-range connections) and integration (i.e., strengthening the long-range connections). These processes lead to a dual-network control architecture that underlies different learning mechanisms (Fair et al., 2007). Despite agreement among researchers about these connectivity outcomes, more recent studies noted artifacts in the data due to participant head movements (Hallquist et al., 2013; Power et al., 2012). Power and colleagues (2012) have recommended using graph theoretical measures to examine segregation and integration processes. Nevertheless, there is evidence that a critical part of cognitive control development is due to the integration of large-scale brain networks. Brain regions that underlie cognitive flexibility must encompass a large number of connections across several brain systems to support multiple cognitive control functions, such as monitoring and updating (Luna et al., 2015).

At the behavioral level, cognitive flexibility shows significant growth during the preschool years (Davidson et al., 2006). Although the Dimensional Change Card Sort task is classically viewed as a measure of cognitive flexibility (Zelazo et al., 2013), children's performance appeared to reflect a more basic, underlying ability to sustain and control attention in the context of changing task demands as performance generally improved when experimental conditions increased attention to current task-goals (Benitez et al., 2017; Moriguchi & Hiraki, 2009). The development of an attentional control network appears to be the driving force behind the age-related changes in cognitive control, although the control components are less distinct or separable in children than in adults, particularly during the preschool years when a more unitary construct of cognitive control can be observed (Nelson et al., 2016; Wiebe et al., 2011). The separability of components becomes more apparent during the elementary school years with the clearest separation of working memory from inhibition and flexible shifting (Brydges et al., 2014; Nelson et al., 2022).

Taken together, the outcomes from behavioral studies suggest a gradual separation of cognitive control functions throughout childhood and adolescence. In the meantime, both segregation and integration of brain connectivity are apparent. However, future research is needed to identify the specific processes in brain networks that determine the developmental course of component differentiation in cognitive control. Using a variety of tasks may show increasingly diverse performance in children, as their brain networks become more task-specific with development.

2.3 Behavioral Paradigms Used to Assess Cognitive Control

Most of the behavioral tasks that have been used to assess cognitive control skills in children are either experimental paradigms or clinical/educational tests. While the former tasks were developed specifically for experimental purposes, the latter were not, yet they are often used in research projects. These clinical/educational tests were created to differentiate between typical and atypical cognitive processing. The early neuropsychological tests were specifically developed to assess frontal lobe functions in individuals with aphasia, stroke, traumatic brain injury, or brain tumors (Absher & Cummings, 1995). The problem with these tasks is that they measure multiple cognitive control components simultaneously and provide global scores (Marton, 2019; Valian,

2015). For example, the Wisconsin Card Sorting Test, originally developed to measure conceptual thinking (Eling et al., 2008), is used today to measure task switching. Moreover, this test was also used to evaluate inhibition (Milner, 1963); implicit learning and working memory (Eling et al., 2008); and learned irrelevance (Owen et al., 1993). Although this test has strong psychometric properties, its specificity is low (Gratton et al., 2018; see a more detailed discussion of task impurity in Chapter 3, "Methodological Issues"). The reason for these mixed reports is that the tests target broadly complex constructs and cannot address specific cognitive control processes.

The "unity and diversity" account (Friedman & Miyake, 2017; Miyake et al., 2000) provides a useful description of the factor structure of cognitive control, and its components are linked to associated tasks. The three main cognitive components in this model are inhibition, updating, and shifting. Even though this is a data-driven classification of the cognitive control components, it is not an exhaustive list. The authors themselves emphasized that their classification provides only a useful reference framework and that a number of complex tasks involve additional control processes.

2.3.1 *Response Inhibition Paradigms*

There are multiple variants of response inhibition tasks that require frequent responses to a particular type of stimuli (e.g., left or right pointing arrows) with infrequent events (e.g., a beep sound) that signals the need to withhold the response. Variations of Go-NoGo tasks, Stop-Signal tasks, or the AX Continuous Performance Tasks all measure response inhibition. However, they also require a great deal of monitoring, sustained attention, and to some extent, working memory updating, particularly the AX Continuous Performance Task. Thus, a weakness in any of those cognitive control skills may have a negative effect on performance efficiency.

From a developmental perspective, it is important to note that there are shared underlying mechanisms behind automatic response inhibition and resistance to interference. However, these functions develop at different rates (Dempster & Corkill, 1999; Friedman & Miyake, 2004). While response inhibition develops typically during the preschool years (Mazuka et al., 2009), interference control improves throughout adolescence (Bjorklund & Harnishfeger, 1990). The distinction between response inhibition and interference control has been further demonstrated by Blackwell and colleagues, who tested six-year-old children's switching and inhibition functions with a card sorting task (Blackwell et al., 2014). Their main finding was that children who were good at switching showed poor

2.3 Behavioral Paradigms

response inhibition compared to children who tended to perseverate in the switch conditions. In contrast, switchers showed better interference control than perseverators. These results suggest a trade-off between these cognitive processes. The two most likely reasons for these phenomena are individual differences in working memory updating and variations in the maturation of the prefrontal cortex. Future studies using more specifically focused tasks involving fewer processes are needed to better understand the nature of this trade-off and to link this trade-off process to the developmental course of these cognitive control functions.

2.3.2 *Working Memory Updating Paradigms*

In order to perform well on a working memory task, current task-goals must be active and previous memory traces must be suppressed, as relevant and irrelevant items compete for the same limited capacity. During recall, participants aim to reconstruct the context linked to the target information, even if it is somewhat noisy (Unsworth et al., 2013). However, as they perform a more extensive inspection, they often include some irrelevant information in their searches as well. Thus, a wider inspection provides them with more opportunities to find the target information on the one hand, with lowered recall probabilities due to increased interference on the other.

The relationship between working memory and interference control strengthens as children get older. They develop stronger working memory representations; more conscious differentiation between relevant and irrelevant items; and intentional suppression of irrelevant memory traces with age (Roncadin et al., 2007). As a result, they demonstrate increased processing efficiency. The most common working memory updating tasks used with children are variations of the N-back paradigm and the Sternberg item-recognition task.

The N-back paradigm is one of the most robust measures of updating. Participants are presented with a sequence of stimuli, and their task is to judge whether the current item (a letter, an abstract shape, a picture of fruits, etc.) matches the one presented "n" steps back. Three item types are typically included in this task; the target that matches the item that was presented "n" steps back in the sequence, a neutral probe that the participant has not seen before, and an interfering lure that is a familiar item in the incorrect position. When n=1, participants may respond based on item familiarity, whereas with n >1, recollection is needed. Performance accuracy may reflect the efficiency of multiple processes, such as the maintenance of content-context bindings between items and their positions, suppression of items that lie further back in the sequence, and the ability

36 Cognitive Control

to update the content-context bindings after each new stimulus (Oberauer, 2005). Intrusion costs express the difference in reaction time between the interference and the neutral (new) probes (see Figure 2.1).

The Sternberg paradigm measures recollection, updating, and resisting interference. Participants are presented with a set of memory items (i.e., items to-be-remembered) that are followed by a probe. The task is to decide whether the probe was a member of the original memory set. In a modified version developed in our laboratory, we use this task as a baseline measure, which is followed by a cue-based retrieval condition. The structure of the trials is similar in these two conditions, but in the latter one, participants are presented with a cue, following the initial memory list. The cue highlights a specific location and indicates the item to be remembered from the list. Participants are instructed to make a judgment about the probe. The only possible target in this case is the item that was presented in the cued position in the original memory list (see Figure 2.1). All other items are various distractors. A new distractor is an item that was not presented before. An interference item is a stimulus that was presented in the original memory list but not in the cued position. A second type of intrusion distractor is an item that was the target in the previous trial but not in the cued position. Finally, a third interference distractor is an item that was the target in the previous trial and was presented in the cued position. These manipulations allow us to better understand whether the errors reflect a weakness with refreshing the contents in working memory or a content-context binding problem.

2.3.3 Switching Paradigms

Switching paradigms are frequently used to test children's cognitive flexibility skills. These tasks target shifting between task-goals or task-sets. Multiple versions of the most common switching task, the Dimensional Change Card Sort task, have been used in the literature (Zelazo, 2006). In most versions of the task, participants are required to sort items according to one of two rules: according to shape or color (see Figure 2.2). When the sorting rule changes, participants must flexibly switch to the new rule. The switch requires the suppression of the old rule and the activation or the strengthening of the new rule's representation. Two robust outcomes are typically reported for these tasks: switching cost and mixing cost. Switching costs or local costs refer to the difference in reaction time between stay trials and switch trials in mixed blocks (i.e., blocks in which the two rules alternate). Switch trials require the reconfiguration of action

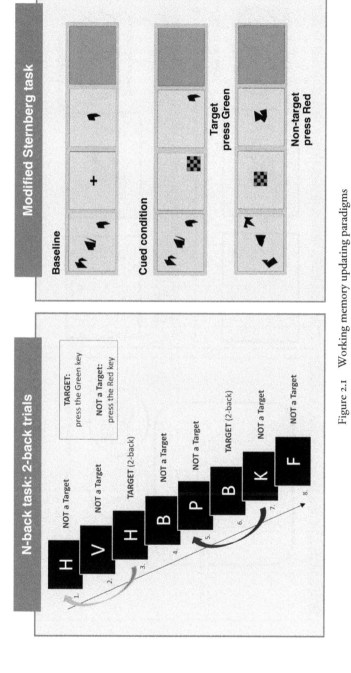

Figure 2.1 Working memory updating paradigms

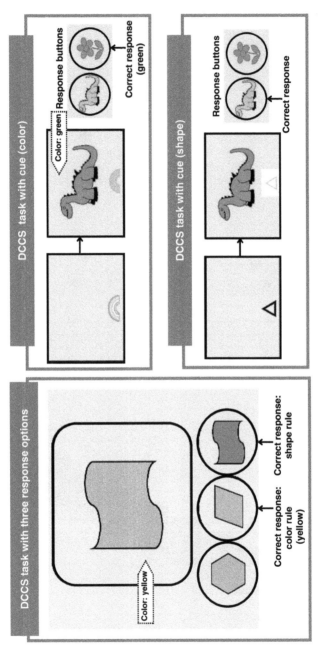

Figure 2.2 Switching paradigms

sets and reflect general response preparation (Rogers & Monsell, 1995). These processes show relatively small age-related changes (Reimers & Maylor, 2005). In contrast, mixing costs or global costs indicate how the different contexts affect participants' responses to stay trials. They refer to the difference in reaction time between stay trials in single blocks (i.e., blocks in which only one rule is followed) and stay trials in mixed blocks. Mixing costs are associated with task-set interference resolutions and show large linear age-related changes (Reimers & Maylor, 2005; Wiseheart et al., 2016). Switching and mixing costs are highly influenced by both changes in task demands and adjustments in context (e.g., changes in switching frequency; Bonnin et al., 2011; Dreisbach & Haider, 2006).

2.4 Conclusions

Although there are a number of theoretical accounts that define and describe the mechanisms of cognitive control from different perspectives, most of them complement each other well (e.g., Botvinick & Braver, 2015; Botvinick et al., 2001; Cohen, 2017; Shenhav et al., 2013). They all seek to answer fundamental questions about the control mechanisms, recruitment of control resources, selection of task-relevant processes, and prevention of interference. However, they also provide distinct explanations about the mechanisms that are involved in detecting when control is needed, as some theories focus more on the regulatory processes, while others on the evaluative mechanisms.

There are many remaining questions about the sources of capacity limitations, the effects of contextual changes, and individual differences, particularly in the developmental literature. Future research is needed to identify the specific processes in brain networks that determine the developmental trajectories of the differentiation processes in cognitive control. The use of a variety of tasks shows increasingly diverse performance in children, as their brain networks become more task-specific with development. A critical issue is that the most widely used cognitive control tasks in the developmental literature provide global scores, target multiple underlying functions (Valian, 2015), show no correlation with one another (Paap & Greenberg, 2013), and do not provide a sensitive measure of the cognitive control construct (Marton, 2019). When weaknesses are observed, it is difficult to identify the target functions because of task impurity. To better understand the developmental course of cognitive control and to provide a more subtle differentiation between typical and atypical control processes, we need to develop tasks with high specificity and sensitivity values. The integration of behavioral and neural data across age groups may also help us to better describe the dynamic processes behind goal-directed behaviors, such as learning and language acquisition.

CHAPTER 3

Methodological Issues

3.1 Identifying the Appropriate Conceptual Framework

The focus in this chapter is on methodological issues in research with particular attention to the bilingualism and the childhood language impairment literatures. In the past few decades, the number of studies examining the cognitive control skills (common term: executive functions) of children with different language abilities and proficiencies has shown significant growth in both bodies of literature, largely because most research questions target complex problems that cut across traditional disciplines. Oftentimes, however, the questions of these studies are not conceptually but educationally or clinically driven. Having no or an unclear conceptual framework appears to be related to issues such as the lack of comprehensive theoretical models integrating cognitive control concepts and language processing theories; the mixed use of terminology across disciplinary literatures; and limited familiarity with other disciplines' literature and conceptual frameworks among scholars who work at the intersections of different fields. Moreover, even those who claim to perform interdisciplinary research, frequently just borrow theoretical constructs rather than integrate concepts and theories from two or more disciplines (CohenMiller & Pate, 2019).

A further issue is that the term "conceptual framework" itself is used with at least three different meanings. It may refer to major ideas and arguments of a study; it may be used as a synonym for "theoretical model"; or it may be the guiding principle for the entire research process, from the general statement through the literature review, research questions, methodology, data analysis, and theoretical, as well as practical implications (Ravitch & Riggan, 2017). Thus, depending on one's scientific approach, the same conceptual framework may play different roles in the research process and may be used with different meanings.

To provide perspectives and constructs for multiple disciplines, integrative models are needed. Recent shifts in focus to cultural and linguistic diversity within both the bilingualism and language impairment literatures has prompted scholars to develop more integrated conceptual frameworks (e.g., Chen & Padilla, 2019; Jiménez-Castellanos & García, 2017; Mistry et al., 2016). A number of these studies included researchers and participants from ethnic and linguistic minority groups, and they added new social constructs to the existing models to integrate such cultural, social-economic, linguistic, and life-experience factors that may help to interrupt educational and social inequality. Traditionally, however, the bilingualism literature focused on children's language background (i.e., level of proficiency, age of acquisition, and frequency of language use), whereas the sociolinguistic literature examined aspects of biculturalism. As of today, when studying cognitive control in bilingual children, demographic factors, such as immigration status, community background, and educational opportunities (e.g., school district), are not typically considered. Thus, specific social constructs are not included in cognitive-linguistic conceptual frameworks, despite having results that link children's cognitive, language, and academic performances to their socioeconomic status (Merz et al., 2019; Sheridan et al., 2017) and cultural background (Grossmann & Varnum, 2011). In future studies, a number of these constructs should be included in conceptual frameworks that are used in the child language impairment literature, especially in studies with bilingual children with developmental language disorder.

3.2 Matching Conceptual Frameworks and Research Designs

Following the selection or development of a comprehensive or integrative conceptual framework, it is important to ensure that it is in line with the study's design. Both the bilingualism and the child language impairment literatures are full of contradictory findings related to methodological issues. One problem is a mismatch between the conceptual framework and the methods. The approaches that researchers select to design their studies reflect the ways they conceptualize the problems they examine. When the methods do not match the conceptual framework, the outcomes are often misinterpreted and explained without any compelling arguments. The most common methodological issues are related to the selection of participants, tasks, and target functions. There is a complex relationship among these variables, and any meaningful research outcome will depend on how they interact within the given research design.

3.2.1 Participant Selection

Both language ability and proficiency are continuous variables reflecting a wide range of knowledge and competencies. Despite the nature of these variables, most studies select participants using a group-based approach (e.g., monolingual, bilingual, typical language development, language disorder). This categorization process contributes to the level of heterogeneity of participant groups, which is a critical issue in both the bilingualism and the language impairment literatures. Even when groups are matched on particular variables, such as age, gender, and education level, they differ in many other aspects that might also affect the cognitive-linguistic outcomes. There is, of course, a limit to the number of variables that can be controlled within each design. Furthermore, the use of discrete groups indicates the assumption of representativity, which is typically not met in research with children who are bilingual and/or exhibit developmental language disorder (Kašćelan & De Cat, 2022). The external validity of most studies in both literatures is relatively weak, and scientists, particularly in experimental research, often prioritize internal over external validity. Thus, they increase specificity over generalizability.

Heterogeneity is further boosted by the dynamic language practices and diverse life experiences of children in the twenty-first century. Cultural and linguistic diversity are present in every setting of our lives – in research, education, and policy making, among others. Children's language socialization is strongly affected by the growth of diversity within their various language communities (García et al., 2011). Variations in children's language socialization and other life experiences may affect their cognitive control performance to a great extent. These other experiences may include making music or art, frequent use of computer games, and participation in sports (Chaddock-Heyman et al., 2014; Colzato et al., 2013; Diamond & Lee, 2011; Pallesen et al., 2010). Children may practice these activities on a daily basis but only in varying degrees. Thus, even if researchers attempt to control for overall language skills, music ability, artistic talent, gaming experience, and physical activities, children will still exhibit individual differences in these areas, which would have differential effects on their cognitive control performance. Moreover, a given experience may exert a stronger effect on the performance of one task over another (Valian, 2015).

With an individual-differences approach, where the heterogeneity issue becomes part of the research question, scholars could replace the group-based approach with a more continuous one (Kaushanskaya & Prior, 2015; Marton, 2019). A study with an individual-differences focus may allow

3.2 Matching Concepts and Designs

researchers to view participants' levels of language, music, art, gaming, and physical skills as a reflection of their own lived experiences (Garivaldo & Fabiano-Smith, 2023). Only a dynamic and flexible approach could capture the cultural and linguistic richness of current communities. Assessing children's abilities along a continuum would allow researchers and educators to evaluate children's cognitive-linguistic skills with more flexibility and greater awareness of potential growth.

3.2.2 Task Selection

In addition to the heterogeneity of most participant groups, task impurity also contributes to the inconsistent findings in the literature. Most of the cognitive control tasks used in the bilingualism and child language impairment literatures measure multiple functions that tap into different underlying mechanisms. This is reflected in the large number of outcomes, including the inconsistent findings (e.g., low replicability), in minimal or no correlation among tasks claiming to target the same functions and processes, and in global scores that are difficult to interpret (Friedman et al., 2008; Marton, 2019; Valian, 2015).

A demonstrative example for the mixed findings from the bilingualism literature is the debate about the existence of a cognitive advantage in bilingual speakers. Some studies reported superior performance in bilingual individuals on specific cognitive control tasks, such as conflict resolution (Costa et al., 2008) or selective attention (Salvatierra & Rosselli, 2011) compared to monolingual controls, whereas others suggested only a general processing advantage for bilingual people across different cognitive control components (Hilchey & Klein, 2011). In contrast to these findings, a number of studies reported no difference in cognitive control between bilingual and monolingual participants (Von Bastian et al., 2016; Yudes et al., 2011). Mixed results related to task impurity can also be seen in the child language impairment literature, for instance, in studies on visuo-spatial working memory. While some authors reported difficulties in visuo-spatial working memory in children with DLD, others showed no evidence for a group difference between children with DLD and their typically developing peers (Archibald & Gathercole, 2006b; Hick et al., 2005; Marton, 2008). These studies used different visuo-spatial working memory tasks, with some targeting the storage and others the control components more heavily.

A further problem related to task impurity in the literature is that a number of tasks are used interchangeably while showing minimal or no correlation with one another. Thus, performance on one test may have little or no predictive value for performance on another test (Chan et al., 2008). For instance, measures of resistance to interference often include the Stroop task, the Eriksen flanker task, and the Simon task (Botting et al., 2017; Wang & Gathercole, 2015; Yeung et al., 2020). Stins and colleagues (2005) compared twelve-year-old children's performance on these three tasks and found minimal or no correlation. The speed of processing data across tasks showed some correlations, but the interference effects did not. Similar findings have been reported by Paap and colleagues, who compared the outcomes with the Simon and flanker tasks in college students (Paap & Greenberg, 2013). One reason for the lack of correlation across these tasks may be that they target resistance to interference through the activation of different cognitive control processes and different brain areas. With regards to the Stroop test, there are various suggestions in the literature about its target functions. While Stroop created the task to measure interference (Stroop, 1935, cit. MacLeod, 1991, p. 164), Houben and Wiers (2009) claim that the task measures automatic response inhibition. Mackin and colleagues (2010), however, used the Stroop task to measure speed of processing. Thus, the Stroop effect may be interpreted as an indicator of interference control, automatic response inhibition, or speed of processing. A further reason for the lack of correlation across these interference tasks (i.e., Stroop, Simon, flanker) may be the relatively low reliability of the interference scores.

A third issue related to task impurity is that a number of the widely used cognitive control tasks, particularly the neuropsychological tasks, provide global scores (Marton, 2019; Valian, 2015). In Chapter 2, "Cognitive Control," there is a demonstration of this problem using the Wisconsin Card Sorting Test. Poor performance on that task may be attributed to difficulties in task switching, working memory updating, or inhibition (Marton, 2008). A weakness in any of these functions may result in perseveration. Moreover, many of these tasks have assorted variants that further increase the sources of variability. Even slightly dissimilar tasks may tap into different underlying mechanisms.

Furthermore, these tasks may measure additional processes that are not directly related to the cognitive control system, such as perceptual encoding and response readiness. Hence, these tasks measure complex and broad constructs, and a number of them demonstrate low specificity and/or sensitivity. The Stroop test is considered to be one of the most reliable tasks among the neuropsychological measures used to assess cognitive control. In a meta-analysis based on 33 published articles including the Stroop test with

3.2 *Matching Concepts and Designs* 45

school-age children with different neurodevelopmental disorders (ADHD, autism, etc.), Homack and Riccio (2004) found medium to good sensitivity but low specificity. Children with different learning disabilities performed more poorly than their typically developing peers, but the Stroop test did not distinguish among the children with different diagnoses. Interestingly, the specificity and sensitivity measures of the Stroop task showed a reversed pattern in adults who were clinically referred for neuropsychological testing (Erdodi et al., 2018). In a sample of 132 participants with psychiatric or neurological disorders, the Stroop test showed high specificity but variable (low to medium) sensitivity with overall low sensitivity for an inverted Stroop effect. Although it is important to note that the children and adult studies used different versions of the Stroop test, they all claimed to target inhibitory functions related to activity in the prefrontal cortex. A similar pattern was found in a study measuring error-related negativity using the flanker task with a large sample (N=457) of adolescent females. Meyer and colleagues (2018) found high specificity but low sensitivity in predicting anxiety disorder among the participants. The findings were in line with outcomes from adults with early frontotemporal dementia, where the flanker task showed fairly high specificity but very low sensitivity (Krueger et al., 2009).

There are plenty of additional examples of issues with specificity and/or sensitivity with these widely used tasks of cognitive control in both the developmental and adult literatures. Thus, when interpreting the mixed outcomes in the bilingualism or in the child language impairment literatures, the specificity and sensitivity values of the cognitive control tasks should always be considered. Unfortunately, only a few studies have examined the psychometric properties of the most widely used neuropsychological tests. Therefore, more research is needed to study the construct validity of these tests, so that we can have a better understanding about the cognitive control components that are measured by the different tasks.

To overcome some of the problems with task impurity, specificity, and sensitivity, we can develop conceptually driven experimental tasks that are well controlled. These tasks may allow us to disentangle cognitive control processes, manipulate and control various components under different conditions, and compare outcomes to baseline measures. Comparisons across conditions, trial and item types may provide more detailed information about the control processes. It is important to note that these manipulations have to correspond to predetermined processes and components based on the study's conceptual framework. Researchers have to ensure a clear match between the targeted cognitive control components and the measures provided by the experimental task.

Furthermore, offline tests that result in "end products" (i.e., global scores) do not reveal information about the processing sequence and strategy use of the participants. However, if they are combined with online methods, such as eye-tracking and pupillometry, electrophysiological measures, the results may reveal details about the decision-making process. Online paradigms may provide more information about individual differences in strategy use, error detection, and post-error behaviors, among others. Even with these combinations of offline and online measures, linking experimental designs with solid conceptual frameworks to answer specific hypotheses is critical because variations in stimulus presentation, in the number of trials, in time intervals, or in response modes may all influence the outcomes.

A paramount criticism of experimental tasks concerns the ecological validity of these measures. Although many studies include a section of educational or clinical implications at the end of their discussion, in most cases, they do not clarify the extent to which performance on experimental tasks predicts everyday functioning. In educational and clinical research, it is essential to consider this issue despite its challenges.

3.2.3 *Target Function Selection*

As discussed in various chapters in this book, cognitive control represents a broad multifaceted construct comprising a wide range of processes and components. There have been attempts in the literature to determine the functional organization of the control processes by identifying higher order functions (e.g., attention) and core functions (e.g., inhibition). Despite the differences in concepts, all models nevertheless operationalize the control system and the underlying neural structures as componential (Baggetta & Alexander, 2016). While the components are separable, they also interact with each other, which makes the assessment of the cognitive control functions challenging. Friedman and Miyake (2017) described this dynamic relationship as the "unity and diversity" of cognitive control components.

When selecting the target functions for a study on cognitive control, it is important to examine the development and functioning level of the individual components. It is equally critical to understand the interactions among the different components to help describe complex human behaviors. Unfortunately, matching tasks with varying demands to specific control processes and components is quite difficult (Badre, 2011; Luna et al., 2015). This fractionation of the components appears to contribute to the low correlations among the cognitive control tasks even within the same construct.

3.2 Matching Concepts and Designs

Studies using latent variable analyses of cognitive control functions across age groups revealed differences in the rate of component development, with more unity in younger children and more differentiation in older ones (Brydges et al., 2014; Huizinga et al., 2006; Wiebe et al., 2011). Karr and colleagues (2018) performed a systematic review and a reanalysis of an extensive body of research, including data from 46 samples (N = 9,756) across the human lifespan. Their results showed one- or two-factor models in preschool-age children, three-factor models in school-age children and adolescents, three-factor or nested-factor models in adults, and two-factor models in elderly people. The results across studies were fairly consistent, with some exceptions, such as the findings of a four-factor model in adolescents, including working memory, shifting, inhibition, and planning (Laureys et al., 2022). Furthermore, Karr and colleagues noted a certain degree of publication bias based on their systematic review. Many studies replicated previously highly cited models and accepted those as standards. It is not clear how much this practice has contributed to the consistencies in findings across studies.

In addition to age, task complexity also affects the clustering of the different cognitive control components. The most general latent variables (i.e., inhibition/common executive function, updating, shifting) have been observed only with a medium level of task complexity. In more complex tasks, different combinations and separations of the components were apparent (Friedman & Miyake, 2017). Further, when evaluating the cognitive control abilities of participants, individual differences in behavioral performance, brain activation, and connectivity must be considered in addition to the age-related and task-complexity factors.

3.2.3.1 Mismatch between Tasks and Targeted Cognitive Control Functions

Mismatches between tasks and targeted functions are quite frequent in both the bilingualism and the language impairment literatures. There are in-depth discussions of this problem with respect to language abilities and levels of proficiency in Chapter 1, "The Language Continuum" and in Chapter 5, "Associations among Language Ability, Language Proficiency, and Cognitive Control." Therefore, here, we focus on the measures of cognitive control.

Issues related to task impurity and to the complexity of different cognitive control constructs may contribute to the mismatches between both task selection and identification of target functions (see Figure 3.1). Mismatches have been reflected by findings from studies using different tasks (that may not correlate with one another) to test the same cognitive control function (e.g., resisting distractor interference assessed with the Simon, flanker, and matching-to-sample tasks) or by outcomes from studies using the same

	Participant selection	Task selection	Target function selection
Methodological issues	• Group-based approach • Minimal consideration to cultural and linguistic diversity	• Task impurity • Global scores • Interchangeably used tasks show minimal or no correlation with each other • Low sensitivity and/or specificity	• Difficulty with matching tasks to specific control processes and components
Suggestions for future research	• More frequent use of individual-differences approaches	• Develop conceptually driven, well-controlled experimental tasks • Combine off-line tests with online methods	• Determine the targeted mechanisms for each task • Consider individual differences in behavioral performance, brain activation and connectivity, as well as age-related and task-complexity factors

Figure 3.1   Methodological issues and suggestions

task to assess different cognitive functions (e.g., the Wisconsin card sorting task to assess task switching, implicit learning, response inhibition, working memory, and conceptual thinking). Variations in age and task complexity further confound the ability to match between task and target function. For instance, in a developmental study using complex linguistic span tasks to measure verbal working memory, Marton and colleagues (2006) found that younger children (7–8 years old) relied more on storage resources and exhibited difficulty in attention switching and flexible adaptation to changing task requirements compared to older children (10–11 years old) and young adults. The latter two groups relied more on their monitoring and working memory updating skills while performing the same tasks. These differences were also reflected in variations in error types. While younger children produced many interference errors, older participants not only made fewer errors, but their errors were simple omissions rather than interference. Thus, to measure the same cognitive control functions, different tasks should be used with different age groups.

The effect of task complexity was clearly demonstrated in a study on processing speed by Cepeda and colleagues (2013). A large variety of tasks were used to test processing speed across the lifespan, including box completions, digit copying, color naming, and others. Additionally, a series of cognitive control tasks were administered to target participants' working memory, inhibitory control, and task switching abilities. This study revealed that the more complex processing speed tasks also target cognitive control functions, particularly in children and older adults. Thus, a number of tasks used in the literature as pure measures of processing speed assess complex cognitive control skills as well. Therefore, these processing speed tasks should not be used as baseline measures in complex cognitive control tasks, which is the current practice, because of their overlapping constructs. Instead, Friedman and Robbins (2022) suggest assessing cognitive control skills across multiple contexts and statistically extracting the common variables to receive purer measures with no or minimal random measurement errors.

3.3 Data Analysis

The first question we address in this section is how much the selected scoring method matters. Beyond the basic measures of overall accuracy and reaction time, many behavioral studies have involved more detailed scoring to better describe their groups' performance profiles, including the examination of the effect of set size, item type, trial order, the application of Z-scores, and partial credit.

Considering the complexity and the popularity of working memory span tasks, we use these tasks to demonstrate how the findings may differ, depending on the scoring method. In an earlier study, Gillam and colleagues (1995) scored each participant's responses with three different methods. With the conservative method, answers were counted as correct only when they were also recalled in the correct serial position (first place, second place, etc.). With the liberal scoring method, credit was given for each correctly recalled item in the proper order, even if they were not recalled in the correct serial position. For example, if the first two items were omitted but the following three items were in the correct order, then the serial positions were all incorrect, but the order of the three words was correct. Therefore, the child received credit for those three items. With the free scoring method, credit was given for each correct item, regardless of its serial position or the order of recall. Although all participants received the highest scores with the liberal scoring method, the presence of the primacy effect (i.e., recalling the first few items with higher accuracy than the following items) was not impacted by the different scoring styles. In contrast, when examining the recency effect (i.e., recalling the last few items with higher accuracy than the prior items), significant interactions with *group* × *task* × *serial* position emerged. Some researchers have incorporated this serial position idea into their working memory model, so they could examine both the content and the binding between the content and its context (e.g., serial or temporal position) when evaluating the outcomes (Cowan, 2005; Oberauer, 2009).

Other modifications to overall scoring were implemented by Leeser et al. (2016), who explored how recall correlated with accuracy, reaction time, and set size using five scoring methods: (1) *recall*, (2) *recall + accuracy*, (3) *recall + accuracy + reaction time*, (4) *set size*, and (5) composite *Z-score*. The five scoring methods were correlated within and across working memory tasks with *set size* showing the weakest correlation, which is an interesting finding, given that set-size manipulations are common in the working memory literature. Set size manipulations are often used to reveal limitations in working memory or attentional capacity (Baddeley et al., 1975; Oberauer et al., 2016; van den Berg et al., 2014). Moreover, when Leeser et al. (2016) compared the working memory outcomes with sentence interpretation, they found interactions across working memory *task type* × *scoring method* × *type of analysis*. Their conclusions included two important points: (1) even if the scoring methods show high correlation, there may still be relevant differences among them, and (2) depending on the manner tasks are scored and how the variables are modelled, completely different results may emerge. Thus, in answer to our first question, we may conclude that scoring methods do matter.

3.3 Data Analysis

In addition to questions about scoring, a number of concerns have been raised regarding manipulations with statistical analyses. Here, we highlight only a few problems from the literature, specifically cognitive biases and issues related to replicability. Two cognitive biases, "dichotomania" and "nullism" (Greenland, 2017), are common issues in the bilingualism and language impairment literatures. Dichotomania refers to the perception of quantities as dichotomous, even when they are not. We have touched upon this problem in our discussion of the measures of language proficiency. When individuals are grouped as monolingual or bilingual speakers, regardless of their level of language proficiency, then a continuous variable is treated as dichotomous. Greenland (2017) demonstrated this issue with regards to the p value and its categorization as "significant" or "nonsignificant." Significancy, as a dichotomous indicator is determined by the use of a fixed cut-off point, instead of reporting the real value of the p. Another cognitive bias, nullism, is about the assumption of "no difference," even when there is no theoretical or conceptual ground for it. This bias is seen in both frequentist and Bayesian analyses. To avoid this issue, Amrhein and Greenland (2022) suggest that the p value should be calculated for multiple values for the effect size and not just for the null hypothesis that is posited with the assumption of no difference between the inspected values.

Replicability is a further problem in the bilingualism and language impairment literatures. According to Baker (2016), more than 70 percent of active researchers have tried and failed to replicate someone else's experiments. The question is whether replicability is really important and whether it can tell us anything about the quality of research. Given the number of issues related to the selection of participants, tasks, and target functions, it seems inevitable that two studies would differ in a number of variables. Baker (2016), however, found some other answers based on a survey. More than 60 percent of the scientists surveyed reported pressure to publish and selective reporting in the literature as the two main reasons for the low replicability rate. With current funding and promotion systems, the pressure of publishing has not vanished, despite reports of scientific misconduct linked to such pressure (e.g., John et al., 2012). Selective reporting or publication bias was identified as one of the factors behind the inconsistent findings on the bilingual cognitive advantage. De Bruin and colleagues (2015) found that the chances for having one's paper published was much higher (68 percent) if the results supported superior performance in the bilingual group compared to less than half that publication rate (29 percent) if the outcomes showed no group difference in cognitive control between monolingual and bilingual speakers.

These few examples demonstrate that there are many issues that we have been unable to solve yet. Advancements in methodology and research techniques also come with new challenges. It is important, however, to be aware of these issues and incorporate these limitations into the interpretations of the results.

3.4 Bridging the Gap between Scientific Research and Clinical and Educational Approaches

Even though the majority of papers published in applied research journals devote a section to the educational or clinical implications of their research, or to the description of their study's broader impact on the society, there is a critical need for more systematic translational and clinical research, and for greater collaboration among educators, clinicians, and scientists. Cognitive control is a favored topic, not only in research but in education and clinical practice as well (in the latter two fields, the term "executive function" is used). Multiple hypotheses have been suggested to explain the existence of this gap between research and practice, including the differences between the kind of knowledge that educators and clinicians need during their daily practice and the kind that researchers produce and share. Researchers and educators or clinicians also seem to speak "different languages"; they use different terminology; create and present arguments within different conceptual frameworks; and prioritize different ideas and goals (Garivaldo & Fabiano-Smith, 2023; McIntyre, 2005; Nye, Jr., 2008; Snyder et al., 2015). This, of course, is not an exhaustive list of issues that contribute to the largely independent paths that researchers and educators, as well as clinicians follow.

When examining the ways this gap could be narrowed, one of the first steps should undoubtably be the expression of mutual respect toward each other's expertise and the acknowledgement of the value of complementarity. It is crucial that professionals from different disciplines and subject fields demonstrate interest and willingness to work toward intellectual coherence, scholarly merit, and true commitment to teamwork (Hruby, 2012; McIntyre, 2005). An openness toward real dialogues and the expansion of everyone's own knowledge base may further strengthen collaborations and interprofessional practice. These examples are general steps that provide a foundation for more specific strategies related to individual areas of research and practice, such as the investigation and clinical application of cognitive control. Snyder and colleagues (2015) recommended the utilization of different cognitive control models in clinical research and practice.

Their suggestions included the careful selection of specific cognitive control components, the use of multiple tasks for each component, and the extraction of the most sensitive and reliable measures from each task. To further strengthen the partnership and enhance practical relevance, these goals and strategies may be complemented by specific, clinically oriented research questions and approaches, as well as with insider perspectives. A recent exploratory study from the bilingualism literature provides an excellent example of how the quality of research may benefit from the involvement of an insider's perspective (Garivaldo & Fabiano-Smith, 2023). The data from three studies were reanalyzed and reinterpreted by a researcher from within the target community. The combination of a novel theoretical framework and the addition of an insider's perspective resulted in the reinterpretation of the language data that reflected some previously hidden sociolinguistic aspects of the participants' natural language practice.

An in-depth review of the literature shows that the gap between researchers and educators and clinicians is a long-standing one, despite continuous efforts to identify the problems and find solutions. It is a complex problem that involves conceptual, methodological, and ethical issues (Hruby, 2012). Surely in the current digital era, however, we can aspire to find new ways to initiate lively dialogues more easily among professionals from different disciplines.

3.5 Conclusions

In this chapter, we reviewed a few examples from a burgeoning number of methodological problems. Without trying to solve all of these issues, the goal was to demonstrate the complexity of the problems and to call attention to the importance of researchers', educators', and clinicians' awareness of the variety of intricate questions. It is essential that we allow researchers and practitioners to report freely even unexpected and diverse results and findings without having to worry about not getting published or funded because of interpretations that may diverge from the mainstream literature. This is particularly important in research, education, and clinical practice involving disadvantaged communities, groups of speakers of minority languages, and participants from ethnically and culturally diverse backgrounds. Both research and education have to respond more sensitively using individual-difference approaches to the dynamic and distinct practices of the communities in the twenty-first century.

CHAPTER 4

The Effect of Age on First Language Acquisition, Second Language Learning, and Cognitive Control Development

4.1 Age and Language Ability

4.1.1 Individual Differences in Monolingual Typically Developing Children

A detailed discussion of language development in monolingual, typically developing children is beyond the scope of the current chapter. In this section, we highlight only important age-related individual variations in monolingual language acquisition to identify patterns that may help us distinguish typical language development from the development of late talkers and developmental trajectories of bilingual children. The primary focus is on variations in the rate of acquisition and learning style. The effects of the social-communicative environment on age-related individual variations in language acquisition are discussed in Chapter 6, "The Impact of Language Input on Cognitive Control."

Variations in the rate of language acquisition in early childhood are well known and linked to the maturation of the brain, the input from the social-communicative environment, and the interactions between these factors (Hoff, 2013). A number of studies with an individual differences approach have focused on vocabulary development in young children because changes in early vocabulary are relatively easy to measure, and they provide researchers with a sensitive index of language development. In a large study, based on data from 1,800 children on the MacArthur Communicative Development Inventories (CDI), Bates and colleagues (2017) examined individual variations in vocabulary comprehension and production rates. Vocabulary comprehension positively correlated with age by sixteen months, but it only accounted for 36 percent of the variance. The results revealed a complex time course for vocabulary production in children during the first three years of life. While relatively little variance was observed within the first year of age, significant individual variations

54

have been reported after thirteen months, with rapid growth of vocabulary in children with more advanced overall language skills. Even at thirty months of age, the skewed distribution of vocabulary was still present.

Findings with the CDI on a different sample of eight–fourteen-month-old infants/toddlers indicated additional rate differences; some children exhibited fast while others showed slow trajectories of vocabulary development, and there were significantly more girls in the fast group and more boys in the slow group (Bauer et al., 2002). These gender differences in the rate of early vocabulary development have been thought to be linked to variations in brain maturation, particularly in the left inferior frontal gyrus (Blanton et al., 2004). Moreover, these gender differences in vocabulary development may also reflect girls' superior processing efficiency of language input (Barbu et al., 2015).

The developmental patterns of vocabulary comprehension largely overlapped with those of vocabulary production in most children. There were, however, children who showed a dissociation between these two: rapid production despite slow comprehension or a reversed pattern (fast comprehension and slow production). Thus, it is important to note that comprehension and production are not always in synchrony, and this asynchronous pattern is more frequently observed in boys (Bauer et al., 2002). These dissociations may be seen because both comprehension and production are highly influenced by other nonlinguistic factors, such as variations in attention functions and memory, as well as in learning styles.

Furthermore, early vocabulary development is remarkably linked to grammar acquisition. Although most children exhibited earlier and faster growth in comprehension than in production in both vocabulary and grammar acquisition, there were a few who indicated a reversed relationship: better production than comprehension (Fenson et al., 1994). One possible explanation for this finding is that these children used more complex forms without analyzing them. They imitated forms that others used around them in the social environment, without fully comprehending them. Alternatively, the gap between comprehension and production reflects these children's cautious and nonimitative behavior (Bates et al., 1994). These contradictory explanations show the complexity of the relationship among age, individual variations in rate of acquisition, and learning styles.

One specific measure of early grammar development is the use of suffixes. Fenson and colleagues found that very few children use suffixes at the age of sixteen months, whereas almost all children do so by the age of thirty months. The individual variations between sixteen and thirty months are extensive. A particular aspect of suffix use is the onset of tense marking. This was studied within the framework of a maturational model in two–three-year-old slowly developing children (Hadley & Holt, 2006). Robust individual differences were observed even at 30 months of age, and the onset and growth of tense marking was strongly related to children's skills for combining words and using different sentence structures. Children with earlier tense marking typically used longer and/or more complex sentences. Thus, these children showed more advanced overall cognitive-linguistic skills.

Similar to the gender differences in vocabulary, almost all measures of sentence length and complexity revealed a gender effect in a study by Fenson and colleagues (1994). Girls outperformed boys, but the gender difference only accounted for 1–2 percent of the variance. Hence, there are consistent findings on gender differences in early language acquisition in the literature, but their contribution to overall individual variations is small, suggesting important roles of other influential factors that might interact with gender, such as social context and learning style.

Learning styles have been interpreted, either in relation to personality traits or as social psychological concepts, that are determined by a number of factors, personality being only one of them (Kolb & Kolb, 2005b). Depending on the child's age, the communicative context, and the parents' education level, children may exhibit different learning styles that represent a continuum of approaches and not a dichotomic system. For instance, children do not approach every learning situation, either analytically or holistically. If speed of processing is relevant in a given task, then a holistic approach might be more efficient, whereas accuracy would be better supported by a more analytic approach (Bates et al., 2017). Thus, these learning styles interact with speed-accuracy trade-offs. An alternative explanation associates these learning styles with children's working memory capacity. Children with better memory functions may manipulate larger linguistic units (Plunkett, 1993). Thus, they may seem to be more holistic in their language acquisition approach but during information processing, they may rely on their analytic skills because they have the memory capacity for it. Both speed of processing and working memory capacity show rapid development during childhood and reflect close links to language acquisition. For example, children with better nonword repetition skills (i.e., phonological working memory) exhibit larger vocabularies across age groups (Gathercole & Baddeley, 1993).

Bates and colleagues (1994) examined the associations between age and learning style in early childhood and noted that the same measures may signal varying underlying mechanisms at different points in life. For example,

4.1 Age and Language Ability

the proportion of closed-class word production in children's vocabulary during the first years of life (before the child produces 400 words) reflects stylistic variations, whereas in children with a vocabulary larger than 400 words, it is an index of productive grammar. This example also shows that separating learning styles from developmental patterns is often very difficult.

Taken together, these studies show that children's language development, from their first words to early grammar, reflects great variability. This period of language acquisition is characterized by strong dissociations and associations. A dissociative example is that most children exhibit a gap between comprehension and production in both vocabulary and grammatical structures. There are multiple explanations for this finding, but the most likely reason is that these language skills are closely linked to other nonlinguistic cognitive abilities, as well as to environmental factors. Nonetheless, these two modalities explain how associations are further reflected by the robust relationship between vocabulary size and children's sentence production. Studies of language development have to take into consideration both the individual differences and overall general patterns when examining the age effect.

4.1.2 Children Who Are Late or Early Talkers

Although a number of criteria have been used in the literature to identify children with delayed onset of language development, the most common criteria are small vocabulary size (less than 50 words) with no word combinations by the age of two years or vocabulary scores below the 15th percentile at eighteen–twenty-three months (MacRoy-Higgins et al., 2013; Rice et al., 2008). Depending on the criteria of identification, 9–20 percent of toddlers exhibit late language emergence (Suttora et al., 2020; Zubrick et al., 2007), but the majority of those children perform similarly to their typically developing peers on different language tasks by the time they enter school. These children exhibit a transient language delay. Children with persistent language delay, however, show language problems even at the beginning of the school years (Matte-Landry et al., 2020). A number of them are already diagnosed with developmental language disorder (DLD) during preschool. Despite these distinguishing features, late talkers form a heterogeneous group, and the outcomes of language measures vary as functions of age of identification and age at follow-up examination (Rescorla, 2011). There are fewer children with persistent language delays among those who are identified as late talkers early, around 18 months, compared to those who are only identified around 30 months of age (Henrichs et al., 2011). This finding highlights the importance of early identification and intervention.

Many researchers and clinicians have tried to determine which factors could predict later DLD in late talkers, but most of the predictors had low sensitivity and specificity values. Therefore, the findings were inconsistent (Dale et al., 2003). While a number of studies identified expressive language skills as critical predictors, the outcomes from a meta-analysis revealed that the receptive language skills of toddlers showed only a medium significant effect on expressive-language outcomes and expressive-vocabulary size with just a small significant effect for socioeconomic status (Fisher, 2017). In addition to different language tasks, several environmental factors, demographic and birth variables, as well as developmental milestones have been used as predictors, particularly in children below three years of age, but most of them have accounted for only a small percentage of variance (Rescorla, 2011). These mixed outcomes on predictors were highly influenced by variations in tasks and selection criteria. Follow-up studies, however, showed more consistent patterns than did early identification studies. While children with persistent language delays exhibited a range of language and academic difficulties during school years, children with early transient language delays typically had no language or learning problems. These follow-up studies have also revealed that about 30–50 percent of children who were identified as late talkers at the age of two continued to exhibit low language skills even between four–ten years of age (Armstrong et al., 2017; Reilly et al., 2010).

In contrast to late talkers, early talkers, children who produced sentences before the age of twenty-four months and who produced around 300 words by two years of age, showed advanced language and literacy skills during school age (Preston et al., 2010). Further, early talkers exhibited different vocabulary composition and structure than late talkers. These two groups of children knew different sorts of words and exhibited different word learning biases (Colunga & Sims, 2017). Thus, the vocabularies of early talkers were not only larger than those of late talkers but qualitatively different. In addition to these behavioral differences, early and late talker status was strongly related to distinct neural activation patterns as well. At the cortical level, differences included variations in activation in the superior temporal gyrus in response to speech and print. At the subcortical level, it was the putamen and the thalamus that signaled group differences during language processing (Preston et al., 2010). These findings further support the notion that age-related differences in the rate of acquisition are linked to variations in brain maturation.

Taken together, research clarifies that early identification of expressive language problems is critical for both children with transient and persistent language delays. Early and late talkers show different neural activation patterns when processing language. Advanced early language abilities allow children to develop superior language skills later during school age, regardless of domain (e.g., children who produce their first sentences early also develop superior written language skills). In contrast, children who show delayed language emergence may either catch up with their typically developing peers by the time they enter school or exhibit language and academic problems throughout their school years. A large number of these children received the diagnosis of DLD. Language development in children with DLD is discussed in Chapter 1, "The Language Continuum" with a detailed review.

4.2 Age and Language Proficiency

4.2.1 Language Acquisition in Bilingual Children

There is converging evidence in the bilingualism literature about an overall link between age and success of second language (L2) acquisition. The more detailed findings, however, are less cohesive, in part, because there are many contributing factors to successful bilingual language acquisition, and age is only one of them. If we disregard these other factors for a moment, there is still a critical question in the literature related to the conceptualization of L2 age of acquisition. A number of criteria have been used across studies: active daily use of two languages (Luk et al., 2011), age of immersion in an L2 environment (Tao et al., 2011), first exposures and inputs to L2 (Kalia et al., 2014), age at which a child begins to speak in L2 (Kapa & Colombo, 2013), and age at which a child becomes fluent in L2 (Pelham & Abrams, 2014). These age of acquisition criteria reflect very different points in early life. Therefore, they show distinct interactions with language performance.

A further problem is that even though age is a continuous variable, most studies in the literature used overall age of acquisition categories, such as native bilingual speaker (i.e., the child who grows up with two or more languages from birth), early bilingual, and late bilingual. While early bilingual speakers are those who acquire both of their languages during childhood, late bilingual speakers learn the second language typically after puberty or anytime during adulthood. These are gross categories, so the bilingual groups that were based on differences in age of acquisition included individuals with various language experiences. A few studies used more specific age criteria for early and late bilingual speakers, but there is still no consensus in the literature about the specific cut-off points. While Luk and colleagues (2011) considered ten years of age as a cut-off point to distinguish between early and late bilingual groups, Kalia and colleagues (2014) used six years of age for the same purpose. Hence, many inconsistencies in findings in the bilingualism literature may be related to the use of different age-of-onset criteria and to the employment of broad age categories. This is particularly problematic in research with children where the cognitive and linguistic skills are constantly changing with increasing gains in bilingual experience and with the maturation of the brain.

Age-related changes in brain activation have been studied extensively in bilingual individuals, although more studies focused on young adults than on children. Overall, late bilingual speakers showed a greater amount of activation for L2 than individuals who acquired a second language early in childhood (Higby et al., 2013). When early and late English-Spanish bilingual speakers were matched for language proficiency, late L2 learners showed increased activation in Broca's area compared to early bilingual speakers during the processing of irregular grammatical items (Hernandez et al., 2007). Moreover, a number of imaging studies have revealed that in addition to showing an increased activation level, late bilingual individuals recruited wider brain regions than early L2 learners when they were processing speech stimuli (Abutalebi, 2008; Vingerhoets et al., 2003). In an electrophysiological study, Ortiz-Mantilla and colleagues (2010) found that late bilingual speakers showed increased brain responses to both speech and nonspeech stimuli compared to early learners. The findings across neurophysiological studies suggest that late bilingual speakers need to exert more effort when performing the same task compared to their early learner peers, even if they are highly proficient in both of their languages.

Gray matter density has been negatively correlated with age and positively with language proficiency. Overall, bilingual individuals showed greater gray matter density than monolingual speakers, and this effect was greater for early bilingual individuals (i.e., L2 acquisition before the age of 5 years) than for late bilingual speakers (i.e., L2 acquisition between 10–15 years of age). Greater gray matter density was found in the inferior parietal lobule and in adjacent regions of the temporo-parietal cortex (Della Rosa et al., 2013; Grogan et al., 2012; Mechelli et al., 2004). These are important areas in phonological working memory performance, vocabulary acquisition, and semantic processing. Changes in gray matter density may occur

4.3 Age and Cognitive Control Development

4.3.1 Age-Related Changes in Cognitive Control in Typically Developing Monolingual Children

As discussed in Chapter 2, "Cognitive Control," research in this area has shown remarkable growth over the last few decades. In this section, we provide examples of age-related changes in those cognitive control skills that play the most relevant role in language development and academic success. These include working memory, and attention control from four years through adolescence across the working memory components that differed in domain. The tasks in this study were relatively simple compared to those used by Marton and colleagues (2006). The latter study used a theoretical account suggesting that individual differences in working memory capacity reflect variations in executive control, specifically in the ability to maintain goal-relevant information in a context of interference (Engle & Kane, 2004). To test this theoretical hypothesis, Marton and colleagues applied two modified listening span tasks with stimuli that varied in both length and linguistic complexity (i.e., simple short sentences, complex short sentences, and complex long sentences combined with non-word repetition and answers to questions). Three groups were examined in this study: children aged seven–eight and nine–eleven and young adults aged nineteen–twenty-two. The age effect was reflected by the number of errors (younger children made more errors), as well as by differences in performance patterns and error types, particularly with linguistically more complex stimuli. Both age groups of children produced significantly more interference errors than young adults. These findings are in line with Cowan's (2016) suggestions about the role of attention-control behind the age-related differences in working memory capacity.

Attention control itself shows important developmental changes between preschool and early school years. Even though attention control is often viewed as a unitary construct, the developmental trajectories of the different attention functions, such as alerting, orienting to sensory events, and executive attention, vary (Rueda & Posner, 2013). Several studies have reported developmental changes in alertness from preschool to school age and to adulthood. The most common paradigms that have been used to assess alertness are tasks that target responses to explicit cues and tasks of visual searching. Although it has been observed that alertness starts developing early in infancy, age-related changes still occur later in school age. Older children (i.e., 5–7 years) showed greater responsiveness to alerting cues and produced fewer omissions than younger ones, even within relatively restricted age ranges (Mezzacappa, 2004). These findings suggest that older children are able to remain vigilant longer during task performance. Moreover, even ten-year-old children performed more poorly than adults in maintaining an alert state when there was no explicit signal (Rueda et al., 2004). The reasons for the late development of these alerting skills and the age at which children achieve the same level as adults remain unclear.

Orienting has an early onset, as well. Although infants are able to orient their attention to different environmental stimuli, the attention system continues developing throughout childhood and adolescence (Rueda & Posner, 2013). Age differences in orienting functions, however, are also task-dependent. While Rueda and colleagues (2004) found no change in orienting after six years of age using a simple flanker task, Schul and colleagues (2003) reported more accurate and faster orienting with age in children between seven and seventeen years of age and in adults with a variant of Posner's cost-benefit attentional cueing paradigm, that included a focused attention and an attention shifting task. Younger children needed longer cue-to-target intervals to orient attention than older participants. The difference in performance with long (800 ms) versus short (100 ms) cue-to-target intervals gradually decreased with age.

The third component, executive attention, shows the latest onset. However, it is important to note that this function is often measured with more complex tasks, such as conflict paradigms. Different versions of spatial conflict tasks have been administered to children as early as two–four years of age. In these tasks, participants had to press a button or point to the target item (e.g., animals, stars) on a screen. The stimuli appeared either on the same side of the screen or on opposite sides. While two-year-old children showed difficulty with the task by exhibiting low accuracy and a significant congruency effect (i.e., more errors when the items were on opposite sides), their three-year-old peers performed with high accuracy and smaller congruency effect, although their speed was slower than that of older children or adults in previous studies (Gerardi-Caulton, 2000). Further development in both speed and accuracy of conflict processing has been observed in children between four and seven and six and nine years of age using variations of the flanker task (e.g., the fish ANT task), in which children had to decide whether the central fish was facing left or right by

4.3 Age and Cognitive Control Development 63

pressing the corresponding left or right arrow key. In the congruent condition, all items faced the same direction, whereas in the incongruent condition, the central item faced the opposite direction from the surrounding items (Rueda & Posner, 2013; Rueda et al., 2004). The results from different conflict paradigms indicate early development (around 3 years) in accuracy; a gradual decrease in speed throughout childhood; and simultaneously, a decrease in the congruency effect. Thus, children become more efficient in performing tasks with conflicts, an outcome which reflects age-related, positive changes in attention control and monitoring skills.

Error and performance monitoring in children are frequently studied with different neurophysiological methods or by calculating post-error slowing in behavioral performance. One common electrophysiological measure of error monitoring is error-related negativity (ERN), that typically peaks around 50–100 ms following an erroneous response in speeded tasks (Hajcak, 2012; Tamnes et al., 2013). Even though a number of studies reported developmental changes throughout childhood in the ERN amplitude, particularly in more complex tasks, the findings were more mixed about the ERN latency (Davies et al., 2004; Wiersema et al., 2007). Davies and colleagues studied the age-related changes in the ERN in seven–twenty-five-year-old participants and documented an increase in the ERN amplitude in error trials with age. The findings linked the ERN to the dorsal and/or rostral part of the anterior cingulate cortex (ACC) and supported the concept of a late maturation of the ACC.

In a recent study, Kang and colleagues (2021) combined error and novelty monitoring using the ERN and the N2, respectively, in eight–sixteen-year-old participants who performed a modified flanker task. At the behavioral level, older children showed higher accuracy rates, faster speed, and smaller variability in reaction time than the younger children. Likewise, the electrophysiological correlates showed age-related differences. While the error-related ERN was larger in the older children, the novelty-linked N2 was larger in the younger ones. In addition to these developmental trends, individual variations in the ERN amplitude correlated with children's behavioral post-error slowing (see Chapter 8, "Processing Speed and Cognitive Control," for detailed discussion). Larger ERN amplitude was linked to larger post-error slowing. Thus, the ERN amplitude reflected the behavioral adjustments in response to an error, and these processes were more mature in older than in younger children. This finding was in line with the outcomes of other studies that also reported major developmental changes in post-error slowing between six and ten years of age (Gupta et al., 2009). The greater N2 amplitude in response to novelty in younger children may suggest a sensitivity in neural processes to irrelevant stimuli. It is well documented in the literature that younger children are less efficient in resisting interference from irrelevant stimuli than their older peers (Cragg, 2016; Marton et al., 2014).

Interference control has been conceptualized differently across theoretical models. According to one of the most widely accepted accounts (Friedman and Miyake, 2004), resistance to interference is an inhibition-related function. In their model, three inhibitory functions are distinguished: inhibition of a prepotent response, resistance to distractor interference, and resistance to proactive interference. While response inhibition refers to the blocking of an automatic behavior in response to a stimulus (e.g., stopping the ongoing activity when a sound is presented), resisting distractor interference is about selectively focusing on the target while avoiding distraction from the surrounding items (e.g., choosing the appropriate picture from a pool that consists of targets and competing distractor items). Finally, proactive interference control is about resisting internal sources (memory traces) that may hinder efficient information processing (e.g., suppressing irrelevant information from previous tasks or items). The degree of correlation among these inhibition-related functions varies (response inhibition shows greater correlation with distractor interference than with proactive interference), and these three functions show distinct developmental trajectories.

Variations of Go-NoGo and Stop-Signal tasks have been used to examine response inhibition across age groups. There is converging evidence of age-related changes in children aged three–five years (Dowsett & Livesey, 2000) and six–eight years (Lewis et al., 2017). The three-year-olds made more errors and indicated slower processing than their four–five-year-old peers. The error rate was also higher for children aged six–seven years than for older participants aged eight–eleven years. In contrast, speed of processing showed continuous development between the ages of six and twelve years (Lewis et al., 2017; Williams et al., 1999).

The most frequently used measures of distractor interference are the Simon, Stroop, and flanker tasks. The Simon and flanker tasks are considered to be conflict paradigms that reflect similar congruency effects (Hübner & Töbel, 2019). The Stroop test also measures conflict, but there is debate in the literature about the functions it reflects. While Stroop himself claimed that the task measures interference (MacLeod, 1991), Houben and Wiers (2009) suggested that the task assesses automatic response inhibition. Task impurity is a common issue with most cognitive control tasks, because they tend to measure multiple functions simultaneously (see

Chapter 3, "Methodological Issues"). In a developmental study with adults and children aged five–fourteen years, Ambrosi and colleagues (2020) compared performance on these three interference tasks (i.e., Simon, Stroop, flanker). Even though these tasks are often used interchangeably in the literature, Ambrosi's study showed that the developmental trajectories of the interference effects differed across tasks. Children as early as five years of age already showed adult-like performance on the Simon task, while age-related changes have been observed throughout childhood for the Stroop and flanker tasks, although for the latter, the findings were less consistent.

The third inhibitory function, proactive interference, is regularly examined using different versions of working memory or short-term memory tasks. Kail (2002) reported age-related decline in proactive interference based on two studies using the Brown-Peterson paradigm. The first study was a meta-analysis of twenty-six published papers including children aged four–nine years, whereas the second study reported findings from a new experiment with adults and children aged nine–twelve years. Findings from both studies indicated that resisting interference from previous items and memory traces develops throughout childhood. Moreover, the second study also showed that the age-related changes in proactive interference are mediated by the development of processing speed. Thus, increases in age are linked to decreases in proactive interference and to increases in the speed of processing.

Altogether, the findings indicate that while the three inhibition-related functions are conceptually linked, they also show dissociations. They differ in the age of maturation and in developmental trajectories. Response inhibition becomes mature toward the beginning of school age, whereas the different interference functions develop throughout childhood and adolescence. Task complexity and the underlying mechanisms that are reflected by the different experimental paradigms interact with age-related changes. The same children perform differently on tasks that are thought to measure the same functions. Moreover, none of these tasks target only one specific function, therefore the differences in developmental changes may also reflect interactions among cognitive control functions and processing speed.

Finally, task switching is typically examined with versions of the Dimensional Change Card Sort task (Zelazo, 2006). Participants are instructed to sort binary cards first according to one dimension (e.g., color) and then according to another dimension (e.g., shape). Children at the age of three are able to sort the cards according to one of the dimensions but fail to switch to the other dimension when instructed. They perseverate with the post-switch items. By the age of five, typically developing children perform with great accuracy on this task, but children with various neurocognitive disorders, including DLD, show inflexibility and perseverate longer. Their diminished cognitive flexibility has been associated with weaknesses in working memory updating (Morton & Munakata, 2002) and delayed or impaired maturation of the prefrontal cortex (Friedman & Robbins, 2022).

While performance on the Dimensional Change Card Sort task becomes highly accurate by the age of five, processing speed continues to develop. Moreover, associations between slower processing speed and greater improvements in accuracy (i.e., speed-accuracy trade-off) have been identified in children between five and six years of age as well as between six and seven years. Besides these trade-offs, higher accuracy rates at six years predicted faster processing speed at seven years of age (Dumont et al., 2022).

Taken together, the development of cognitive control functions is neither unitary nor linear. There are both associations and dissociations among the different functions that are also reflected in the variations in developmental trajectories of these cognitive control skills (see Figure 4.1). Age-related changes are influenced by a number of factors, in addition to brain maturation, such as task complexity and task impurity, individual variations in processing speed, and language status.

4.3.2 Cognitive Control in Late Talkers

The focus in this section is primarily on preschool-age children because by school age, late talkers either catch up or are diagnosed with DLD. Age-related changes in cognitive control in typically developing children (i.e., children who catch up with their peers) have been discussed above, whereas cognitive control in children with DLD is discussed in detail in Chapter 5, "Associations among Language Ability, Language Proficiency, and Cognitive Control."

The cognitive control skills of late talkers were examined to see whether they differed from those of preschool-age children who received an early diagnosis of DLD (Dodd, 2011). Even though both groups performed with low accuracy on a number of language tasks (phonology, vocabulary, etc.), children with DLD produced more severe errors than the late talkers. Furthermore, the groups differed in certain cognitive control functions, such as flexibility. Cognitive flexibility was measured with a card sorting task that included color, shape, and size as set rules. Children with

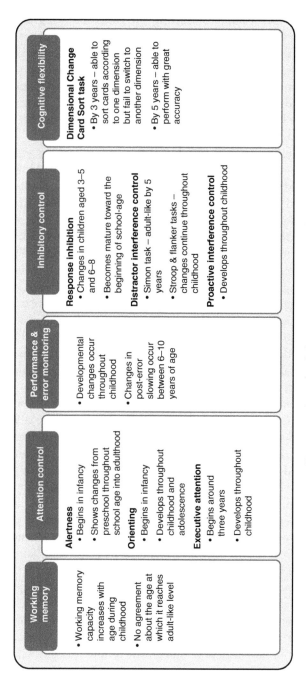

Figure 4.1 Age-related changes in cognitive control

DLD showed more difficulty sorting the cards following a rule switch than children with language delay. Children with DLD did perseverate on the first rule that they were presented with, while children with language delay performed the task with more flexibility. These findings support the idea that cognitive control tasks, particularly the ones with minimal language demands, may help to differentiate between children with DLD and children with language differences, such as delayed language development or low English L2 proficiency (Marton et al., 2019).

With a similar idea in mind, Kautto and colleagues (2021) tested whether the inhibitory functions at school age would distinguish between children who had a history of delayed language development but exhibited typical language skills in school age from those with a history of language delay and a later diagnosis of DLD. In addition to language testing, children were examined with a flanker task. Although the accuracy data did not show the expected interactions among early language status, flanker performance, and late talker outcomes, the reaction time data revealed overall slower processing in children with DLD. More efficient processing speed in the flanker task was associated with more advanced language skills. The authors listed many limitations of the study that may have contributed to the lack of group difference in accuracy on the flanker task. Therefore, future research is needed to see whether certain cognitive control skills in preschoolers could predict later language status.

Working memory performance proved to be a better measure for distinguishing among groups of children with typical language development, DLD, and a history of delayed language development but typical language outcomes by the age of five years (Petruccelli et al., 2012). Working memory was tested using six different tasks across the domains of phonological memory, visuospatial memory, and linguistic span. Although children showed different performance patterns across modalities, the outcomes on nonword repetition and sentence recall clearly distinguished the groups. Both typically developing children and their peers with a history of language delay but no later language impairment performed better than the children with DLD. The former two groups performed similarly on every working memory measure. Although these data are promising, the question remains whether nonword repetition and sentence recall can distinguish late talkers at the age of three. Thus, future research should determine whether these tasks can be designed to predict who among the late talkers will catch up in language development by school age and who will continue showing language problems.

4.3.3 Interaction between Age of Language Acquisition and Cognitive Control in Bilingual Speakers

As demonstrated above, it is not easy to determine the age of second language acquisition because of the variations in the criteria that have been used in the literature and the individual differences in children's bilingual experience. It is well known that the age of L2 acquisition interacts with other aspects of the bilingual experience, such as the frequency of language use or the amount of exposure. Given these challenges, there are only a few studies that have focused on the relationship between the age of L2 acquisition or the age of becoming bilingual and the development of cognitive control.

In a cross-sectional study, Carlson and Meltzoff compared (2008) three groups of kindergarten children on a number of cognitive control tasks (attention and interference control; task switching; and short-term memory). Children were either monolingual, Spanish–English bilingual from birth (i.e., native bilingual), or participated in a bilingual immersion program with a six-month exposure to the L2. While the native bilingual children outperformed the monolingual children on the cognitive control tasks, particularly on tasks that involved conflict, participants in the immersion program, who were emerging bilingual children, did not exhibit this cognitive advantage compared to their monolingual peers. Although the findings suggest an effect of age of language acquisition on cognitive control, it is important to note that the emerging bilingual and native bilingual children also differed in the amount of exposure and L2 language use. This study provides another example of how difficult it is to disentangle the different aspects of the bilingual experience.

Luk and colleagues (2011) provided further evidence for the effect of age of L2 acquisition on cognitive control. They compared early and late bilingual individuals' performance on a flanker task, in which participants had to indicate whether the direction of a red chevron in the center was the same as the directions of surrounding black chevrons. The flanker task is typically considered to measure resistance to distractor interference and sustained attention. In this study, early bilingual participants had become actively bilingual before the age of ten years, while late bilingual participants had acquired their L2 after ten years of age. Even though the early bilingual and monolingual college students exhibited similar levels of language proficiency in English, the two groups differed in the flanker effect. Early bilingual students showed better resistance to distractor interference than their monolingual peers. In contrast, late bilingual students showed

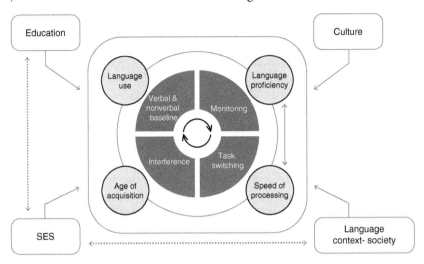

Figure 4.2 Interactions among language acquisition and proficiency, cognitive control, and environmental factors in bilingual speakers

lower language proficiency in English than the monolingual students, but the two groups performed similarly on the flanker task. Hence, early acquisition of two languages resulted in higher language proficiency and better resistance to interference than late L2 acquisition.

Interestingly, Tao and colleagues (2011) found a more complex relationship between the age of language acquisition and cognitive control. In their study, early versus late bilingualism was determined by the age of arrival to the country. Early bilingual speakers arrived before the age of six years, whereas late bilingual individuals arrived after twelve years of age. Both early and late bilingual speakers showed superior performance compared to their monolingual peers on a task of monitoring and attention control. Furthermore, late bilingual speakers, who showed a high level of proficiency and language use, outperformed the early bilingual participants in conflict resolution. In contrast, early bilingual speakers exhibited better monitoring skills than their late bilingual peers. These outcomes are particularly interesting given that efficient conflict resolution requires good monitoring. These findings further confirm the complex relationship among the different aspects of the bilingual experience and their interaction with cognitive control (see Figure 4.2). Age of acquisition interacts with language input, frequency of language use, and language proficiency, and their cumulative effect on cognitive control results in different patterns of performance.

4.4 Conclusions

Language acquisition is characterized by strong associations and dissociations among the different linguistic rule systems and other cognitive functions during the early years. Individual differences in language acquisition are linked to the development of other nonlinguistic cognitive abilities, brain maturation, and environmental factors. Hence, there is no single cut-off point that could be used to determine the specific age of L2 acquisition or that at which a language delay predicts the presence of a language disorder. Early identification of expressive language problems, however, is critical for children with both transient and persistent language delays. When specific cognitive control components and processes are examined, it becomes clear that the development of cognitive control functions is neither unitary nor linear. Nevertheless, various developmental trajectories can be observed in children with different language skills, as the age of language acquisition shows an overall interaction with cognitive control functions.

CHAPTER 5

Associations between Language Ability, Language Proficiency, and Cognitive Control

5.1 Conceptual Background, Terminology, and Measures

The terms "language proficiency" and "ability" are often used interchangeably in the literature (see Chapter 1, "The Language Continuum" for a detailed discussion of the issue). The focus in this chapter is on the relationship between cognitive control and language proficiency and language use in monolingual and bilingual children with different language abilities. While we use the term language ability in reference to children's language and communication skills that are typically measured with standardized language tests with the goal of detecting the presence or absence of a language disorder, we discuss language proficiency with regards to bilingual children's functional language use, that is their overtly observable language performance (Jilka, 2009). This use of terminology is consistent with Birdsong's (2014) definition, which specifies proficiency as individual language skills used across different domains (e.g., conversations, listening to speech). These skills have been assessed with both subjective (questionnaires, "can do" lists) and objective measures (standardized language tests). The problems related to the use of standardized tests as a measure of language proficiency rather than language ability have been discussed in the previous Chapters 1 and 3, "The Language Continuum" and "Methodological Issues," so here, we only reiterate the findings of Bedore and colleagues, whose research has shown that tests often used interchangeably to measure children's various language skills were developed for other purposes. Tests of language proficiency have not been designed to identify children with language disorders, and tests that were developed to determine the presence of language disorders do not provide appropriate measures to quantify language proficiency (Bedore et al., 2012). A further problem in the literature is that language talent is often measured by the number of languages a person acquires and how native-like their accent in their second language (L2) is rather than by their ease of L2 acquisition.

5.1 Concepts, Terminology, and Measures 73

Nevertheless, our goal in this chapter is to examine the associations between the different language skills and children's cognitive control skills. To do so, we first examine the interactions between language ability and proficiency (e.g., language proficiency in children with language talent) and then, we discuss appropriate measures for children with different language skills. Even though the term bilingual is often used synonymously with multilingual in the bilingualism literature (see Higby et al., 2013), we distinguish between these terms in this chapter because the brain networks of people who speak at least three or more languages differ from those who speak only two languages (Cenoz et al., 2003b), and this may affect their cognitive control skills. Moreover, in this chapter, it is also important to distinguish between multilingualism and language talent because many multilingual individuals speak their languages at varying proficiency levels across different contexts, and not all individuals who speak three or more languages exhibit language talent. Even among children with language disorders, there are some who grow up speaking three languages (e.g., English at school, Spanish and French at home).

In the L2 acquisition literature, language talent is defined as aptitude, in reference to unusual cognitive strengths that an individual demonstrates during language acquisition across different settings (Robinson, 2005). Studies interested in language talent typically take an individual-differences approach to identify the specific characteristics in aptitude in individuals with and without language talent and to determine those aptitude components that predict more efficient language acquisition and higher language proficiency. This question can be examined by exploring individual differences in information processing during the performance of L2 tasks with varying cognitive demands. Studies taking this approach typically include traditional measures of phonetic and grammatical sensitivity, rote memory, lexical access, as well as more recently, working memory tests, measures of emotional responses to learning (e.g., anxiety level), emotional intelligence, motivation, and self-regulation (Moyer, 2014; Sparks et al., 2011; Wen & Skehan, 2011).

In children at the other end of the language ability continuum, those with DLD, measuring language proficiency is very challenging, and it typically requires a within-subject approach. It is important to distinguish between errors that are related to the child's language disorder and their level of functional language use. When working with children with DLD, the measures of proficiency cannot be substituted with measures of ability. For example, using a standardized vocabulary test to assess a bilingual child's language proficiency is not appropriate in children with DLD because the results may reflect the child's limitations related to the

74 Language Ability, Proficiency, and Cognitive Control

disorder. Language proficiency in children with DLD may be better determined based on the outcomes of semi-structured interviews conducted in both languages of the child by bilingual speech-language pathologists. A set of conversational topics could be used to elicit speech samples that offer a view of the communicative exchanges relevant to the child's social-interactive and academic experiences.

5.2 The Relationship between Language Proficiency, Exposure, and Language Use

This section is focused on the utilization of subjective and objective methods of language proficiency with regards to language exposure and the frequency of language use. While some scholars make no distinction between the terms exposure and language use, interpreting both terms as the time that a person is engaged with a specific language (Bedore et al., 2016), others differentiate between active use of language, such as engaging in conversation, and passive exposure to language, such as having a certain language spoken in the vicinity (Hoff et al., 2012; for more details, see Chapter 6, "Impact of Language Input on Cognitive Control").

In a recent study, we examined whether the measures of language proficiency that have been used interchangeably in the literature provide similar outcomes in groups of bilingual students (young adults) experiencing different degrees of exposure to English in their daily lives (Gehebe et al., 2023). We defined exposure within the theoretical framework of Grosjean (1989), who described a continuum of language modes referring to different activation levels of language. Language modes are highly influenced by various contextual factors, such as the conversational partner or the language context of the activity. The central notion in Grosjean's theory is that, regardless of modality, bilingual individuals activate both of their languages immediately when they are exposed to any activities involving elements of either language. Therefore, we used the term language exposure in reference to the time during which individuals focus their attention on processing either spoken or written language. We compared language proficiency by using objective and subjective measures in three groups. Our results showed that participants with high English exposure (80–95 percent daily) exhibited similar proficiency levels with each type of language measure (i.e., subjective questionnaires and "can do" lists or objective vocabulary tests and sentence completion tasks). Conversely, the different measures of proficiency showed only a moderate correlation in participants with medium (50–70 percent daily) and low exposure (20–40 percent daily). It appears that these subjective and objective measures target distinct language skills that may undergo varying levels of development in individuals with medium and low language exposure. Therefore, the use of both subjective and objective measures is necessary in bilingual speakers with medium or low language exposure. These findings suggest complex interactions between language proficiency and exposure across different modalities.

Several studies have also shown a strong relationship between language proficiency and the frequency of language use (Luk & Bialystok, 2013; Ribot et al., 2018). Luk and Bialystok performed a factor analysis to examine the factors contributing to the bilingual experience. The two strongly related and most relevant factors were language proficiency and the frequency of language use. Consistent with these findings are the results of Ribot and colleagues (2018), who studied preschool-age Spanish–English bilingual children. Their results revealed that children's frequency of language use affected their language proficiency level as measured by an expressive vocabulary test. Those children who used one of their languages more frequently showed greater expressive vocabulary in that language. This finding adds further information to the existing literature on the positive relationship between expressive vocabulary and the diversity of language input (Chondrogianni & Marinis, 2011; Hoff, 2003).

5.3 Language Proficiency and Cognitive Control

In this chapter, we sidestep the debate prevalent in the literature regarding the "bilingual cognitive advantage" because the majority of those studies focused on performance differences between bilingual and monolingual individuals, and the bilingual groups often involved individuals with differing proficiency levels. Here, we are interested specifically in the interactions between language proficiency variations and performance differences in cognitive control. Both behavioral and neurophysiological studies suggest that language proficiency modulates the engagement of cognitive control processes. Thus, bilingual individuals with higher language proficiency outperform their peers with lower language proficiency in cognitive control tasks, such as tasks of cognitive flexibility and interference control (Abutalebi et al., 2013; Ibrahim et al., 2013; Kheder & Kaan, 2021). For example, bilingual listeners' processing of auditorily presented sentences often involves phonetic and phonological similarities between the target and distractor languages, but the extent of interference experienced by the speakers is modulated by their level of language proficiency (Kim et al., 2019). Unfortunately, most of the studies examining this relationship involved adults, so there are few studies in children. Yet, the results appear to be consistent across age groups.

Iluz-Cohen and Armon-Lotem (2013) studied cognitive control in subgroups of four–seven-year-old, English–Hebrew-speaking bilingual children, balanced across *high proficient bilingual, L2-dominant, L1-dominant,* and *low proficient* in both languages. Children with high language proficiency outperformed their peers with low language proficiency in resisting interference and task switching but not in concept generation. The results suggest that the modulatory effect of language proficiency may vary, depending on the target function. One critical issue related to this study is that there was no differentiation between language proficiency and language ability. Children's language skills were measured with standardized language tests in both English and Hebrew. Children in the first three groups performed within the typical range in at least one of their languages, so those were classified as bilingual children with average language ability who differed in language proficiency. The fourth group, performing below average in both languages, was thus considered to exhibit low proficiency in addition to low language ability. Despite confounding issues with the low proficiency/ability group, this study remains important as one of the first studies in children to call attention to the modulating role of language proficiency in cognitive control.

Similar results have been reported by Marton (2019), who measured language proficiency as a continuous variable in eight–eleven-year-old bilingual children, all of whom had English as their primary language while their non-English language varied (Spanish, Russian, Hebrew, Urdu, and Portuguese). Cognitive control was measured with a verbal categorization task, including different conditions (e.g., targeting proactive interference). Language proficiency was positively correlated with a number of cognitive control skills. More proficient bilingual children performed faster and more accurately than their less proficient and monolingual English-speaking peers in resisting proactive interference (i.e., interference from previous memory traces; see Figure 5.1). Highly proficient bilingual children showed smaller intrusion costs (the difference in response to neutral vs. interfering distractor items) than children with lower language proficiency. In tasks that measured performance monitoring and implicit learning, children with higher language proficiency performed faster than their low proficient peers but showed similar performance patterns in accuracy. Another component that further affected the relationship between language proficiency and cognitive control was the frequency of language use. Even among the highly proficient bilingual children, there were variations in language use. Some of these children used both of their

5.3 Language Proficiency and Cognitive Control

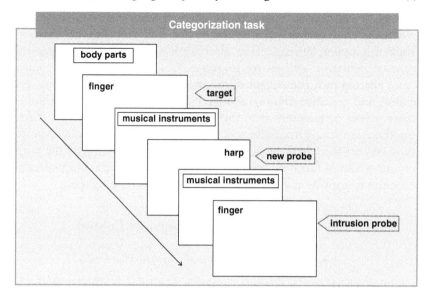

Figure 5.1 Conflict paradigm: Verbal categorization task

languages 50 percent of the time on a daily basis, whereas others used their non-English language as little as 10 percent of the time. The former group showed better resistance to interference and more efficient performance monitoring than the latter group. Hence, this study also confirmed that the relationship between language proficiency and cognitive control is influenced by children's bilingual language use, by the target cognitive control function, and by the type of measurement.

Based on these findings, Marton (2019) further examined how language proficiency and processing speed interact with different cognitive control functions using path analysis (Loehlin, 2004). The results showed that language proficiency and cognitive control interact in multiple ways. Language proficiency had a direct effect on children's intrusion errors and on their processing speed in a task measuring interference control, but in a monitoring task, the effect of language proficiency was mediated by the speed of processing (see details about this analysis in Chapter 8). These findings strengthen the notion that language proficiency, processing speed, and cognitive control show complex interactions, and future research is needed to further our understanding about this relationship.

The link between language proficiency and processing speed was also studied in ten–eleven-year-old multilingual children in tasks targeting attention control (Videsott et al., 2012). All the children went to schools where they were taught in Italian half of the time and in German for the other half, with Ladin as a support language. Thus, all children spoke all three languages with varying proficiency levels across languages. Children's multilingual competence affected each component of the attention network (i.e., alerting, orienting, and executive control), and the highly proficient children exhibited faster overall performance than their peers with lower proficiency. Taken together, the existing studies involving children suggest that cognitive control functions are modulated by language proficiency. Depending on the target cognitive control function, language proficiency may have a direct effect on cognitive control, or its effect may be mediated by processing speed.

5.4 Language Ability and Cognitive Control

5.4.1 Language Talent and Cognitive Control

Children with language talent are not often identified as gifted in the bilingualism literature. Instead, they are characterized as bilingual children with high language proficiency. More attention has been given to language talent in the second language acquisition rather than the bilingualism literature, even though the definitions of talent and proficiency remain inconsistent. While some scholars have suggested that motivation, practice, and experience contribute to the degree of language proficiency but not to talent (Jilka, 2009), others have linked talent and the core concept of foreign language aptitude to different learning contexts, attitude, and experience (Moyer, 2014; Wen & Skehan, 2011).

In the last two decades, research on language learning aptitude has expanded and has become associated with information processing. At the lower level of information processing, it is phonetic and phonemic coding and production that have been linked to language learning aptitude in individuals with a language talent, whereas at the higher level, working memory, attention control, and implicit learning have been related to the construct of aptitude (Mercer & Ryan, 2010; Wen & Skehan, 2011). Similar to the positive findings on the relationship between working memory and language acquisition and processing in monolingual children (e.g., Archibald, 2017; Baddeley, 2003; Gathercole & Baddeley, 1993), individuals with language talent, who have acquired multiple languages, have also exhibited more efficient working memory performance and superior attention control compared to their peers (Dörnyei & Skehan, 2003). Earlier studies have already shown better performance in students with language

5.4 Language Ability and Cognitive Control

talent in verbal working memory measures, such as nonword repetition and auditory digit span (Papagno & Vallar, 1995), and the results have shown correlations with enhanced word-learning skills (Baddeley et al., 1998). Thus, children with language talent exhibited more efficient word learning than typically developing children. More recent research has integrated these findings at a conceptual level with advanced language aptitude, including phonological coding, grammatical sensitivity, and attention control. Future synthesis of these constructs at the conceptual level still requires empirical evidence. Therefore, more research is needed to compare language learning aptitude in typical bilingual children and in children with language talent.

Another critical component of cognitive control is monitoring because it helps to prevent and/or reduce interference between the competing language systems in multilingual individuals. Children with language talent exhibited enhanced monitoring skills measured by an attentional network task, and these behavioral findings were complemented by changes in brain structures (Della Rosa, 2013). In a longitudinal study with nine-year-old children speaking German, Italian, Ladin, and English, Della Rosa and colleagues found brain adaptations in the lower parietal region (LIPL) that has been called the "language talent area" in the literature. These plastic changes in the LIPL region have been linked to improved attention, memory, and phonological categorization that support monitoring and control of the competing languages. The study confirmed that children with language talent are not only able to acquire multiple languages, but also exhibit specific changes in the brain that are associated with potential cognitive benefits, such as enhanced attention control.

Taken together, very few studies have differentiated between language talent and high language proficiency in bilingual and multilingual individuals. Most studies that attempted to do so were theoretical in nature. Hence, there is scarcity in empirical studies examining the interaction between language proficiency and ability, particularly in children. In future studies, the differentiation between language ability and proficiency in multilingual children may help us to clarify some questions related to the existence of the bilingual cognitive advantage.

5.4.2 Developmental Language Disorder and Cognitive Control

5.4.2.1 Cognitive Control in Monolingual Children with DLD

Information processing limitations have been widely researched in children with DLD, and weaknesses were reported across modalities and domains. It is important to study cognitive control in children with DLD because it plays a critical role in working memory updating and language processing (Van Dyke & Johns, 2012), as well as in children's academic performance (St Clair-Thompson & Gathercole, 2006). Major weaknesses in information processing and cognitive control have been associated with difficulties in working memory, attention skills, and inhibitory control. Working memory research of the past two decades has shown extensive growth, including the child language disorder literature. Given the magnitude of the working memory literature and the consistency in findings across studies including children with DLD, we summarize here only the main outcomes. Working memory studies focusing on children with DLD have been framed using various theoretical accounts, such as the resource theories (e.g., Just & Carpenter, 1992), decay theories (e.g., Baddeley, 2003), and interference theories (e.g., Oberauer et al., 2012). The employment of these different conceptual approaches resulted in the use of various methodologies across modalities and domains. In the verbal domain, both preschool and school-age children have been tested using nonword repetition, digit- and word span, sentence span, and N-back tasks. There is converging evidence in the literature that children with DLD perform more poorly than their typically developing peers on these verbal working memory measures (e.g., Archibald & Gathercole, 2006a; Ladányi & Lukács, 2019; Marton & Schwartz, 2003; Montgomery, 2003) and produce different error patterns than their peers (e.g., more interference errors; Marton, 2006; Marton et al., 2007). Fewer studies have examined visuospatial working memory in children with DLD, and the findings are not as robust as in the verbal working memory literature, but the overall results indicate weaknesses in this domain too, regardless of age (Hick et al., 2005; Marton, 2008; Vugs et al., 2013). Taken together, the findings across studies suggest a critical working memory problem in children with DLD that is not modality or domain specific.

Another extensively studied area of cognitive control in the DLD literature is attention control. Given that attention is not a unitary construct, it is unsurprising that children with DLD exhibit weaknesses in certain attention skills but not in others. In both simple nonverbal vigilance tasks and in tasks measuring attention shifting, children with DLD performed similarly to their age-matched peers (Henry et al., 2012; Im-Bolter et al., 2006; Marton et al., 2012). In sustained attention, however, the outcomes were different. Children with DLD (4–7 years old) exhibited difficulties in visual sustained attention using the visual Continuous PerformanceTask with epoch (i.e., first through fifth minute of testing) and rate manipulations (i.e., fast and slow stimulus presentation rates; Finneran et al., 2009).

Children with DLD produced fewer hits and more false alarms than their typically developing peers. Thus, children with DLD were less attentive but more impulsive than their peers, particularly with the fast rate of stimulus presentation. A slightly different result was found by Marton and colleagues (2012) with older children (10–14 years old) using a different visual sustained attention task in which children had to detect target sequences in a stream of digits that were presented in pseudo-random order on a computer screen. The number of hits were similar for the children with DLD and their peers, but the number of correct rejects differed. Children with DLD rejected fewer error items, suggesting that these children had difficulty deciding whether an item was relevant or not, even though they were attending to the stimuli. Based on these two studies (Finneran et al., 2009; Marton et al., 2012), attentional focus shows improvement with age in children with DLD during the school years, but sustained attention remains problematic because of these children's difficulties in distinguishing relevant information.

Spaulding and colleagues (2008) studied sustained attention in four–six-year-old children with DLD across different stimulus conditions: visual, nonverbal auditory, and linguistic. Unlike the other studies (Finneran et al., 2009; Marton et al., 2012), Spaulding and colleagues found no group difference in visual attention, but they did identify weaknesses in the nonverbal auditory and the linguistic attention tasks in children with DLD. All three studies used different tasks to examine visual attention; while the Finneran and Marton studies used more abstract stimuli and had more complex conditions, the Spaulding study employed a more holistic and more child-friendly task. Given the group differences in nonverbal auditory and linguistic attention in the latter study, all studies reported difficulties in sustained attention in children with DLD, but the findings indicate that children's performance may differ across modalities and domains and is highly influenced by the nature of the task. Age-related differences may also contribute to the mixed results in attention control.

In line with the findings of Spaulding and colleagues were the outcomes from an audio-visual speech perception study in an eye-tracking experiment that examined five–nine-year-old children's attention to people's mouths as they were talking. Children with DLD paid significantly less attention to an individual's mouth than their peers. Moreover, typically developing children spent more time attending to a person's mouth than to their eyes, whereas children with DLD looked at mouths and eyes equally, showing no preference to either (Pons et al., 2018). Even though several studies identified weaknesses in attention control in children with

82 Language Ability, Proficiency, and Cognitive Control

DLD, taken together, these difficulties are less general than the working memory problems. As we have shown, children with DLD perform similarly to their peers in simple attention tasks, such as vigilance, or in tasks with less complex conditions, but they do exhibit problems with more complex tasks, particularly in the auditory modality.

The third cognitive control construct related to information processing problems in children with DLD is inhibitory control, including both distractor and proactive interference (i.e., resisting environmental or memory trace distractions), as well as response inhibition (Friedman & Miyake, 2017). Distractor interference has been studied in both auditory and visual modalities, in verbal and nonverbal domains, and in preschool and school-age children with DLD. Proactive interference has been studied only in school-age children with visual verbal tasks.

Spaulding (2010) investigated resistance to distractor interference in preschool-age children with verbal and nonverbal auditory stimuli (i.e., distracting sentences and environmental sounds), as well as with visual distractors. All children were susceptible to distraction, but this negative effect on performance was greater for children with DLD than for their typically developing peers. A comparison across modalities and domains revealed that typically developing children performed better on the task with linguistic distractors than on the others, whereas children with DLD performed similarly across modalities and domains. These children showed difficulty suppressing any irrelevant information regardless of the nature of the stimuli.

Im-Bolter and colleagues (2006) used a mental attention memory task to measure distractor interference in the verbal domain. Their task design included three conditions with different degrees of interference. The highest degree of interference was targeted with a modified Stroop task. All children, aged seven–twelve years, performed more poorly as the degree of interference increased, but children with DLD exhibited more difficulty than their typically developing peers across task conditions. Interestingly, with the increase in interference, the group differences decreased, meaning that the typically developing children also showed significant difficulties at the highest levels of interference.

For a visual nonverbal task in children aged ten–fourteen with DLD, we also found weaknesses in resisting the distraction from irrelevant items. In this task, children had to find a matching pair of a visual stimulus (abstract shapes) among similar items. Children with DLD performed more poorly than their age-matched and their younger, language-matched peers (Marton et al., 2012). The language matched children were two–three years

5.4 Language Ability and Cognitive Control 83

younger than the children with DLD. Therefore, this finding suggests more robust difficulties in children with DLD.

Based on the findings on resistance to distractor interference, we designed a series of studies examining proactive interference across groups of children with different neurocognitive disorders and adults with acquired language disorders using a verbal conflict paradigm, in which previous target items became distractors (Marton et al., 2014, 2016, 2018; see Figure 5.1). Here, we report only on proactive interference in school-age children with DLD. Children with DLD failed to suppress previous memory traces and did not remove irrelevant information from their working memory. Different explanations may be offered for this finding, however, the most likely one is related to the activation and binding theory of Oberauer and Lange (2009). Children with DLD responded to the interfering items based on their familiarity. Familiarity arises from an item's activation level, and if children with DLD do not update their working memory regularly during task performance and keep previous items active during subsequent trials, then those previous items interfere with the current targets. This explanation would be in line with the neural network model of perseveration by Morton and Munakata (2002). It also suggests that proactive interference occurs when the working memory representations of previous items are stronger than those of the current item.

While group differences in resistance to interference are common in the literature, differences in response inhibition, the active suppression of an automatic or prepotent response, are not. Although preschool-age children with DLD differed from their age-matched peers in response inhibition on a Go-NoGo task (Spaulding, 2010), school-age children with DLD showed similar error rates and reaction times to their age-matched peers (Epstein et al., 2014). Likewise, children with DLD performed similarly to their peers on a Stop-Signal task that also measured response inhibition in the presence of an auditory cue. Children were instructed to press a button to indicate the direction (right or left) of an arrow presented on the computer screen but never when accompanied by an auditory beep signal. The delay between the visual and the auditory stimuli was adjusted using a staircase procedure, where correct answers increased the delay (making the task more difficult), and incorrect answers decreased the delay (Marton et al., 2012). These findings suggest that even though younger children with DLD perform more poorly than their peers in response inhibition, this group difference disappears by school-age. The difference in performance accuracy between interference control and response inhibition in school-age children with DLD may be related to distinct developmental

84 Language Ability, Proficiency, and Cognitive Control

patterns of each skill. Age, however, is not the only contributing factor. Findings with typically developing children suggest that cognitive flexibility plays a major role in the interaction between the different inhibitory functions (Blackwell et al., 2014).

Overall, the findings in the DLD literature suggest that in addition to the language problems, children with language disorders also exhibit weaknesses in different cognitive control functions, particularly in working memory, sustained attention, and interference control. The results, however, are highly influenced by the nature of the task, including task conditions; item and response types; as well as by participants' age and prior experience.

5.4.2.2 *Cognitive Control in Bilingual Children with DLD*

Most studies on bilingual language disorders have focused on children's language performance to examine whether bilingualism has a negative effect on language acquisition or on the severity of the language disorder (Gutiérrez-Clellen et al., 2009; Rothweiler et al., 2012). Converging evidence has shown no negative effects. The literature on cognitive control in bilingual children with DLD, however, is scarce and inconsistent. The two critical questions in this literature are whether bilingualism attenuates the effects of DLD in cognitive control in bilingual children with DLD and whether cognitive control performance contributes to the diagnosis of DLD in bilingual children.

To answer the first question, Engel de Abreu and colleagues (2014) used a series of cognitive control tasks to compare three groups of eight-year-olds: Portuguese and Luxembourgish bilingual children with DLD; Portuguese and Luxembourgish typically developing bilingual children; and Portuguese typically developing monolingual children. The bilingual children with DLD showed weaknesses in verbal working memory but not in visuospatial working memory or visual selective attention. In resisting distractor interference, measured by a flanker task, the bilingual typically developing children outperformed both their monolingual peers and the bilingual children with DLD. Moreover, the bilingual children with DLD did not differ from the monolingual typically developing children in interference control. These latter results are promising because monolingual children with DLD typically show weaknesses in resisting distractor interference. Hence, these results and the good visuospatial working memory outcomes in bilingual children with DLD suggest that bilingualism may attenuate the effects of DLD, but we have to be cautious with any conclusions because the study did not involve monolingual children with

5.4 Language Ability and Cognitive Control

DLD. Therefore, no direct comparison between monolingual and bilingual children with DLD can be made based on these findings.

Our preliminary findings are in agreement with these results (Marton et al., 2019). We studied cognitive control in monolingual and bilingual children, with and without DLD, using tasks with minimal language demands (visual N-back task and visual cue-based retrieval task with abstract shapes; see Figure 2.1 in Chapter 2). The results indicate a complex interaction between bilingualism and language impairment. In simple task conditions (smaller set sizes, less interference), bilingualism had a positive effect on children's performance; bilingual children with DLD performed as well as monolingual typically developing children and better than monolingual children with DLD. In tasks with more complex conditions, bilingual and monolingual children with DLD performed similarly to each other and more poorly than their typically developing peers. Hence, in simple tasks, bilingualism had a positive effect on performance in children with DLD but in more difficult task conditions, language disorder had a stronger effect than bilingualism.

To answer the second question, whether cognitive control performance may be used for diagnostic purposes in bilingual children with DLD, Laloi and colleagues (2017) examined response inhibition in six–eight-year-old monolingual and bilingual children with and without DLD. The outcomes suggest no strong link between response inhibition and language, particularly not in older children. Therefore, tasks of response inhibition are inadequate for diagnosing DLD in bilingual children. This is not surprising based on the findings on response inhibition in typically developing bilingual children and monolingual children with DLD. Bilingual and monolingual typically developing children perform similarly on response inhibition (i.e., no bilingual advantage). Likewise, monolingual school-age children with and without DLD show similar performance (Bialystok & Viswanathan, 2009; Bonifacci et al., 2011; Marton et al., 2012).

In our ongoing research (including over 100 school-age children), we select tasks of working memory updating and interference control with no or minimal language demands (i.e., abstract shapes) to distinguish between emerging bilingual students and bilingual children with DLD. We use diffusion models to identify the underlying processes that are reflected in variations in reaction time and accuracy in these cognitive control tasks. Preliminary findings from two recent studies are encouraging because distinct performance patterns are emerging for the different groups (unpublished data). While bilingual typically developing children perform the most efficiently on the selected cognitive control tasks compared to monolingual children with and without DLD and to bilingual children with DLD, the least efficient performance is exhibited by monolingual children with DLD. These children show complex patterns of weaknesses, including difficulties in encoding the cognitive control tasks, problem-solving and decision-making, and strategy use.

5.5 Conclusions

Cognitive control shows a complex interaction with both language proficiency and ability. Most cognitive control skills, such as working memory, attention, and inhibitory control are positively linked to language ability and proficiency. Thus, better language abilities and higher bilingual language proficiencies are associated with superior cognitive control performance, whereas language disorder and low bilingual language proficiency are linked to lower performance on cognitive control tasks. However, not all cognitive control components show this pattern. For example, response inhibition does not have a close link to language skills; children with different language abilities and proficiencies may perform similarly in response inhibition. Age, prior experience, and variation in task types may all influence these relationships.

CHAPTER 6

The Impact of Language Input on Cognitive Control

6.1 Language Input, Intake, and Exposure in Monolingual and Bilingual Children

In this chapter, we explore the relationship between language input and cognitive control, particularly in children with reduced language input. Reduced input in one particular language may occur because of a lack of environmental input or exposure to multiple languages. Even though the literature on the relationship between language input and children's cognitive-linguistic development is flourishing, there is no agreement among scholars about the most critical components of this relationship, particularly in bilingual children. Recent debates on language input reveal contradictory views about the nature of language learning and the mechanisms that enable children to process information from the environment (Carroll, 2017).

Usage-based theoretical models emphasize the importance of both quantity and quality of language input on children's development. Recent findings suggest that in their early years, bilingual toddlers' language skills are highly influenced by the amount of language input, while during the preschool years, the quality of input becomes more relevant (Anderson et al., 2021; Surrain et al., 2021). Attuned dyadic behaviors, including the parent's supportive guidance and the child's active engagement were linked to children's expressive and receptive language skills, as well as to their verbal reasoning skills (Jokihaka et al., 2022). Other studies measured quality by the diversity and complexity of the linguistic features in the parents' speech (Anderson et al., 2021). Moreover, in a study on Russian gender acquisition in a Turkish-Russian bilingual child, findings revealed that despite a reduced amount of input, the acquisition of form-related gender was achieved at a high level, indicating the critical role of quality over quantity in language input (Antonova Ünlü & Wei, 2018).

It is important to note, however, that the effect of language input on children's language skills cannot be understood without studying the

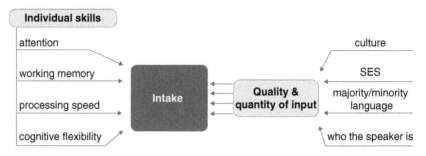

Figure 6.1 Individual and global components influencing language intake

child's intake from that input (Badger, 2018). It is the intake that signals the amount of information that the listener derives from the language environment (Wong, 2001). This process, however, depends on a number of factors (see Figure 6.1). There has been a debate over the years about the specific functions that are needed for a child to derive relevant information from the input. An earlier view, the "Noticing hypothesis," suggested that it is the person's awareness that is needed for input to become intake. Thus, the difference between input and intake was associated with consciousness (Schmidt, 1993, 2001). More recent studies suggest the contribution of multiple components to intake, including the child's perceptual skills, attention, and language knowledge (Rowe, 2015). Further, intake will also depend on the nature of the input, such as the frequency of certain linguistic elements in a given language and the discriminability of the items (Wijnen, 2000).

As children mature, there is an expansion in their language knowledge and an increase in the number of opportunities to practice their language skills that lead to variations in intake (De Houwer, 2017). Children with more advanced intake produce higher-level output, which, in turn, leads to improved input. For example, mothers talked more and used more diverse and complex language with their older children than with the younger ones (De Houwer, 2014). These child-to-parent effects were also evidenced in a large-scale twin study (Dale et al., 2015), as well as in research with children who exhibited a language delay. Although parents of children with a language delay provided as much input as the parents of typically developing children, the quality of their input showed differences. Parents of children with language delays adjusted their conversational style to what they perceived as the child's language abilities and

6.1 Language Input, Intake, and Exposure

took fewer conversational turns than the parents of typically developing children (Vigil et al., 2005).

In addition to quantity and quality, a further aspect of language input is the length of exposure. Although the terms "input" and "exposure" are often used interchangeably in the literature, in certain disciplines, these two terms are used with slightly different meanings. For example, in the bilingualism literature, the terms "quality" and "quantity" typically refer to the current input, while the term "exposure" is used when the child receives particular language experiences over time. As children age, they participate in different communicative acts across linguistic environments, and receive different quantity and quality of language input from the other speakers. Given the variability of all of these factors, there is a need for integrating the different language input elements when examining children's language experiences. This task, however, is further complicated by the large variety of methods used across studies. Many scholars used surveys to assess parental language input, such as the Multilingual Infant Language Questionnaire (Liu & Krager, 2017); the Parents of Bilingual Children Questionnaire (Tuller, 2015); and the Maternal Mental State Input Inventory (Peterson & Slaughter, 2003), among others.

To provide a more integrated view of parental input, Ågren and colleagues (2014) developed a language profile measure with French-Swedish bilingual children by using a combination of input components. The input variables for French included the parents' language proficiency, proportion of French spoken at home, number of weeks per year spent in French-speaking countries, contact with other native speakers of French, access to French TV and computer games, and reading habits in the target language. Each component was graded on a 3-point scale. This method allowed the authors to analyze input from both qualitative and quantitative perspectives, as well as to develop an index to distinguish among groups of children (e.g., children with bilingual native language and early successive bilingual children).

The currently used, most objective measure of input is the LENA "talk pedometer" system. It includes a small device that children carry with them all day long to record the speech they hear and that which they produce. At the end of the day, the audio files are sent to a cloud-based processing system that uses algorithms that are trained to differentiate the adult input from the child's output and from other noises, such as TV (www.lena.org). A meta-analysis of studies using LENA technology (Wang et al., 2017) revealed that the system can be used efficiently in families speaking various languages (e.g., English, French, Korean). An important finding across studies was that the number of conversational turns between the parent and the child is at least as predictive of the child's language development as is the number of words spoken by the adult. This result highlights the significance of the child's active participation in communicative acts with the parents. The more engaged the child, the more involved and responsive the parent. The outcomes across studies also revealed that parents of children with communication disorders greatly benefited from parent-focused intervention in association with the use of the system. Professional guidance and parental-group support resulted in decreased parental stress; increased well-being and communication competence; and more efficient strategy use (Moseley Harris, 2021; Rutherford et al., 2019).

Taken together, the relationship between input and intake is dynamic in nature, and shows individual variations in speakers. Input should always be considered with regard to intake and vice versa. The more we understand about children's cognitive functions and learning mechanisms, the better we comprehend their interactions with the quality of language input. A deeper understanding of these effects may contribute to more efficient communication between caregivers and their children.

A major challenge for child language development theorists, however, is to explain children's productions of structures for which there is no environmental input (Lieven, 2014; Tomasello, 2003). These questions are often explained with productivity and abstraction. Behavioral and neurophysiological methods have been applied to examine the cues that children use as they process particular structures, including the preferential looking paradigm, electrophysiological measures, and eye-tracking studies (e.g., Stone & Bosworth, 2019; Waldman DeLuca et al., 2023). Detailed error analysis data may provide another useful source to answer these questions. Children's errors may reflect their level of abstraction and their creative use of language. It is important to note, however, that even after careful consideration of all the influential linguistic factors, including the language environment, there are individual differences that indicate the role of domain-general cognitive contributors in the relationship between language input and development.

6.2 The Relationship between Language Input and Cognitive Control

Both the quantity and quality of language input interact with a number of cognitive control functions. One of the most widely studied components is working memory. Studies on language processing and working

6.2 Language Input and Cognitive Control

memory provide multiple conceptual frameworks to explain the relationship between language input and processing capacity. Although many scholars approached the relationship between working memory and language by studying the working memory skills of children with different language abilities (typically developing monolingual children, children with language impairment, etc.), it is important to note that the relationship between language and working memory is bidirectional. Relevant to our topic are the connectivist-based efficiency accounts with the suggestion that processing capacity is related to both the linguistic features of the language input (experience) and individual characteristics (architecture) of the speaker (MacDonald & Christiansen, 2002). Working memory performance is affected by the linguistic complexity of the input (word frequency, morphological and syntactic complexity, etc.), as well as by the child's language skills (Mainela-Arnold & Evans, 2005; Marton et al., 2006). This interaction between architecture and experience is reflected in individual differences within groups.

There is consensus in the literature that during language development, children need to process complex language inputs that require a strong and efficient information processing system to store and evaluate the incoming information (Gathercole & Baddeley, 1993). Processing verbal input in working memory is critical in order to develop long-term representations of words and linguistic structures. It allows the learner to analyze and to determine the structural properties of the language input. Its capacity is determined by the amount of information that can be kept active in the face of interference. Verbal working memory has been linked to vocabulary acquisition in both first and second language learners (Gathercole, 2006; Martin & Ellis, 2012); to language comprehension (Just & Carpenter, 1992); syntactic processing (King & Just, 1991); and to reading comprehension (Daneman & Carpenter, 1980; Gathercole & Baddeley, 1993; McVay & Kane, 2012b).

Working memory is also viewed as a system that operates in strong interaction with attentional control (Meier & Kane, 2017). Outcomes from structural modeling have revealed that the relationship between working memory capacity and higher-level cognition is mediated by attentional control, including the discriminating selection of specific processes for engagement (Unsworth et al., 2014). Studies describing the relationship between working memory and attentional control have shown that individuals with high working memory spans exhibit better abilities in attention control; they are able to maintain information more efficiently and retrieve it more quickly than others with lower working memory spans (Unsworth & Engle, 2006). Thus, children with better attention and working memory skills process language input more efficiently and resist interference with greater success.

Cross-language interference has been studied extensively in the bilingualism and second language acquisition literatures (Hsin et al., 2013; Kaushanskaya & Marian, 2007; Prior et al., 2017). However, only a few studies looked at the relationship between language input and interference control for irrelevant lexical items; for competing sentence interpretations (e.g., in sentences with syntactic ambiguity); or for simultaneously active languages. Ye and Zhou (2009) examined the different brain areas that were activated in response to potent but irrelevant items compared to competing stimuli. While the ventral lateral prefrontal cortex, particularly the Broca's area, controlled interference from irrelevant information, the parietal cortex signaled the lateral prefrontal cortex when there was a conflict between competing representations in response to multiple inputs. These are important findings because conflict resolution and interference control are often discussed in the behavioral literature as similar or interchangeable processes. The neurophysiological outcomes reveal a difference between these processes, and they show how interference control relies on a dual-network system, which supports distinct adaptive control and more stable functions (e.g., to ensure set-maintenance; Dosenbach et al., 2007). These findings have significant implications for children processing multiple language inputs.

6.3 Delayed or Reduced Language Input and Cognitive Control

6.3.1 Cognitive Control in Children from Families with Low Socioeconomic Status

Socioeconomic status (SES) has been linked to children's cognitive, language, and academic performance, as well as to their brain functions (Farah et al., 2006; Merz et al., 2019; Sheridan et al., 2017). In a large-scale study examining brain structures associated with disparities in parental education and family income, the regions of language development, cognitive control, and memory were identified as the most critical areas in the brain (Noble et al., 2015). Similar findings were reported by Farah and colleagues (2006), who assessed seven different neurocognitive systems by administering multiple cognitive control (i.e., inhibition, resistance to interference, and monitoring), language ability

6.3 Delayed or Reduced Language Input and Cognitive Control 93

(i.e., phonological awareness, vocabulary, and syntactic knowledge), and nonexecutive tasks. SES did not affect all cognitive skills across the board, but did impact children's language skills, cognitive control, and memory functions. It did not influence the outcomes on reward processing or visual cognition, such as face perception and shape detection. Thus, when studying different cognitive functions, researchers need to be aware that SES may highly influence the outcomes on cognitive control and various memory functions.

Children in families with low SES typically receive decreased quantity and quality of language input compared to children from mid- and high-SES families (Schwab & Lew-Williams, 2016). Even though low- and mid-SES mothers showed the same number of social goals in play situations with their infants, they differed in their language goals. Mid-SES mothers incorporated more language goals into their play activities than low-SES parents. The lexical and grammatical diversity of the input, as well as the mean length of utterances of the mothers predicted their children's language development, including their vocabulary knowledge, as well as their grammatical skills (Hart & Risley, 1995; Hoff, 2003). Upper- and middle-class parents spoke more, used more word types, and attended more to their children's initiatives than lower-SES parents, who tended to direct their children's behavior more often. In addition to differences in language outcomes between children from low- and high-SES families, cognitive functions were also affected by mothers' verbal input (Chang et al., 2009). However, mothers who participated in parental intervention increased the language and cognitive stimulation of their children, which, in turn, had a positive effect on the children's development.

Mothers' verbal input was a strong predictor of cognitive development, independent of maternal sensitivity in a large sample of eight–twelve-month-old infants (Page et al., 2010). While maternal sensitivity showed no link to cognitive development, it did influence children's social-emotional outcomes. In contrast, verbal input had a great impact on children's cognitive performance, and it was measured by parents' verbal statements such as those that encouraged the infant, described the task, or provided supportive feedback to motivate the infants to achieve their goals. Furthermore, the effect of parental language stimulation on cognitive development grows with an increase in children's age. Cognitive flexibility was observed in a longitudinal study (at ages 6, 9, and 12 months) in low- and high-SES families who differed in their language input. Cognitive flexibility was measured with the perseverative reaching task. The groups differed across all three sessions, demonstrating that the delays observed in low-SES children compared to their high-SES peers persists over time without intervention (Clearfield & Niman, 2012).

In addition to the behavioral differences related to SES and parents' verbal stimulation, there are observable variations in brain structures across these groups. Low SES has been linked to reduced gray matter and decreased integrity of white matter tracts in both language and cognitive control regions of the brain, such as the left perysilvian area and the prefrontal cortex (Merz et al., 2019). In a working memory study using the N-back and count span tasks, children from higher income families exhibited both greater working memory capacity and greater functional brain responsiveness with increased working memory demands compared to children from low-income families (Finn et al., 2017). There were significant differences in brain activation in the prefrontal cortex and in the parietal regions between the groups, even when performance differences were matched across working memory loads and children were matched for nonverbal IQ. A similar pattern was observed in adolescents with a delayed match-to-sample working memory task. With an increase in working memory demands, participants' performance showed a linear relationship with parental SES; adolescents' working memory performance improved with an increase in parental education level.

The relationship between SES, language input, and working memory was further evidenced by neuro-imaging data. Children from families with low SES exhibited less efficient neural recruitment in the superior parietal cortex and in the prefrontal cortex on working memory trials with higher cognitive demands (Sheridan et al., 2017). It is important to note that none of these participants had experienced physical or sexual abuse or any other form of violence. However, the parents provided reduced language input and cognitive stimulation to their children, and the children had fewer books and learning opportunities. The study by Sheridan and colleagues clearly showed that parental language and cognitive stimulation play an important role even in older children's cognitive performance, and the lack of complex language input has a long-lasting effect into the adolescent years. These findings also raise concerns about these children's schooling and the expected compensatory effects of education. The gap in working memory performance between adolescents from low- and high-SES families (ages 13–20 years) was still present following eight–twelve years of education.

Taken together, parental education and income are closely linked to the quantity and quality of the language input that children are exposed to in families with disparities in socioeconomic status. Children from low

6.3 Delayed or Reduced Language Input and Cognitive Control 95

SES families perform more poorly than their more affluent peers on various language, cognitive control, and memory tasks. The gap in cognitive and language performance between children from low- and mid-high-SES families persists through adolescence. These cognitive and language weaknesses have a negative effect on children's academic achievements, including literacy skills and performance in mathematics. Such behavioral patterns are also associated with specific functions and structures of the brain. Differences in brain structures that were linked to SES status were particularly prominent in areas of language processing and cognitive control.

6.3.2 Interaction between Language Input and Cognitive Control in Children with Developmental Language Disorder (DLD)

The literature on the relationship between language input and language development in typically developing children highlights the relevance of both the quantity and quality of language input and underscores how these properties affect children's cognitive-linguistic behavior. Considering the dynamic nature of this relationship, there is evidence that parents may adjust the quality and quantity of their language input based on their children's age and communicative abilities. This was evidenced in families with children experiencing language delays (Vigil et al., 2005). Parents of typically developing children responded more often to their children and used more elaborated language than did the parents of children with language delay, even though the number of utterances and the number of words in their utterances were similar in the two groups of parents. In contrast, parents of children with language delay produced more initiations than the parents of typically developing children, which resulted in more frequent topic changes in the former group. Thus, parents of typically developing children responded more to what their children were saying and stayed on topic longer following their children's lead compared to the parents of children with language delay, who switched topics more often to engage their children in the conversation. This was probably done because the children with language delay used fewer utterances than their typically developing peers.

In children with DLD, a discrepancy has also been found between parental input and children's intake as a result of these children's limitations in processing capacity, especially in working memory (Laloi et al., 2017; Leonard et al., 2007) and sustained attention (Boerma et al., 2017). Thus, even when the parents provided rich and linguistically diverse language input, children with DLD were able to process only parts of that information because of their weaknesses in processing capacity. From the perspective of emergentism, the working memory limitation or the reduced processing speed in children with DLD could lead to difficulties in mapping certain aspects of the language input, such as the statistical properties of low-frequency information (Evans, 2001). A number of studies on the learning mechanisms of language development emphasized the importance of statistical learning (Hsu & Bishop, 2010). In the case of typical development, as children receive more language input, they detect regularities that facilitate the development of specific linguistic structures. In children with DLD, however, the working memory limitations may result in a negative impact on statistical learning. In order to detect regularities in the language input, children need to store and process a number of elements to memorize a sufficient amount of information for specific cognitive-linguistic patterns to emerge. Children with DLD need more language input compared to their typically developing peers to develop these patterns. Thus, the working memory limitations and the associated weaknesses in statistical learning necessitate increased language input for children with DLD to develop specific cognitive-linguistic structures.

The relationship between children's working memory performance and parental language input was further evidenced in a study with two subgroups of children with DLD and their typically developing peers (Kalnak et al., 2014). One subgroup of children with DLD had parents who themselves demonstrated spoken and/or written language problems, whereas the other subgroup of children with DLD had parents with good language skills. Children in the DLD subgroup with parents who demonstrated weaknesses in language processing, received less diverse language input than children in the other two groups. Children's nonword repetition performance, which is a measure of working memory and a marker of DLD, differed across groups. Nonword repetition in the subgroup of children with parents with poor language skills was not only one standard deviation below the scores of their typically developing peers but was also significantly lower than that of the other children with DLD, who had parents who exhibited good language skills and provided their children with rich language input. These findings demonstrate how in families with language impairment – language difficulties in both parents and children – the social interactions are negatively affected by the limitations in language production in both parties. In these families, both parents and children adjust their communicative behaviors to some lower standards in response to each other's language production. In addition to

6.3 Delayed or Reduced Language Input and Cognitive Control   97

the parents' less diverse language input, their lower level of education and genetic transmission might also contribute to the children's poor nonword repetition performance.

While most studies have focused on the interaction between language input and processing capacity by examining performance on working memory and attention tasks in children with DLD, Farrant and colleagues (2012) studied the relationship among language input, theory of mind, and cognitive flexibility. The authors tested the hypothesis that children's acquisition of sentential complements would mediate the relationship between language input and children's understanding of explicit false belief. The amount of maternal language input for children with DLD and their typically developing peers did not differ in this study. The results showed a strong relationship between maternal language input and children's theory of mind and cognitive flexibility development. Traditional correlation analyses showed that the language input was clearly associated with both cognitive flexibility and theory of mind. However, outcomes from structural equation modeling revealed that theory of mind development was mediated by memory for false complements and cognitive flexibility. Memory for false complements facilitated the development of explicit false belief understanding, as well as cognitive flexibility. Children with DLD exhibited significantly poorer memory for false complements, weaker cognitive flexibility, and lower explicit false belief than typically developing children. Weaknesses in memory and cognitive flexibility contributed to their delayed theory of mind development.

Based on the findings on slower information processing in children with DLD compared to their typically developing peers, Montgomery (2005) examined the effect of input rate (i.e., normal, slow, and fast speaking rates) on children's performance in a word recognition task measured by reaction time. He found that children with DLD exhibited slower reaction times than their typically developing peers when the sentences were presented at normal or fast rates, but they processed information faster when the presentation rate was slow. The two groups showed opposite patterns, and their performance was associated with their attentional capacity. Children with DLD needed more time to allocate their attentional resources to process the sentences, whereas increased time had a negative effect on typically developing children's language processing performance. These children processed information less efficiently when the input rate was slowed down.

In addition to input rate, the frequency of input and its spacing were also examined in children with DLD (Riches et al., 2005). These children benefited from more frequent inputs in a verb learning study, particularly when the words were widely spaced. The same manipulations did not have a positive effect on typically developing children's performance. Spacing had a larger impact than frequency on children's performance in the DLD group, a pattern that suggests that the repetition of information is insufficient if it is not widely distributed in the language input.

Taken together, there are consistent findings in the literature indicating that children with DLD do not benefit as much from parental language input as typically developing children do. There is a complex interaction between language input and these children's processing capacity limitations, including weaknesses in working memory and attentional capacity. On the one hand, these cognitive problems limit the intake from the language input in children with DLD; on the other hand, limited intake leads to further difficulties in language processing and cognitive flexibility. The outcomes of these studies, however, also revealed that children with DLD may benefit from the language input if it is presented more slowly, more frequently, and with a wider distribution of items compared to typical parental language input.

6.3.3 Multiple Language Input: Interaction between Language Input and Cognitive Control in Bilingual Children

The amount of language input in bilingual children can be presented as the quantity of the overall language input or as the quantity of input in each language separately. Even in balanced bilingual children, the quantity of input per language is never the same, and may change over time because it is highly associated with the language context (e.g., home language vs. school language). The amount of time that children spend in one language environment over the other frequently shifts with age and results in changes in the amount of language input. For example, as children get older, they tend to spend more time in school and among their peers than at home with family.

Early studies in the bilingualism literature emphasized the disadvantages of bilingualism and argued that dual-language input leads to confusion and poor performance (for a review, see Hakuta, 1986). This view is no longer accepted among scholars, but the number of studies that have examined the bilingual child's entire linguistic repertoire is still small and often limited to children's vocabulary development (Bedore et al., 2005; Monsrud et al., 2019). Although there has been a positive shift over the years in opinions and attitudes towards the effect of dual-language input on children's language development, many studies still compare bilingual

6.3 Delayed or Reduced Language Input and Cognitive Control 99

children's performance in one language to that of their monolingual peers (Bialystok et al., 2010; Vagh et al., 2009). This approach puts bilingual children at a disadvantage because, unlike monolingual children, bilingual children cannot use their entire language knowledge when tested in one language only. For example, bilingual children's vocabulary is distributed across their languages, so when their lexical knowledge is tested in just a single language, they are limited in using their resources. In addition to the language context, a number of other variables affect children's quantity of input, among which the languages spoken by the parents are particularly important. Children's input at home will depend on whether both parents are bilingual, whether they use different languages with the child, and whether they are minority language speakers.

The length of children's exposure to each of their languages is frequently associated with the age of acquisition of that particular language (for more details, see Chapter 4, "The Effect of Age on First Language Acquisition, Second Language Learning, and Cognitive Control Development"). There is evidence that the development of certain linguistic structures may be more closely associated with age of acquisition than the amount of language input. For example, in Turkish-English sequential bilingual children, vocabulary was affected by both age of acquisition and language input, whereas tense morphology was only influenced by age of acquisition (Chondrogianni & Marinis, 2011). These results were in line with findings suggesting that measures of language input are good predictors of phonology and vocabulary, but they do not predict grammatical development, particularly the acquisition of syntax (Armon-Lotem & Meir, 2019). Thordardottir (2011) provided an even more nuanced analysis, which clarified how the relationship between the amount of language input and receptive vocabulary differs from that of expressive vocabulary. Although both types of vocabulary showed a strong correlation with the amount of language input, when bilingual children's vocabulary performance was compared to that of monolingual children, bilingual children needed a larger amount of input to meet the expressive vocabulary norms than the receptive ones. The amount of input was also related to children's speed of language processing, and these two variables positively affected vocabulary knowledge (Hurtado et al., 2014).

Young children, who are exposed to multiple languages, need to develop a complex cognitive control system allowing them to extract patterns from each language and to switch between the languages. Taking in multiple language inputs requires different adaptation processes. For example, infants developing two languages simultaneously need to allocate attentional resources from one language to the other. In most cases, the language input differs between the two languages, causing infants to establish a stronger and a weaker language. In order to develop the weaker language, children need to allocate more attentional resources to that language (Kovács, 2015). The frequent switches between the two languages on a daily basis may contribute to further adaptation in the cognitive system. In a series of eye-tracking studies, infants who received input in two languages demonstrated more cognitive flexibility than monolingual children by suppressing their previous responses more efficiently and updating their predictions according to changes in task requirements (Kovács & Mehler, 2009).

Another type of attention skill that contributes significantly to children's language development is joint attention. Joint attention provides the child with substantial nonlinguistic scaffolding during parent–child interactions, which are periods when the child is highly attentive and motivated to learn by using social cues (Tomasello & Farrar, 1986). Early joint attention experiences are related to children's later language abilities. Therefore, the quality of input that the child receives during these interactions with the parent is critical. Parents' input typically involves two different joint attention strategies, (1) following the child's attentional focus and commenting on the objects and events that the child is engaged with, or (2) redirecting the child's attention, shifting attentional focus to a new object or event.

Moreover, there are different cultural-linguistic elements that impact joint attention activities in bilingual families. Several studies have shown that when a minority language is spoken at home, then parents tend to use more redirecting strategies to ensure that they engage the child in those interactions, whereas they are more willing to follow their child's lead when the majority language is used (Vigil et al., 2006). Further, parents who speak the child's weaker language typically speak more, using more repetition and more directives than parents who speak the child's stronger language (Pearson & Amaral, 2014).

Fathers and mothers also differ in how much child-centered input they provide. Mothers tend to use more child-centered language, while fathers use more directives. In bilingual families, where one parent speaks one language and the other parent speaks another language, these qualitative differences in language input may lead to differences in the child's development of the two languages. In association with variations in language input, Yow and Markman (2011) found heightened aptitude toward joint attention in bilingual children compared to their monolingual peers, which

6.3 Delayed or Reduced Language Input and Cognitive Control 101

was reflected by more efficient use of referential cues. Bilingual children were better at predicting the speakers' intent from their use of nonverbal referential gestures. Even when their monolingual and bilingual parents provided the same amount of parental input, bilingual children exhibited more vigilant behavior in monitoring and assessing the communicative cues. These outcomes indicate a bidirectional relationship between dual-language input and joint attention. Bilingual children tend to be more vigilant in joint-attention activities than monolingual children, and the parents of bilingual children seem to use different communicative strategies when speaking the stronger versus the weaker language. The interactions among these factors appear to have a facilitative effect on bilingual children's language development.

Even though there are not many studies linking variations in language input to differences in overall cognitive control, there are findings suggesting that dual-language input is associated with children's cognitive flexibility, and this relationship may be moderated by children's language skills. Children with strong language skills showed better cognitive flexibility with an increase in dual-language input (Crespo et al., 2019). This pattern was not observed in children with lower language scores. Cognitive flexibility was measured with the Dimensional Change Card Sort task (Zelazo, 2006), which required sorting binary cards based on specific rules. Children sorted the cards, first according to color and then by shape. As discussed in Chapter 2, "Cognitive Control," the two most common measures in this task are switching cost and mixing cost. While the switching cost reflects the time difference between stay and switch trials, the mixing cost is calculated by comparing participants' responses to stay trials – in which no switching is involved – between a single block and a mixed block. Single blocks include stay trials only, whereas mixed blocks include both stay and switch trials. Thus, the mixing cost indicates how the different contexts affect participants' responses to stay trials. The increase in dual-language input had a positive effect on the mixing costs (i.e., increased language input was associated with smaller mixing cost). The same relationship was not observed with the switching cost. Thus, children who had more language input were less affected by the global context of the task. Language input showed a strong relationship with global sustained attention and overall monitoring skills (mixing cost), but it did not show a positive relationship with children's local response inhibition (switching cost). These findings suggest a bidirectional relationship between language and cognitive control development, and provide support to previous research suggesting that mixing and switching costs rely on different neural mechanisms and reflect different sustained and transient control processes. While sustained attention and monitoring in mixed designs are supported by the activation of the right anterior prefrontal cortex, the maintenance of task-set information is related to the lateral prefrontal cortex, and task-set reconfiguration and updating following a switch reflects the activation of the superior parietal cortex (Braver et al., 2003).

A further question is whether language input could have a similar effect on cognitive control if bilingualism is acquired through a second language immersion program. Eight-year-old monolingual and bilingual children were compared on a number of cognitive control tasks. The bilingual children had three years of bilingual immersion education experience. Children in this latter group were significantly faster than their monolingual peers on most cognitive control tasks, including alerting, auditory selective attention, divided attention, and mental flexibility, but the groups did not differ on inhibition (Nicolay & Poncelet, 2013). The findings on inhibition are consistent with other studies (e.g., Kautto et al., 2021; Laloi et al., 2017). Response inhibition develops relatively early during childhood, and inhibition tasks typically do not distinguish between monolingual and bilingual children or children with typical and atypical language development.

The effect of school-based language input was also studied by He and colleagues (2020) from the perspective of code-switching. Bilingual children's cognitive flexibility was enhanced by their teachers' frequent code-switching practices, particularly with intra-sentential switches. Compared to inter-sentential code-switching, intra-sentential switches are more difficult to predict and therefore are more demanding on the control system. The children needed to monitor the language input, separate the codes according to the different languages, and switch between them continuously. The findings suggest that children who are exposed to frequent intra-sentential switches in the language input exhibit better cognitive flexibility, even in nonverbal tasks, than children who are not exposed to frequent intra-sentential code-switching.

Overall, despite some inconsistencies in the bilingualism literature, the findings across studies suggest that children who are exposed to multiple languages learn to monitor the different language sources and variations within the linguistic environment early on. They exhibit enhanced vigilance and cognitive flexibility in both verbal and nonverbal domains. Furthermore, dual-language input seems to affect certain cognitive control functions to a greater extent than others, and these differences are linked to distinct neural mechanisms in the brain.

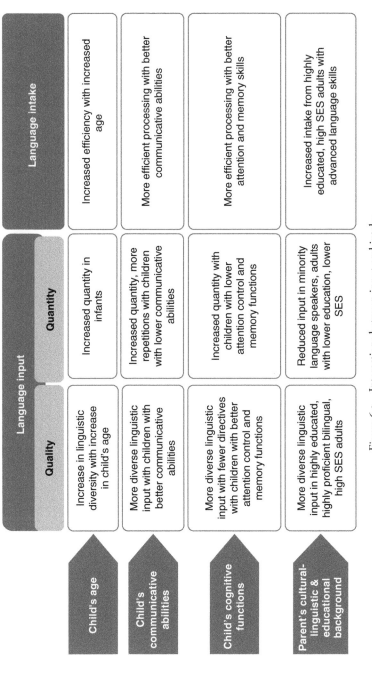

Figure 6.2 Interactions between input and intake

6.4 Conclusions

The quality and quantity of language input across populations show multiple interactions with both cognitive and language development in children. The interactions among parental input, language environment, and the child's age, as well as communicative abilities, are bidirectional, resulting in complex patterns. Communicative abilities are also associated with children's cognitive control skills. Therefore, cognitive control abilities may show either a positive or a negative correlation with children's intake, depending on the child's individual skills. The interactions among language input, parental background, the child's individual skills, and language intake are summarized in Figure 6.2.

CHAPTER 7

Cognitive Control and Social Context of Language Use

7.1 Social Context: Conceptual Foundations

How does the social context, more specifically the presence of other people, affect children's cognitive-linguistic control? The focus in this chapter is on the interactions between language and cognitive control across different social-communicative contexts. Used broadly in the literature, the term "social context" refers to different situations where other people are present socially and information about the social environment is processed to guide behavioral decisions (Wyer & Srull, 2014). Typically, two levels of social context are distinguished: local and global (see Figure 7.1). The local level is specific to a given social-communicative interaction and to language use, while the global context is associated with culture, age, and socioeconomic status (Bazzanella, 2004). Although these two levels interact with each other, the local level is more dynamic and less foreseeable, whereas the global one is more predictable with less rapid changes. These differences in levels of social context have a strong effect on the development of cognitive control.

From a young age at the local level, children use different language registers across social contexts as they adjust their speech according to the various interactional partners and changing topics, as well as to the environment. Register use is reflected by a variety of linguistic elements, such as variations in lexical items, syntactic structures, and prosodic features (Wagner et al., 2010). These variations in register use are also accompanied by changes in cognitive control functions, such as enhanced attentional focus in the presence of others (Klauer et al., 2008). The partner's social role further influences children's responses; they react differently in the presence of an observer compared to a competitor. These role variations across social contexts are associated with different cognitive control processes that either facilitate or inhibit certain responses (Fischer et al., 2018). For example, children rely on different cognitive control functions

105

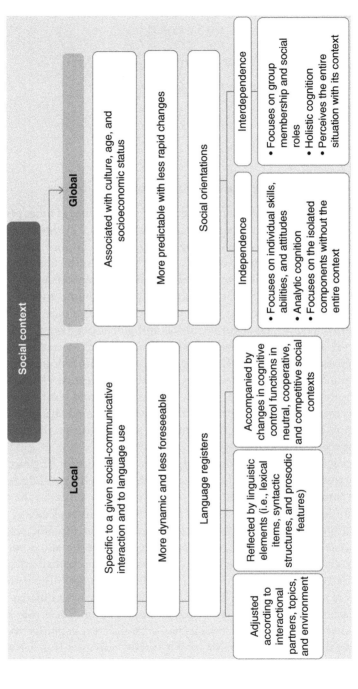

Figure 7.1 Levels of social context

7.1 Social Context: Conceptual Foundations 107

in neutral, cooperative, and competitive social contexts. They adapt their cognitive system more efficiently in cooperative and competitive contexts, compared to a neutral one. This is reflected by fewer errors and faster response times. Interestingly, children's pupil dilation, which is an indicator of engagement, also differs between the cooperative and competitive contexts as a function of age. Preschool-age children show greater pupil dilation (more engagement) during competition, whereas school-age children show greater pupil dilation in the cooperative context. Younger children enjoy more competition, whereas older children prefer cooperation with others (Fischer et al., 2018). Moreover, these two social contexts show distinct interactions with different cognitive control functions. While cooperation has a direct facilitative effect on cognitive control, as it promotes the maintenance of socially shared goals in working memory (Qu, 2011), competition can boost enjoyment and motivation and lead to an increase in cognitive control through positive emotions (Cagiltay et al., 2015; Plass et al., 2013).

At the neurophysiological level, there are variations in prefrontal cortex activation across these social contexts – neutral, cooperative, and competitive. Contextual variations are associated with activation levels in different cortical areas. In the competitive context, activation levels are higher in the left pre-frontal cortex, whereas in cooperative and neutral contexts, activation is higher in the right pre-frontal cortex. Furthermore, this pattern is more pronounced in older (8–9-year-old) children than in younger (5–6-year-old) ones (Chevalier et al., 2019).

These outcomes are in line with previous behavioral findings that have shown an age effect in children's engagement of control. In response to increasing cognitive demands, older children utilize more differentiated control processes (e.g., inhibition control, working memory, monitoring, etc.) and use various strategies (e.g., verbalization and proactive strategies), compared to younger children (Camos and Barrouillet, 2011; Chatham et al., 2009). These findings suggest that more flexible and more efficient cognitive control is available for use among older rather than younger children.

The results from these studies also highlight the role of motivation. Competition and motivation have been closely linked in studies with serious games, video games, and artistic creativity. In serious games, competition enhanced motivation and increased response accuracy (Cagiltay et al., 2015), whereas in video games, competition facilitated learning by eliciting increased interest and enjoyment that lead to a stronger goal-oriented behavior (Plass et al., 2013). Thus, an increase in motivation exhibits a facilitative effect on cognitive control. Finally, children's intrinsic and extrinsic motivations were also measured while performing an art project. Intrinsic motivation was positively correlated with creativity, while competition heightened intrinsic motivation as it added to the challenge of the task and to children's level of excitement (Conti et al., 2001). Taking these findings together, competition increases children's interest, excitement, enjoyment, and motivation, and these emotional factors lead to more goal-oriented behavior with enhanced cognitive control.

7.2 Social Context, Emotions, and Cognitive Control

A frequently asked question in the literature concerns the extent to which cognitive control depends on emotions in different social contexts. Social situations are typically emotionally charged, so it is essential to understand the influence of emotions and how they affect cognitive control across different social contexts. In recent years, it has been suggested that emotions play a critical role when recruiting cognitive control to perform goal-directed behavior or solve a conflict (Inzlicht et al., 2015). Behavioral regulation involves both emotional and cognitive control. For example, the control of negative emotions may lead to a limitation in expressive actions; it does not reduce unpleasant experiences, but it does decrease memory performance, and it increases the activation of the sympathetic nervous system. In contrast, cognitive control neutralizes negative emotions without impairing memory functions, although it might decrease physiological arousal (Gross, 2002; Ochsner & Gross, 2005). There is a large body of literature discussing emotion regulation and cognitive control in different social contexts in adults, while only preliminary findings have emerged in the literature on children and adolescents. Children's emotion regulation is closely linked to their social relationships with peers and to the parent–child relationship within the family. Only a few studies have examined the links among social context, emotion regulation, and cognitive control, and most of them were focused on the effect of parental support on children's cognitive control.

The quality of family relationships has a clear effect on children's cognitive control abilities. This has been supported by both behavioral and neurophysiological studies. In families with negative parent–child relationships, adolescents were less able to allocate cognitive control resources efficiently, and poor cognitive control led to risk-taking behaviors (McCormick et al., 2016). In contrast, higher parental control in low-chaos households predicted enhanced cognitive control in adolescents. In chaotic environments,

7.3 Cultural Background and Cognitive Control

children showed more neurocognitive vulnerability based on outcomes from a flanker task and a spatial interference task. However, in families with high-quality parent–child relationships, children performed better on the same cognitive control tasks. Hemodynamic correlates of cognitive control were assessed during task performance to support these behavioral findings at the neural level (Kim-Spoon et al., 2017).

The quality of the parent–child relationship may have a buffering effect on the interaction between socioeconomic status (SES) and cognitive control. Supportive parental behavior mitigates the negative effects of low SES on adolescents' cognitive control skills. Lower cognitive control performance was observed in children from low-SES families only where there was a negative parent–child relationship (Li et al., 2022). These findings are in line with the resilience theory (e.g., Brody et al., 2019; Zimmerman et al., 2013) that focuses on the positive aspects of adolescent development in negative social contexts and reveals the protective factors, such as parental warmth and support, that modify the effects of negative social contexts on cognitive and behavioral control. These outcomes already show a certain level of interaction between local and global level contexts (i.e., parent–child relationship and SES), and these results are further influenced by other global level components, such as cultural background.

7.3 Cultural Background and Cognitive Control

Changes in cognitive effort and control are also linked to global level variations in cultural background and social class (Grossmann & Varnum, 2011). Countries and cultures have been characterized by different cognitive styles, either more analytic (e.g., USA) or more holistic (e.g., Japan; Varnum et al., 2010), and these styles are associated with specific social orientations, such as independence and interdependence. In independent cultures, the self is separate from others, and the focus is on individual skills, abilities, and attitudes, whereas in interdependent cultures, the self relies more on social relationships, and the focus is on group membership and social roles (Kafetsios, 2019). Thus, independent cultures are characterized by analytic cognition and field independent attention – that is, the individual focuses more on the isolated components without the entire context – whereas interdependent cultures show more holistic cognition and field dependent attention, as they perceive the entire situation with its context. These variations are reflected in both behavioral and neurophysiological changes. For example, while watching pictures of natural scenes, the eye movements of American and Chinese students were compared in an eye-tracking study. The American students fixated sooner and longer on objects in the foreground, and they encoded more visual details than the Chinese students. In contrast, Chinese students showed more balanced fixations between the objects in the foreground and those in the background and exhibited more holistic processing of visual images. These differences in eye movements reflected differences in students' cultural experiences and socialization. While in independent cultures, the focus was on objects, in interdependent cultures, it was on contexts (Chua et al., 2005).

To further explore the relationship between cognitive control and cultural background, Canadian and Japanese children's cognitive control skills were compared across studies. Moriguchi and colleagues (2012) examined task switching using two different versions of the Dimensional Change Card Sort task (DCCS). In the social version, a person who served as a model was introduced to a child. The model started sorting the cards according to one of the rules (i.e., either shape or color), and the child was asked to observe the model. After a certain number of trials, the model left the room, and the child was asked to sort the cards according to the other rule. In the traditional version, children were asked to sort, first according to one rule, then according to the other rule. While in the traditional version of the DCCS, Canadian and Japanese children performed similarly, in the social version of the task, the Japanese children performed more poorly than the Canadian youngsters. The Canadian children were able to follow the rules they were given, regardless of the behavior of the model, whereas the Japanese children were more highly affected by the behavior of the model, so they made more errors. The results suggest that children from cultures that are characterized by interdependence may become more attuned to the actions of others in their social environment than children who are socialized in cultures that are more independent.

Similar differences were found in a study on selective attention using variations of the flanker test with children from Canada and Japan (Senzaki et al., 2018). In the social version, children were instructed to detect the emotion (happy or sad) of the central figure that was surrounded by four other faces expressing different emotions. In the nonsocial version, children were presented with the widely used fish flanker task. In this latter task, children had to respond to the direction of the central fish, that was surrounded by flankers that either faced the same or opposing directions. In the nonsocial, fish-flanker task, all children made more errors in the incongruent conditions (i.e., where the central fish was surrounded by others facing the opposite direction) than in the congruent ones (i.e., the central fish was surrounded by others facing the same direction). Both the

Canadian and the Japanese children showed an interference effect in this traditional task. In contrast to these findings, in the social, facial emotions flanker task, only the Japanese children showed an interference effect, indicating that these children were more strongly affected by the expressions of the faces that surrounded the central figure than the Canadian children were. The Canadian children were less distracted by the social context of the target. These findings provided further support for the interactions between local- and global-level components and their impact on cognitive control, including cultural differences in social orientation. It is important to note that many participants in these cultural studies spoke multiple languages. Therefore, we do not know whether the number of languages spoken affected the relationship between the social context and cognitive control.

7.4 Social Context and Cognitive Control in Children with Different Language Skills

7.4.1 Bilingual Social Contexts and Cognitive Control

Children from different cultural backgrounds often speak multiple languages; therefore, the social context is closely linked to both cognitive and language control – two systems that are interdependent. In their seminal work, Green and Abutalebi (2013) explored the cognitive-linguistic demands of three social contexts: single-language use, dual-language use, and dense code-switching. Bilingual speakers in the single-language context typically communicate with a monolingual person. Therefore, they must suppress one of their languages to prevent cross-language intrusion and maintain the current language goal. From a cognitive flexibility perspective, this context requires mostly stability, strengthening the current language representations by increasing attentional focus, monitoring, and resistance to interference. In a dual-language context, however, the bilingual speaker uses one language with one person and another language with a different person within the same social context. This situation also requires goal maintenance and monitoring but additionally, the speaker also needs to be ready to switch to the other language when addressing the other conversational partner. Thus, both languages have to be highly activated, and attention has to be focused on the conversational partners to switch from one language to the other when needed. This context requires increased stability while focusing on one partner and enhanced flexibility when switching to the other partner. Thus, this social context is highly demanding on cognitive control. Finally, dense code-switching contexts involve communicative partners that speak the same languages and are ready to switch between them frequently. A bilingual individual who is involved in a dense code-switching context must identify conversational cues and engage or disengage in one language or the other accordingly. This context requires intense monitoring, highly focused attention to the conversational cues, and a great amount of flexibility. Taken together, these three social contexts require different levels of control and flexibility to adapt the cognitive system to the changing task demands. Moreover, the same speaker may be involved in all three situations to varying extents.

To specifically target the cognitive control skills across these three bilingual social contexts, Hartanto and Yang (2020) administered nine cognitive control tasks to participants across these contexts and performed a latent variable analysis. Their data revealed that the dual-language context significantly predicted task switching, whereas the dense code-switching context predicted inhibitory control and goal maintenance. Although this latter finding was in contrast to the authors' original hypothesis, which predicted an association between performance in task switching and the dense code-switching context, the results are in line with the predictions of various cognitive control models (e.g., Botvinick & Cohen, 2014; Cohen, 2017). When a certain behavior, such as switching occurs frequently, as in the dense code-switching context, less control is needed, and switching becomes more automatic than in light-switching conditions where switching occurs less frequently. However, the dense code-switching context still requires the management of coactivated language structures. Therefore, inhibitory control is still needed to ensure rule-based switching.

The adaptation of the cognitive system across these bilingual contexts may further vary, depending on whether the dominant or nondominant language is being used by the bilingual speaker (Timmer et al., 2019). Timmer and colleagues applied a common language-switching paradigm, but the frequency with which the dominant and the nondominant languages were used was manipulated. This variation in language context revealed the following pattern. When the switching task involved mainly the dominant language, a symmetric switch cost (i.e., the difference in reaction time between the stay and switch trials) and global slowing of the dominant language were observed. In contrast, when the switching task involved mainly the nondominant language, an asymmetric switching cost with larger costs for the nondominant language and no global slowing down of the dominant language were observed. These results show that the

7.4 Social Context and Cognitive Control

language context has a clear effect on how the cognitive system functions; it reveals that the system adapts flexibly to contextual changes. These outcomes suggest that the activation levels of the two languages are not the same and are altered by the language context.

The above findings show that the cognitive system adapts flexibly to changing conditions whether they are cultural (e.g., cultural orientation) or linguistic (e.g., dominant vs. nondominant language). To follow up on these results, Liu and colleagues (2019) examined the combined effects of language context and social cultural identity on the control system by using a language-switching paradigm as well. The authors were particularly interested in the impact of nonlinguistic factors, such as faces, on the control system. In everyday life, faces help us to decide which language to use. For example, a Chinese-English bilingual child may choose to speak Chinese with someone who has an Asian face and English with someone who has a Caucasian face. Previous research with young adults has shown that the visual cue of a sociocultural face may stimulate language selection (Li et al., 2013). Liu and colleagues (2019) tested the social-cultural identity and language control across three conditions in college students. In the baseline condition, language-switching occurred with no faces; in the congruent condition, Asian faces were presented with the Chinese (dominant) language; and in the incongruent condition, Caucasian faces occurred with the Chinese (dominant) language. In contrast to the baseline condition, where a symmetric switch cost was found, there was an asymmetric switch cost, with a larger cost for the nondominant language than the dominant one in the congruent condition. The presentation of an Asian face while switching to Chinese facilitated the reactivation of the suppressed dominant language, which reduced the switch cost compared to that of the nondominant language (English). The switch cost in the incongruent condition was somewhat similar to the baseline. However, the overall response time was slower, indicating an interference effect. Thus, when the social face and language matched each other, language-switching was facilitated, whereas an interference effect (i.e., overall slowing) was observed when the face did not match the language. The cognitive system adapted to the changing conditions in both cases, but this adaptation was stimulated in the congruent context and hindered in the incongruent context.

These examples show a complex but quite consistent relationship among language control, cognitive control, and the social context in neurotypical children and young adults. A further question is whether these interactions differ in children with language impairment.

7.4.2 Social Context and Emotional and Cognitive Control in Children with Developmental Language Disorder (DLD)

While a rich social context is needed to facilitate language and cognitive development, particularly in children with DLD, it is difficult to develop and maintain appropriate social relationships without having adequate language skills (Andrés-Roqueta et al., 2016). Indeed, children with DLD exhibit a weakness in forming successful social interactions, including peer relationships (Conti-Ramsden & Botting, 2004). They often perform at the extreme ends of the behavioral continuum; they are either quiet and withdrawn, they do not initiate conversations, and tend to play alone, or they are disruptive, occasionally even aggressive with others. These children more often employ nonverbal coping strategies, regardless of their appropriateness to the social situation (Marton et al., 2005), and they use fewer conflict resolution and negotiation strategies than their typically developing peers (Brinton et al., 1998; Stevens & Bliss, 1995). A number of these behavioral patterns indicate that in addition to language impairment, children with DLD also exhibit weaknesses in understanding why other people behave in certain ways in different social contexts. This problem is particularly relevant during the school years, when peer relationships become more complex, and children need to compete and collaborate with one another. It has been shown in the developmental literature that peer relationships play a critical role in both children's social and emotional development (van der Wilt et al., 2019).

Very few sociometric studies have involved children with DLD, and the findings have been mixed (Andrés-Roqueta et al., 2016; Gertner et al., 1994; McCabe & Meller, 2004). Nevertheless, children with DLD tend to receive more negative nominations and show lower social acceptance than their peers. The correlation between peer acceptance and children's social cognitive skills increases with age. Rejection by peers often leads to anxiety, loneliness, and depression (Conti-Ramsden & Botting, 2004; Reijntjes et al., 2010) or to conduct problems and substance abuse in adolescents (Dodge et al., 2003). Anxiety and depression have well-known negative effects on cognitive control, particularly on attention, memory, and processing speed. In highly demanding cognitive conditions, anxiety causes a slowdown in processing reflected by difficulties with attention shifting within and between tasks, resulting in a decrease in processing efficiency (e.g., Derakshan et al., 2009; Eysenck et al., 2007). Depression has a negative effect on cognitive control, too, but depression-related impairments are primarily linked to motivational components, in addition to attention and memory problems (e.g., Gotlib & Joormann, 2010; Grahek

7.4 Social Context and Cognitive Control

et al., 2019). These negative effects of anxiety and depression on cognitive control, however, have not been examined in children with DLD.

Given that friendships serve as protective factors for children (de Bruyn et al., 2010), negative peer acceptance is often associated with bullying and victimization in adolescents. Peer victimization is more frequent in children with DLD than in their peers; these children are subjects of both physical and verbal bullying and unlike in typically developing children, friendships do not serve as buffers in children with DLD (Conti-Ramsden & Botting, 2004; Redmond, 2011). This finding might be related to a number of factors. First, bully victimization is directly associated with weaknesses in social competence, powerlessness, low self-esteem, peer rejection, depression, and anxiety (Evans et al., 2014), which behaviors are frequently observed in children with DLD (Marton et al., 2005). Second, the quality of friendships that children with DLD have is not strong enough to serve as a protective factor. Results from typically developing children indicate that friends who are rejected by their peers do not provide the same buffering effect in their friendships as children who are well accepted by others (Schwartz et al., 2008). Thus, children with DLD may not only have fewer friends than their peers, but their friends may be children who exhibit lower social status among their peers.

These findings show that the difficulties with peer relationships that children with DLD experience are related to multiple cognitive, linguistic, and social issues. This notion was further supported by the results from school-age children who were presented with hypothetical social scenarios to assess negotiation and conflict resolution skills, as well as to identify children's coping strategies (Marton et al., 2005). Children with DLD performed more poorly in every aspect than their peers; their social cognitive scores were significantly lower than their language scores, indicating that their social relationship problems exceeded their language difficulties. Children with DLD tended to use nonverbal means in place of speech; these reactions included physical aggressive behavior, such as pushing and shoving, and withdrawn reactions, such as relinquishing to the partner and avoiding the negotiation process. Notably, a number of these problems were associated with these children's poor cognitive control skills. The error analysis data revealed that children with DLD exhibited difficulties with analyzing the social context and setting goals to either resolve a conflict or to initiate an interaction. They struggled with planning and monitoring the social situation to negotiate and/or collaborate with their peers. Similar to the findings of Brinton and colleagues (1998), children's remarks reflected their weaknesses in recognizing the perspectives and needs of their partners within the social context.

Considering previous findings in five-year-old, typically developing children who indicated a strong relationship between affective perspective taking and cognitive control, the lack of perspective taking in children with DLD might be related to their weaknesses in cognitive control. In typically developing children, affective perspective taking showed a correlation with children's empathy. Those children who showed more empathy were able to take the cognitive and the emotional perspectives of others more efficiently. The outcomes further supported the hypothesis that cognitive control and emotion regulation are integrated systems that underlie empathic responses in children (Hinnant & O'Brien, 2007). Thus, children with DLD show multiple handicaps in initiating and maintaining peer relationships and friendships. In addition to their language impairment, they also show difficulties in perspective taking that seem to be related to their weakness in cognitive control. These findings have significant implications for clinical intervention; it is not enough to focus on these children's language abilities; other cognitive and social skills must be considered during intervention as well.

7.5 Conclusions

There is a close relationship among social context, emotion regulation, and cognitive control. Social context at the local level (e.g., register use) is more dynamically changing than the context at the global level (e.g., culture, SES, age), which is more predictable. Both local and global changes have significant effects on children's cognitive control and language performance. Moreover, these contexts interact with one another, and may either facilitate or interfere with children's cognitive-linguistic functions. These effects are reflected at both the behavioral and neural levels. The adaptation of the cognitive system in different social contexts is also influenced by the language skills of children. While typically developing bilingual children may show more flexibility across contexts than their peers, children with DLD may exhibit weaknesses in forming successful social interactions. Their language and cognitive control problems may be intensified by particular social contexts (e.g., peer interactions). Taken together, children react differently to the presence of other people in social situations, and the social context affects their cognitive linguistic performance. Children's behavior across social situations is most strongly influenced by their age, cultural background, socioeconomic status, language skills, and emotion regulation. Research and clinical work targeting children's cognitive-linguistic skills must consider the effects of these contextual influences.

CHAPTER 8

Processing Speed and Cognitive Control

8.1 Behavioral and Neural Correlates of Processing Speed

Why are various people faster than others when performing the same task?[1] Moreover, why is a single person faster with only certain tasks? To answer these questions, we need to explore both inter- and intra-individual variations in processing speed and cognitive control, across different conditions and tasks. Processing speed can be measured at the neurophysiological and behavioral levels using distinct tasks that may differ in modality, length, and complexity. Therefore, individual variations in processing speed reflect differences in both skills and tasks. For example, perceptual speed is typically measured with simple tasks, whereas decision speed is assessed with more complex ones (Salthouse, 2000).

Simple processing speed tasks involve motor or sensory-motor exercises and measure simple reaction time (RT) to reflect the participants' perception of the stimulus and their motor reaction to it. However, the perception of the task, the early phase of information processing, may be measured separately from the motor reaction. The indicator of this early phase of information processing is the inspection time, which has been closely linked to individual IQ scores and shown to vary with age (Jensen, 2005; O'Connor & Burns, 2003). In contrast to simple RT measures, more complex tasks, such as choice reaction time tasks, require that participants discriminate among items and make a decision, in addition to perceiving the task and producing a motor response. Processing load differs significantly between simple RT measures that require a quick response and

---

[1] The content of this chapter is based, in part, on Marton, K., & Gazman, Z. (2019). Interactions among speed of processing, cognitive control, age, and bilingualism. In I. A. Sekerina, L. Spradlin, & V. Valian (Eds.), *Bilingualism, executive function, and beyond. Questions and insights* (pp. 281–293). John Benjamins Publishing Company.

more complex tasks that require mental manipulations and the involvement of control processes (Chiaravalloti et al., 2003). Thus, performance on more complex processing speed tasks is more demanding on cognitive control skills, such as goal maintenance, attention shifting, and inhibition (Cepeda et al., 2013). When researchers use complex speed of processing tasks to assess individual differences in RT, they measure their participants' cognitive control skills, in addition to their processing speed.

Individual differences at the behavioral level are also associated with neural processing speed. Neuroimaging studies suggest that the relationship between processing speed and neural speed reflects individual differences in white-matter tract integrity (Schubert et al., 2019). High-level cognitive functioning requires widespread brain networks with well-connected white matter that may allow for faster and more efficient information processing (Penke et al., 2012). White-matter integrity is not a tract specific but a brain-wide property. White matter pathways support information processing across brain networks and facilitate the integration of activities carried out by different brain areas. Variations in the microstructure of white matter tracts that interconnect the brain areas supporting high-level cognitive functioning account for the individual differences in behavioral processing speed (Turken et al., 2008). Thus, people with widely connected white matter show improved speed of processing compared to those with less integrated brain networks. Given the interconnectivity of brain areas, weaknesses in one brain tract affect other brain tracts, and this is reflected in an overall slower processing speed, even though neurons might compensate for the connectivity loss with an increase in synaptic response (i.e., less wiring, more firing; Daselaar et al., 2015). Thus, greater brain activity compensates for declines in white-matter connectivity.

8.2   Processing Speed and Cognitive Control

Processing speed and cognitive control show strong interactions; there is a negative correlation between them. The more automatic a behavior, the less cognitive control is needed and the information is processed faster. With faster processing, more content may be integrated efficiently within the same timeframe because fast processing allows one to analyze and interpret more information before the relevant memory traces fade (Demetriou et al., 2013). If, in addition to fast speed, working memory capacity is also increased, then information processing can be further enhanced, and more complex concepts can be more easily analyzed and integrated. Two well-established phenomena in the cognitive control literature are flexibility and

8.2 *Processing Speed and Cognitive Control*

adaptation (Botvinick et al., 2001). If there is multiple presentation of the same item or problem in a task, then performance becomes faster and less controlled as a result of repetition-based practice (Shiffrin & Schneider, 1977). The cognitive system adapts to task-related contextual changes and performance becomes more automatic. Processing speed increases with consistent practice, regardless of the cognitive load, but variations in cognitive load may affect the rate of acquisition. Other examples of the cognitive system's adaptability are related to post-error adjustments, such as post-error slowing, post-error reduction of interference, and post-error improvement in accuracy (see the explanation further on).

Error detection studies also revealed negative correlations between processing speed and cognitive control. Following an error production, the cognitive system recruits more control (e.g., attention) and slows down to focus on the task and improve performance accuracy by carrying out more careful response selection. This results in an increase in cognitive control, with a decrease in processing speed (Notebaert et al., 2009). According to the cognitive control account, these post-error adjustments are triggered by the performance monitoring system. However, the cognitive control account may also be linked to the inhibition account suggesting reduced motor activity in post-error trials (Danielmeier & Ullsperger, 2011). Once participants make an error, they receive top-down signals from the monitoring system, consequently they start focusing more attention on the task and slow down their motor responses to avoid making further errors.

Alternative explanations of post-error slowing are provided by the orienting hypothesis (Notebaert et al., 2009) and the disengagement account (Carp & Compton, 2009). The orienting hypothesis suggests that post-error slowing is a response to an unexpected event (i.e., an error). The authors used an oddball paradigm to demonstrate that people slow down in response to infrequent stimuli, even if the response is correct (post-correct slowing). This account is further supported by neurophysiological findings; EEG studies revealed a correlation between post-error reaction time and the P3 component, which is specifically linked to orienting responses when novel stimuli are processed (Nunez Castellar et al., 2010). This finding, however, does not contradict the interpretation of the cognitive control model because the P3 component reflects attentional resource allocation. Thus, both the cognitive control and the orienting model associate post-error slowing with refocusing attention, but the two accounts emphasize different aspects of this process. The disengagement hypothesis, however, is based on the observation that following an error, individuals do not disengage from the task as quickly as they do following a correct response (Carp & Compton, 2009). Interestingly, the observed reduction in alpha power following an error may signal an orienting response. Taken together, the cognitive control model, the orienting account, and the disengaging hypothesis all point to the role of attention in post-error slowing, even if they do so to varying degrees.

The findings on post-error slowing are also influenced by variations in task and stimulus type, as well as complexity level. According to the cognitive control account, task complexity is determined by both information load and information diversity. Thus, different task features determine the amount of cognitive control needed to perform a given task (Campbell, 1988). For example, if the time interval between the stimuli or between a cue and a stimulus is short, then there is little cognitive control involvement. However, more control would be recruited if the instructions emphasized accuracy over speed, but only if the task is not too difficult for the participants. If the task is too difficult, then regardless of the instructions, individuals may not benefit from recruiting further cognitive control (Danielmeier & Ullsperger, 2011).

Nevertheless, task, item, and instruction types are not the only factors that influence the amount of cognitive control one recruits to improve task performance. Individual differences in skills play a major role as well, and they may lead to a trade-off between processing speed and cognitive control. For example, in a study examining task switching and working memory, children who demonstrated more flexible switching between rules showed better performance on a working memory task than children who tended to perseverate. However, children's increased flexibility came at a cost in speed. Flexible switchers performed more slowly than perseverators on these tasks when there was distraction. Flexible switchers used more proactive control, while perseverators relied on reactive control. In the presence of a distractor, children seemed to revert back to reactive control, in which perseverators were more efficient than flexible switchers (Blackwell & Munakata, 2014). Why did flexible switchers perform more slowly in the presence of a distractor? These children had relied more on proactive control which was disrupted by shifting their attention to the distracting task. Thus, children's strategy use – even if it is implicit – plays an important role in their performance on more complex speeded tasks. Certain strategies (e.g., memory retrieval) are faster and more efficient than others (e.g., counting aloud). Hence, the relationship between processing speed and cognitive control is influenced by individual skills, task types, and complexity, as well as strategy use. Cognitive skills in children, however, are also modulated by age because cognitive control develops throughout puberty.

8.3 Age-Related Changes in Processing Speed during Childhood and Adolescence

Processing speed changes in RT can be depicted by a "u" shape over the lifetime. Processing speed is slower during childhood and adolescence than in adults, even though it gradually increases. Young adults show the fastest processing, while older adults exhibit a slow decline in processing speed (Kail & Salthouse, 1994). Increases in processing speed during childhood and adolescence are linked to improved information processing and the development of higher-level cognitive functions that are associated with the maturation of the prefrontal cortex (Kail, 2008). Adolescence is typically defined as the age range between ten and nineteen years (WHO, 2021), and it is a period of behavioral transitions that are reflected by sensitivity to social cues, increased risk taking, and improved cognitive control (Brenhouse & Andersen, 2011). At the neuronal level, this period is characterized by synaptic refinement, specifically by pruning the dendritic branching, which helps to streamline processing (Purves & Lichtman, 1980). As the neuronal networks become more mature, existing redundancies create inefficient processing, so certain synapses are pruned to increase speed and processing efficiency.

Children's behavioral outcomes on cognitive control tasks are closely linked to these biological maturational factors. A central question of the mental speed theory of cognition (Jensen, 2006) is whether children's greater distractibility and more limited attention and working memory span are causes for their slower processing speed or rather manifestations of a limited system that is also responsible for their slower processing. According to the resource theories, older children perform faster on the same tasks as younger children because they need fewer resources to perform a particular activity; therefore, they have more resources available for memory operations (Case et al., 1982), so this account supports the idea of a limited system that is responsible for both capacity constraints and slower processing speed.

An alternative explanation of age-related changes in working memory and processing speed is provided by the task-switching model (Towse & Hitch, 1995). In linguistic span tasks, where participants have to process sentences and remember their final words, children may use the sentence context to help reconstruct the list of words that have to be remembered. If the task is too complex (processing syntactically complex sentences; recalling exact word order; increasing set length, etc.), then this reconstitution process may be too demanding for the cognitive system, and processing may take so long that pieces of information get lost. The reconstitution process is associated with attention control, so the outcomes of complex working memory span tasks may reflect the ability to control attention, while response times may signal retrieval speed (Hitch et al., 2001; Kail & Salthouse, 1994). Younger children's attentional capacity is more limited than that of older children, and this is reflected in their working memory performance.

The relationship between processing speed and cognitive control is further influenced by the fact that children of different ages may perform the same tasks using different control functions and different strategies (Kail, 1991). This is often reflected in their errors. For example, while performing the same linguistic span tasks, younger children (7–8 years) produced more interference errors than omissions, even in simple sentence conditions, whereas older children (9–11 years) produced interference errors only in complex sentence conditions but more omissions in simple sentences. Younger children also relied more on storage resources than their older peers and showed more difficulty in attention switching, as well as in flexible adaptation to changing task requirements (Marton et al., 2005). These error productions reflected the developmental trajectory of interference control, which improves throughout puberty. Changes in inhibitory control support children's regulation of their motor behavior, attention, and thought processes and, therefore, play a central role in cognitive development (Bjorklund & Harnishfeger, 1990; Harnishfeger & Bjorklund, 1993).

Another critical factor behind children's slower processing in cognitive tasks is their lack of experience and practice. This was demonstrated by Kail and Park (1990), using mental rotation tasks with children and young adults (11–20 years of age). Without any practice, the young adults outperformed the children, but those children who had enough practice performed faster than the adults with no experience. As discussed above, practice leads to more automatic performance, which is signaled by higher accuracy and faster processing speed. To better understand the mechanisms that allow practiced individuals to become faster, master chess players' moves were also analyzed (Sheridan & Rheingold, 2014). Eye-tracking data revealed that chess masters found the relevant regions on the chess board much faster than the novices because masters showed more efficient detection as a result of a practice-related perceptual coding advantage and enhanced memory skills. The eye-mind link hypothesis (Reingold et al., 2012) suggests that higher-level cognitive skills, such as memory, have a strong effect on eye-movement control, facilitating perceptual coding.

8.3 Age-Related Changes in Processing Speed

An additional widely accepted component behind age-related changes in cognitive development is the so-called *common factor* in processing speed, that was suggested by the mental speed theory of cognition (Jensen, 2006). Findings across studies revealed that this common factor is similar to the psychometric *g* of intelligence, and reflects a general mental aspect of cognitive development. The outcomes from a comprehensive review of 72 published studies showed that this is a domain-general, nonlinear, and nontask-specific factor that rapidly changes during childhood (Kail, 1991). However, further research is needed to better understand the nature and role of this common factor.

This was the goal of Demetriou and his colleagues (2013), who decided to integrate the findings on age, processing speed, working memory (i.e., higher-level cognitive function), and fluid intelligence (*gf*) by using structural equation modeling. Their findings indicate two levels of mental organization: efficiency and representation. While efficiency is closely linked to processing speed, representation is associated with cognitive control. Processes within levels (i.e., efficiency and representation) are more strongly related than processes across levels. Different processes emerge as the result of cycles of differentiation and integration. Processing speed and cognitive control show a dynamic relationship within these cycles from early to late childhood, as the cognitive processes begin to differentiate. These functional changes are also related to cyclical changes in the neuronal network. For example, there are cyclical changes in cortical thickness during childhood and adolescence, as phases of thickening are followed by pruning (Shaw et al., 2006). The findings suggest that cognitive development is more about these dynamic changes in cortical maturation than about the amount of grey matter.

Although there are many questions remaining about the age-related changes in processing speed, particularly about the common factor, there is agreement in the literature about the interaction between processing speed and cognitive control. It has become clear that more complex speeded tasks require the involvement of more control processes. Thus, their results reflect both children's processing speed and cognitive control skills. The interaction between task complexity and their demands on cognitive control might lead, on the one hand, to an overestimation of age-related changes in processing speed in complex tasks and, on the other, to an underestimation of age-related changes in cognitive control (Cepeda et al., 2013). Thus, if we want to focus on age-related changes in processing speed, we need to use simple speeded tasks that do not tap into cognitive control as much as complex tasks do because these control functions show significant development during childhood and adolescence.

8.4 Language Status and Processing Speed

Although it is generally accepted in the literature that there is a relationship between processing speed and language development, there is no clear answer about the direction of this relationship. Does processing speed have a significant effect on language development or does the child's language learning experience affect the overall processing speed? Both questions have been explored, but no consensus has been reached. However, there are findings in typically developing preschool-age children suggesting that processing speed can predict language development, particularly vocabulary acquisition (Fernald & Marchman, 2012). This link was explained within the resource theory suggesting that children who process information more quickly have more resources available to attend to relevant language features than children who process material more slowly. Processing speed along with working memory have predicted different aspects of children's language development. While processing speed at two years of age predicted children's receptive language skills at four years of age, working memory was a predictor of both receptive and expressive language abilities at four (Newbury et al., 2016). This finding on working memory is in line with other studies pointing to the role of working memory in language development (e.g., Gathercole, 2006).

Developmental scientists also found a similar time course for processing speed, working memory, and fluid intelligence, suggesting that these skills develop together (Fry & Hale, 2000). However, the direction of these associations is not clear. Some findings suggest that processing speed and working memory together affect intelligence (Schatz et al., 2000). Others propose that age-related changes in IQ are mediated by the effect of processing speed on working memory (Fry & Hale, 1996, 2000), while a third group of scholars imply that variations in performance IQ may contribute to processing speed development (Miller et al., 2001). In addition to its theoretical relevance, this question is also important because processing speed and working memory predict academic achievements, such as reading efficiency and mathematic performance in school-age children (Mulder et al., 2010).

Even though the directional links among processing speed, working memory, and other cognitive control functions, as well as different language skills, are not clear, there is a rich literature on school-age children's processing. There are studies examining these relationships in children with different cognitive, motor, and language impairments (Piek et al., 2007); in children with emotional and behavioral disorders (Mayes & Calhoun,

8.4 Language Status and Processing Speed

2007); and in children with various health problems, such as leukemia (Schatz et al., 2000). Considering our interest in processing speed and cognitive control along the language continuum, we focus on monolingual children with language impairment and on bilingual children, including bilingual children with language impairment.

8.4.1 Processing Speed in Monolingual Children with Developmental Language Disorder (DLD)

Children with DLD often respond more slowly than their typically developing peers on different cognitive tasks, and this slowness has been associated with a weakness in rapid temporal processing (Benasich et al., 2002; Kail, 1994). According to the generalized slowing account, children with DLD exhibit slowing across all aspects of mental processing in both linguistic and nonlinguistic tasks (Miller et al., 2001; Windsor & Hwang, 1999). However, there are significant individual differences within the groups of children with DLD (Windsor & Hwang, 1999). Even though the majority of children with DLD perform slower on cognitive tasks than the controls, there are a few children with DLD in almost every study who perform similarly to their typically developing peers.

Furthermore, weaknesses in processing speed could not be linked to the severity of children's language impairment, as measured by standardized language tests (Lahey et al., 2001). Thus, children with more severe language impairment are not necessarily slower than children with milder language problems. There may be several reasons for this finding. The standardized tests may not be sensitive enough to capture the relationship between processing speed and language ability (i.e., the severity of the impairment). Alternatively, the information-processing tasks are often quite complex, with relatively high cognitive demands, particularly in attention, working memory, and interference control. Hence, these tasks may reflect children's weaknesses in cognitive control independent from the severity of their language impairment. Furthermore, nonlinguistic processing speed appears to be a better predictor for ruling in DLD than for ruling out DLD. Slow processing has hardly ever been seen in typically developing children, but it is common among children with DLD (Park et al., 2015). It is also possible that slow processing is linked to the presence of language impairment, but regardless of severity.

Further research on the relationship between processing speed and cognitive control is needed to explain these inconsistencies in outcomes. Current findings in the literature regularly show weaknesses in various cognitive control functions in children with DLD. These children perform more poorly than the controls in tasks, including attention control (Finneran et al., 2009; Marton, 2008); working memory (Archibald & Gathercole, 2006a; Marton & Schwartz, 2003; Montgomery, 2003); planning and goal maintenance (Henry et al., 2012; Roello et al., 2015); task switching (Dibbets et al., 2006; Marton, 2008; Vissers et al., 2015); and interference control (Marton et al., 2014; Seiger-Gardner & Schwartz, 2008). Poor performance is often reflected in both accuracy and processing speed but in some cases, there is a trade-off between the two. Overall, there is a link between processing speed and cognitive control in children with DLD, similar to that in typically developing children and adults. A remaining question is whether children with more severe language impairment exhibit more severe difficulties in cognitive control.

There is one cognitive control function, inhibition, for which the findings are less consistent. Some authors found no difference between children with DLD and their typically developing peers on inhibition tasks (Laloi et al., 2017; Marton et al., 2012), while others reported group differences (Spaulding, 2010). There are a number of explanations for these mixed outcomes. First, most inhibition tasks measure multiple components of inhibitory control; therefore, they do not necessarily reflect the same underlying mechanisms, and researchers have used a number of different tasks across studies. Further, inhibition is a multicomponent construct, and its subcomponents show different developmental patterns. For example, response inhibition develops earlier than resisting interference (Ridderinkhof et al., 1999). Finally, children with DLD appear to be younger in those studies where a group difference in response inhibition was found compared to studies with no group effects. Thus, the findings suggest that during the preschool years, children with DLD perform more poorly than their typically developing peers in response inhibition, but this difference disappears by school age. Given that most inhibition tasks are nonlinguistic in nature (e.g., Stop-Signal tasks, Go-NoGo tasks), this age-related difference is in line with findings from developmental studies with typically developing children, indicating that the age-related changes in processing speed are greater for nonverbal tasks than for language tasks (Kail & Miller, 2006).

Whether these developmental changes in response inhibition reflect the changes in processing speed and whether the processing speed differences in nonverbal tasks between children with DLD and their typically developing peers are larger during the preschool years than in school age is unknown. Overall, children with DLD are slower in processing information across domains (i.e., verbal and nonverbal) than their typically developing peers, and they also exhibit weaknesses in most cognitive control functions. These difficulties are often beyond the processing speed differences. Individual differences in processing speed within the group of children with DLD also contribute to the complexity of the relationship among processing speed, cognitive control, and language. Therefore, more research is needed to clarify these questions. One particular area of interest is bilingual children with language impairment. This is an exciting new direction of research that might help us to understand more about the relationship among processing speed, cognitive control, and language.

8.4.2 Processing Speed in Bilingual Typically Developing Children

One of the most widely debated questions in the bilingualism literature is whether individuals who speak more than one language show a cognitive advantage compared to monolingual speakers. A further question is whether this advantage is limited to processing speed or is related to different cognitive control skills as well. Some authors reported an advantage in specific cognitive control functions, such as conflict resolution (Costa et al., 2008); selective attention (Salvatierra & Rosselli, 2011); and interference control (Engel de Abreu et al., 2012), while others suggested that bilingual individuals only show a more general processing speed advantage compared to their monolingual peers (Hilchey & Klein, 2011). A third group of investigators argued that there is no difference in cognitive control between bilingual and monolingual participants (Valian, 2015; Yudes et al., 2011).

Even though a large number of studies have been published on this particular issue across the lifespan, the results are not conclusive. A number of factors contribute to these mixed outcomes, such as the age of the participants (i.e., children, young adults, elderly people); their bilingual experience (i.e., age of acquisition, frequency of language use, level of proficiency, etc.); the particular cognitive function studied (interference control, task switching, working memory, attention, inhibition, etc.); and the nature of the tasks (level of complexity; targeted domain and modality; validity and reliability of the measures, etc.).

Bilingual language processing is characterized by bidirectional interactions between the two languages that are associated with both domain-general cognitive mechanisms and domain-specific language functions (Kroll & Bialystok, 2013; Kroll et al., 2015). In the Adaptive Control Hypothesis,

Green and Abutalebi (2013) linked different control processes to distinct communicative contexts and suggested that bilingual speakers exercise various control mechanisms as they adapt their cognitive systems to different communicative contexts (e.g., dense language-switching vs. monolingual situations). Thus, during daily interactions, bilingual individuals activate different control processes, depending on their communicative partners. With monolingual speakers, they need to select one language as target and suppress the other. With a pair of bilingual speakers who share both of their languages, they may switch from one language to the other, according to pragmatic needs. The idea behind the bilingual cognitive advantage is related to the continuous use of different control mechanisms during language selection and language-switching. Thus, bilingual individuals' superior performance on cognitive control tasks has been attributed to these cross-language interactions and to the associated operations of domain-general cognitive processes (e.g., Costa et al., 2008; Salvatierra & Rosselli, 2011).

A frequently recurring question in the bilingualism literature is whether the bilingual cognitive advantage is limited to faster processing speed or also entails qualitative differences in specific control functions. Differences in processing speed between bilingual and monolingual groups are particularly noticeable in children and older adults. (We only focus on children in this chapter.) Six-year-old bilingual children exhibited superior processing speed in the Global–Local and Trail Making tasks compared to their monolingual peers (Bialystok, 2010). These tasks were highly demanding on several cognitive control mechanisms. The bilingual children outperformed their monolingual peers in both the most difficult incongruent conditions, which required inhibitory control, as well as in the congruent conditions that did not involve any conflict. However, these conditions were demanding on different cognitive control processes because children had to maintain two sets of responses and switch between conditions in the mixed blocks. In contrast to their performance on these complex tasks, the groups did not differ in simpler processing speed tasks, such as the box completion task. Thus, the groups did not differ in basic processing speed, but the bilingual children performed faster than their monolingual peers in the more complex conditions that were more demanding on cognitive control.

Bilingual children (5–7 years of age) performed faster than their monolingual peers in working memory tasks with varying memory load and with manipulations of conflict, too (Morales et al., 2013). Bilingual children were more efficient in holding two or four rules in memory

8.4 Language Status and Processing Speed

while ignoring distracting stimuli. Bonifacci and colleagues also showed that bilingual children outperformed their monolingual peers in an anticipatory task with a higher cognitive control load but performed similarly to their monolingual peers in working memory tasks with minimal language load and low cognitive control demands (Bonifacci et al., 2011). The findings from these studies indicate that processing speed differences between bilingual and monolingual children are more pronounced in tasks with high than with low cognitive control demands. Thus, the bilingual advantage is more noticeable in complex conditions than in simple tasks.

In addition to task complexity, participants' language proficiency may also influence the outcomes (see details in Chapter 5, "Associations among Language Ability, Language Proficiency, and Cognitive Control"). In four subgroups of four–seven-year-old, English-Hebrew speaking bilingual children (balanced high proficient bilingual speakers, L2-dominant, L1-dominant, and children with low proficiency), children with high language proficiency outperformed their peers with low language proficiency in resisting interference and switching but not in concept generation across different nonverbal tasks (Iluz-Cohen & Armon-Lotem, 2013). Similar results were produced by eight–eleven-year-old, bilingual children in resisting interference and in performance monitoring using a simple verbal task (i.e., a categorization task using single high frequency words). Highly proficient bilingual children showed smaller interference effects and faster processing speed than children with lower language proficiency (Marton, 2015). Language proficiency was measured along a continuum in this study. Based on the findings, we examined the relationship between processing speed and language proficiency using path analysis and found different patterns. Whereas language proficiency had a direct effect on children's interference errors and on their processing speed in the interference task, the effect of language proficiency was mediated by processing speed in the performance monitoring task (see Figure 8.1). Thus, processing speed contributes to the interaction between language proficiency and cognitive control, and this interaction varies depending on the given cognitive control component. In some cases, language proficiency's effect is mediated by processing speed, in other cases, it has a direct effect on the cognitive control function. Processing speed, however, does not affect cognitive control functions independently from language proficiency. These are preliminary results and more research is needed on the relationship between children's language proficiency and processing speed.

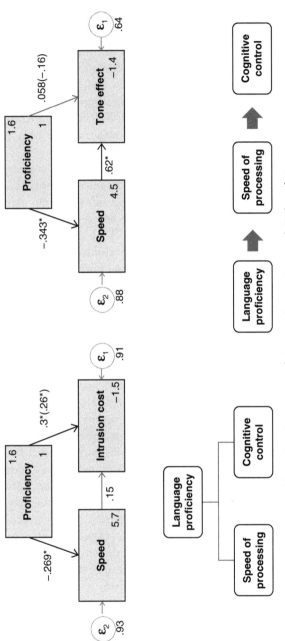

Figure 8.1 Language proficiency and processing speed: Path analysis

8.4.3 Processing Speed in Bilingual Children with DLD

The critical question here is whether the bilingual experience attenuates the weaknesses in cognitive control in bilingual children with DLD. This is a relatively new field of research that has developed as the need for disentangling the effects of bilingualism and DLD on cognitive-linguistic performance have increased (Armon-Lotem & de Jong, 2015), so the literature on cognitive control and processing speed in bilingual children with DLD is scarce and the findings are mixed.

Engel de Abreu and colleagues (2014) compared Portuguese and Luxembourgish bilingual children with DLD to bilingual typically developing children and to Portuguese monolingual typically developing children on measures of verbal and visuospatial working memory and distractor interference. The bilingual typically developing children performed significantly faster than their monolingual peers on the flanker task that measured resistance to distractor interference, and the bilingual children with DLD showed similar processing speed to the monolingual typically developing children. These results are intriguing because the findings indicate that in tasks with minimal language demands, bilingual children with DLD perform with similar processing speed than monolingual typically developing children. This is in contrast to findings from monolingual children with DLD, who often perform more slowly than the typically developing children on tasks measuring nonverbal working memory or interference control (Marton, 2008; Marton et al., 2014). Unfortunately, Engel de Abreu and colleagues' study did not involve a group of monolingual children with DLD.

Laloi and colleagues (2017) also examined cognitive control in bilingual children with DLD by using a Stop-Signal task. The bilingual and monolingual children performed similarly in this study, but the children with DLD were slower than their typically developing peers. These findings contradict some of the previous results. As discussed above, response inhibition does not clearly distinguish children with different language skills, even though influential models of bilingualism are based on inhibitory control for adults (e.g., Green, 1998).

Marton and colleagues' (2019) preliminary findings from monolingual and bilingual children with and without DLD indicate a complex interaction between bilingualism and language impairment. Performance on the N-back task revealed that bilingualism may attenuate the negative effects of DLD, especially in simple task conditions. With smaller set sizes and no interference conditions, bilingual children with DLD showed similar processing speed to monolingual typically developing children. An increase in task complexity (i.e., set size and interference condition), however, resulted in a growing gap between children with DLD and their typically developing peers, regardless of bilingual status. The findings are similar to those by Engel de Abreu and colleagues (2014) and suggest that bilingualism may have a positive effect on processing speed in children with DLD when the task conditions are simple, but in more difficult contexts, language impairment has a stronger effect than bilingualism on cognitive control and processing speed.

8.5 Conclusions

Processing speed and cognitive control show a complex interaction that is influenced by a number of factors, such as age, task complexity and modality, targeted cognitive functions, and children's language ability and proficiency. The age-related (maturational) factors are closely linked to children's behaviors and experiences with different cognitive control tasks. Although within-group performances are highly influenced by individual differences, monolingual children with DLD generally perform more slowly than their typically developing peers, whereas bilingual children often outperform their monolingual peers in processing speed. Bilingual children with DLD provide an unparalleled opportunity to study the joint effects of bilingualism and DLD on processing speed. The preliminary findings suggest that bilingualism does attenuate the negative effects of DLD but only in simple task conditions. Future research is needed to better understand the relationship between processing speed and cognitive control in children with different language abilities and proficiencies.

CHAPTER 9

Cognitive Training and Language

9.1 Conceptual Foundations

Over the past two decades, research on cognitive training has greatly expanded in a number of disciplines (e.g., experimental psychology, education, neuroscience). The burst of cognitive training studies in the literature has also created ongoing debates regarding the effectiveness of training. Some of the most challenging topics include individual differences in responsiveness to training, transfer effects, and measurement issues. The focus in this chapter is on the effects of training in children, with special attention to those with different language skills (e.g., second language learners, children with developmental language disorder). Therefore, leaving aside other widely targeted domains in the general training literature, our discussion centers around a few selected training domains most often associated with language acquisition and language processing.

9.1.1 Cognitive- and Neuroplasticity

The technical advances of the twenty-first century have had a great impact on brain studies, including research on plasticity. Advances in noninvasive imaging techniques have allowed researchers to examine functional and structural changes in the brain in response to environmental modifications. While earlier studies focused primarily on age-related changes in children, more recent research has also examined the functional and structural changes in response to training in both children and adults (for reviews see e.g., Erickson et al., 2013; Kolb et al., 2003; Mahncke et al., 2006). Measures of functional brain plasticity, for instance, have predicted individual differences in response to training (Iuculano et al., 2015).

Progress in neuroscience research has resulted in a greater understanding of brain functions during learning, brain lateralization, and sensitive periods of brain development when the neural system is most receptive to environmental influences. While these sensitive periods are typically associated with the first couple of years of life, sensitive periods of brain development for higher cognitive functions extend into adolescence. Moreover, there is evidence for brain plasticity beyond these periods and into adulthood (Rice & Barone, 2000; Shaw et al., 2008). A number of studies found that activities, such as exercising, typing, juggling, playing video games, and mindfulness often culminate in changes in gray matter, even in adults (Driemeyer et al., 2008; Hamzei et al., 2012; Hölzel et al., 2011; Kühn et al., 2014).

Such changes in gray matter are dynamic in nature with overproduction and regression in different areas of the brain, peaking at varying ages. The developmental trajectories of gray matter in children also differ across those brain regions that support the development of various cognitive skills. These trajectories indicate a strong association with gender, intelligence, and overall functioning. For example, females typically reach peak gray matter volumes one to two years earlier than males (Giedd et al., 1999), and children with higher IQs demonstrate a more dynamic pattern of brain plasticity than children with lower IQs within the average range of intelligence (Shaw et al., 2006). In addition to these changes in gray matter, the white matter myelination process also continues beyond childhood and adolescence (Rapoport & Gogtay, 2008). Thus, current findings show that besides age, many other factors influence changes in the brain, and this needs to be considered when interpreting and translating the outcomes from neuroscience research into educational practices.

The initial excitement over the new findings on cognitive and brain plasticity contributed to the rapid development of various brain training products that quickly became popular among educators and within the general public. This trend was in line with the increasing spread of new technologies within society. Unfortunately, a number of these brain training techniques were not rigorously studied prior to becoming commercially available and consequently led to the development of some questionable teaching strategies and inefficient educational methods in the past (Alferink & Farmer-Dougan, 2010). Despite the lack of evidence about these products' effectiveness, a growing number of educators and clinicians started using them with different populations (Rossignoli-Palomeque et al., 2018). During the last decade, however, researchers from both neuroscience and education have given increasing efforts to narrow the gap between basic research and theory and practice in education (Hruby, 2012). These interdisciplinary advances have offered great support to neuroscience-based approaches to educational and clinical practices. Nonetheless, it is essential that educators and clinicians work together with neuroscientists to avoid the oversimplification or misinterpretation of basic neuroscience outcomes within their practices.

9.1.2 Generalization – Transfer

One of the most critical features of training is generalization or transfer. "Transfer" is a term that has been widely used in the literature but with inconsistent meaning. Some scholars refer to three dimensions within this concept: tasks, contexts, and transfer across time, while others consider only one or two aspects of this notion (Klahr & Chen, 2011). Moreover, along these dimensions, we find a variety of combinations across studies. In some research, the target training tasks and contexts may be very similar to the testing conditions with only the time intervals varied, whereas in other studies, task features may differ, while the contexts remain the same. The temporal features may also vary to different degrees. The distance between the training task and the transfer battery can be minimal (near transfer) or rather large (far transfer).

Previous research has shown that improving one's performance on specific tasks is relatively easy, regardless of domain (Green, 2020). Study participants get better on the skills they practice, and their improved performance may transfer to other contexts. This is considered near transfer, as long as the same skills are needed during practice and testing. Near transfer can be very useful in certain cases, such as dynamic assessment, which is a test-teach-retest situation. In other cases, such specific changes may indicate a limitation in generalizability. In superficial cases, the literature sometimes refers to the narrow specificity to training tasks and stimuli as the "curse of specificity" (Bavelier et al., 2012). Katz and Shah (2020) distinguished between superficial versus real transfer instead of near and far transfer based on the notion that the ultimate goal of training is to find improvements in measures that are not explicitly targeted in the training paradigm (real transfer). This occurs, for example, when practicing some basic skills (e.g., sustained attention, working memory updating, etc.). Real transfer leads to improvements in more complex behaviors because of changes in the underlying mechanisms (e.g., academic achievement in children; Titz & Karbach, 2014).

However, studies that have examined the effect of training on various functions, including some nontargeted ones, have shown mixed results. Some researchers have found no evidence of transfer (Thompson et al., 2013), while others suggested robust transfer effects (Blacker et al., 2017).

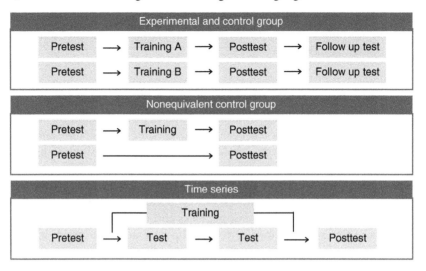

Figure 9.1   Training designs

This discrepancy in outcomes is, to some extent, related to the variability in design of the training and transfer tasks (Shipstead et al., 2012). The following are examples of problems that have been identified in developmental studies with respect to methodological issues: (1) most studies used a pre-and post-test design that seems to be less sensitive to changes than time-series experiments (see Figure 9.1), and they do not allow for detection of effects that occur over time following training (Cepeda at al., 2006; Glass et al., 2008); (2) they did not systematically vary the transfer distance (i.e., near and far) or type of training (Karbach & Kray, 2009); (3) the materials for intervention were not age appropriate (Diamond & Lee, 2011); (4) participants developed different strategies as a mechanism for transfer (Katz & Shah, 2020); and (5) researchers used a limited number of outcome measures, primarily accuracy and reaction time, without considering other outcomes, such as error detection and adjustment, strategy use, or switching and mixing costs in task switching paradigms.

When some of the above variables were controlled, cognitive training, specifically task switching training, resulted in increased real transfer effects, including better interference control, improved working memory performance, and higher scores on fluid intelligence tasks (Kray et al., 2012). The findings of successful training studies have revealed that it is critical to have outcome measures that are more sensitive to changes in the underlying mechanisms than the most common methods (e.g., post-error

9.1 Conceptual Foundations

slowing, post-error reduction of interference, mixing cost, strategy use, etc.). Accordingly, to increase learning and transfer, we need to facilitate different mechanisms that promote brain plasticity, such as multisensory facilitation, reinforcement, multi-stimulus practice, among others (Deveau et al., 2015). Most recent findings suggest that we may also rephrase our research questions; instead of asking whether a training method works, we should identify the individuals who can benefit the most from the given training and focus on answering the question of why some individuals improve their skills significantly, while others show minimal change in response to the same training procedures (Jaeggi et al., 2011).

9.1.3 Individual Differences: Age, Socioeconomic Status, Motivation, Baseline

Even though the outcomes from cognitive training studies are quite mixed, the variations in individual responses to training can be traced to a number of common factors, including age, socioeconomic status, motivation, and baseline performance, as well as the interactions of these variables (Katz et al., 2021). Individual differences in training studies have been noted since the earliest years of research, yet the literature on factors that contribute to these differences contains very few systematic analyses even today. Nevertheless, what follows are some examples demonstrating the contributions of these factors on outcomes in responsiveness to training.

In a large study involving over 600 adolescents and young adults, Knoll and colleagues (2016) found that older adolescents benefited more from training than the younger ones. Training in this study involved complex cognitive tasks and procedures that are believed to support math education, including numerosity discrimination, relational reasoning, and face perception. While face perception did not show any age effect, older adolescents and young adults showed greater improvement in numerosity discrimination and relational reasoning than the younger participants (no one was younger than 11). The authors commented that these data suggest continued brain plasticity for certain cognitive skills, and that the older participants might have used more efficient strategies (Knoll et al., 2016). However, it is important to note when interpreting these findings that the underlying mechanisms for some of these complex cognitive skills continue to develop during adolescence. Neuroscientists consider adolescence as a transitional period of time that is full of transformations. Imaging (i.e., MRI) studies have revealed that neurocircuitry and myelinogenesis are still changing in response to hormonal fluctuations and environmental factors. As the neurocircuitry strengthens, complex cognitive skills, such as problem-solving, multitasking, and processing of complex information, show improvement during adolescence (Arain et al., 2013). Further, the prefrontal cortex reaches maturation during this period; thus, a number of cognitive control skills that are needed to perform complex cognitive tasks, like relational reasoning, are still developing between the ages of ten and twenty-four years (Casey et al., 2008).

In addition to age, socioeconomic status (SES) has also been linked to neurocognitive functions that support language development, cognitive control, and social-emotional processes (Ursache & Noble, 2016). Following evidence showing that cognitive skills, such as attention, are more vulnerable in children from low-SES families, a number of training studies focused on families with low SES (Hackman & Farah, 2009; Stevens et al., 2009) to examine the direct effects of training and the associated engagement of the parents on participating children. The outcomes of these studies are inconsistent. While Neville and colleagues (2013) reported that their family-based training had a positive effect on both children's brain functions supporting selective attention and the parents' behaviors, Romeo and colleagues (2021), who replicated this family-based training, did not find the same results. In the latter study, children's performance in the experimental group differed from the control only in fluid reasoning, but the two groups performed similarly in a number of other outcome measures, including different cognitive control functions and additional aspects of nonverbal IQ. Thus, the training did not improve children's performance in areas other than reasoning. Previous research also showed a positive effect for cognitive training on the reasoning skills of children from disadvantaged families (Mackey et al., 2011). A possible explanation for these positive outcomes is that the training studies targeted problem-solving and encouraged children to choose from various alternatives. Thus, performance on these tasks required focused reasoning from the participants.

The difference in findings between the two similarly designed family-based training studies (Neville et al., 2013; Romeo et al., 2021) is most likely related to distinctions in methodology. Even though they assessed similar skills (e.g., language, problem-solving), they used dissimilar tasks and therefore measured different underlying functions (e.g., receptive vocabulary vs. recall; interpreting verbal material; executing verbal directions). Further, Neville and colleagues (2013) used more rigorous selection criteria, which created a relatively homogeneous group; participants were monolingual and ethnically and racially less diverse, in addition to being

9.1 Conceptual Foundations

a year younger than participants studied by Romeo and colleagues (2021), who had an ethnically and linguistically more diverse sample, including children with developmental disorders, children on medication, and participants who were enrolled in individualized education plans. All of these variables might have contributed to the inconsistent results. These findings show that training studies using the current methodologies most likely produce divergent findings, given the number of distinctive factors that affect the outcomes. These data further support the idea that we need to better understand the factors that affect individual responsiveness to training, develop measures that are more sensitive to changes in the underlying mechanisms, and use multiple outcome measures to get an accurate and comprehensive picture of the training effects.

Children's responsiveness to training is further influenced by motivational factors. A number of constructs have been highlighted in the literature through which extrinsic rewards and expectancy effects have been more widely studied. Although the findings regarding the impact of extrinsic rewards on children's performance are mixed in the literature, there seems to be a consensus among scholars suggesting that frequent and tangible rewards may undermine intrinsic motivation (Deci et al., 2001; Ulber et al., 2016). In contrast, verbal rewards are generally seen to boost intrinsic motivation. While tangible rewards may create a feeling of outside control, verbal rewards are perceived to have an informational function. This is particularly so when rewards are used as incentives compared to behavioral consequences. In the latter case, the reward functions as reinforcement, which is not associated with a loss in intrinsic motivation (Cameron & Pierce, 2002).

Children's perception of rewards is also influenced by the expectancy factor, that is, whether the reward is expected or unexpected. In training studies, this is often determined by the initial information that participants receive. Specifically, whether they are told that the training may improve certain functions, such as cognition or whether they are promised a monetary reward prior to their participation in training. In these cases, participants expect the reward. When no reward is promised prior to participation but is given following completion of the study, that reward is unexpected. Lepper and colleagues' early study has already shown that expected rewards diminish children's intrinsic motivation, whereas unexpected rewards have no such effect (Lepper et al., 1973).

More recent theories of cognitive control, such as the Expected Value of Control model (Shenhav et al., 2013), provide a more nuanced analysis of reward-based decision-making. This theory suggests that when performing a task, motivational factors, such as performance-contingent rewards, modulate how much effort participants will deploy. Exercising control during task performance is costly, and this cost affects how much effort a participant is willing to exert. According to this reward-based perspective, two distinct networks (reward value and control functions) are implicated in encoding those motivational signals to play an essential role in cognitive control (Botvinick & Braver, 2015). During task performance, several competing control signals are compared, and the signal that simultaneously optimizes the potential rewards and benefits while reducing the associated costs is selected. This reward-based decision-making is a critical component of the individual differences detected (Shenhav et al., 2017), and contributes to variations in baseline performance.

The initial behavior prior to training, baseline performance has been widely studied to determine the effectiveness of training methods, and it has been demonstrated that baseline performance and general cognitive resources positively correlate with training gains (Lövdén et al., 2012). Performance at baseline and gains in transfer following training are also linked, but the findings in the literature are mixed. Some outcomes suggest that lower performance at baseline correlates with larger transfer gains, that is, participants who start out with the lowest performance show the greatest improvement following strategy instruction (Johann & Karbach, 2021). Conversely, superior baseline performance associated with better outcomes has also been reported, implying that individuals with better initial cognitive skills show more efficient learning and experience greater gains (Katz et al., 2021). Although the explanations for these two scenarios differ, the role of baseline measures is emphasized in both of them. It is also possible that gains are primarily related to performance at the two ends of the accuracy continuum; participants with the lowest and highest baseline measures benefit most from training. The differences in outcomes might further be related to interactions between baseline performance and other contributing factors, such as SES and motivation.

Baseline behavior plays a critical role in evaluating the response following training and in distinguishing between plasticity and flexibility. An immediate change in performance strategy is viewed as an indication of flexibility rather than a manifestation of plasticity (Wenger et al., 2021). While flexibility is reflected in immediate changes in the targeted behavior, plasticity is exhibited in extended performance changes once conditions are altered. The latter case indicates overall improvement in performance. An accurate assessment at baseline is necessary to clarify the source of improvement. Individual differences in the above components have been explored across various training domains, including domain-specific (e.g., working memory) and multidomain (e.g., music) training that are the two most relevant training types to our topic on cognitive control and language.

9.2 Training to Improve Cognitive Control

9.2.1 Working Memory Training

Working memory training is the focus of a growing line of research with the overall aim of improving cognitive abilities through different brain training programs (Hicks & Engle, 2020). Although there is a debate in the literature about the effectiveness of working memory training, the discussion among scholars is theoretically important and clinically/practically relevant for education, rehabilitation, job training, and aging studies, among others. A critical question is whether transfer occurs due to enhancement in individual working memory capacity or to an increase in efficiency when using the existing capacity following training (Könen et al., 2021). Enhancing working memory capacity is the goal for many training studies with the assumption that enhanced capacity reflects training-induced cognitive plasticity (Lövdén et al., 2010). Several theoretical frameworks, such as that offered by Lövdén or the cognitive routine framework by Gathercole and colleagues (2019), suggest that working memory tasks must create challenges and require novel cognitive routines in order to foster plasticity. One way to achieve this goal is to design adaptive task conditions that keep the working memory demands near the individual's limit. Such adaptive tasks could vary in trial types and testing modes (Könen et al., 2021).

A number of meta-analyses have been performed showing a certain degree of consensus among scholars regarding transfers to other non-trained working memory tasks (near transfer), but there is no agreement about far transfer effects (Könen et al., 2021; Melby-Lervag & Hulme, 2013; Sala et al., 2019). Numerous explanations have been provided for the mixed results. Some are related to theoretical questions, others to methodological ones, such as task selection; matching target functions in training to post-test measures; the length and frequency of the training sessions; and the type of control group.

These critical problems may have contributed to the low percentage of positive findings across studies. In their systematic review, Diamond and Ling (2020) reported data from studies using the two most widely researched training methods: Cogmed and the N-back task. Only 33 percent of studies using the popular computerized Cogmed training found even suggestive evidence for far transfer. Similarly, only 30 percent of studies using the well-established N-back paradigm revealed far transfer following training. The near transfer rates were noticeably higher, particularly for the Cogmed data, but it is important to note that most outcome measures were very similar to the training tasks in the Cogmed studies, and very few N-back studies included children as participants (Diamond & Ling, 2020).

Another criticized aspect of training research is the persistence of improvement. Many working memory training studies did not include long-term follow-up tests. For the ones that examined persistence of benefit, two distinct patterns were found in both behavioral and neurophysiological studies. Some findings showed that without practice, performance returned to baseline, which is the same as the fade-out phenomenon. Others revealed that at least near transfer effects persisted between three and eighteen months following training (Green, 2020; Kuchinsky & Haarmann, 2020). These outcomes are quite contrary. Therefore, a general suggestion for future research is to design behavioral booster training to see whether increased retraining performance could be achieved more consistently.

Despite these issues, Katz and Shah (2020) argued that if the near transfer in these working memory training studies was real and not superficial, then there should be some far transfer as well, even if the evidence for it is elusive. They provided an example related to reading comprehension. If we assume that working memory is a critical component in reading comprehension, and our participants show significant gains in working memory performance following training, then we could expect improvement in reading comprehension as well. However, if the same participants have low vocabulary scores which persist over time, then despite their working memory gains, they may show no improvement in reading comprehension, due to the negative impact imposed by their limited lexical knowledge (Katz & Shah, 2020).

The results from our Cognition and Language laboratory call attention to a further issue. Following a working memory updating training using the N-back task with neutral and proactive interference conditions with college students who were second language learners of English, we found far transfer for certain language tasks but not for others. Specifically, the training that focused on working memory updating and resistance to interference resulted in far transfer to a sentence processing task with

9.2 Training to Improve Cognitive Control 143

lexical ambiguity (adapted from Norbury, 2005). Participants showed significant improvement from pre-test to post-test in resolving interference caused by the sentences with multiple plausible meanings. In contrast, the same participants showed no improvement in reading comprehension. Even though working memory is implicated in reading comprehension, this was an expected outcome because the reading comprehension task was not demanding on updating and interference control where the effects of this particular training could have been manifested (Wadhera, 2020; Wadhera et al., 2018).

Our findings are in line with other scholars' arguments (e.g., Dahlin et al., 2008), emphasizing that it is critical to determine the specific cognitive or linguistic skills that we intend to target with a given training method and with the specific tasks that are being used during training.

9.2.2 Music Training

While working memory training is a domain specific method, music training is a multidomain approach that has an effect on various nonmusical cognitive and speech-language functions, such as memory, cognitive control, and speech encoding (Bugos et al., 2022; Ho et al., 2003; Patel, 2011). Moreover, music may serve as a motivator in any training study for its positive emotional effects. Music training may incorporate music comprehensively or with a focus on one or more elements, such as meter, rhythm, melody, harmony, pitch, tonality, or volume.

A number of studies have examined the specific aspects of musical activities that may affect changes in different cognitive control functions, including visuo-motor skills, focused attention, and memorization, among others (De Dreu et al., 2012; Pallesen et al., 2010). Similar to other types of training, the findings on transfer following music training are mixed. However, more consistent benefits have been seen in studies that targeted cognitive functions associated with auditory information processing and verbal working memory (Moreno et al., 2011; Roden et al., 2014). For several verbal working memory tasks, such as word span and nonword repetition, during natural science activities, Roden and colleagues (2014) reported that children in the music training group outperformed the controls. In contrast, the two groups were equal in visuospatial working memory (Roden et al., 2014). Similarly, Ho and colleagues (2003) studied both the short- and long-term effects of music training on verbal and visuospatial working memory. In their follow-up study, one year after their baseline measures, children who had continued their music training showed further improvement in verbal working memory but not in visuospatial working memory, whereas children who had stopped their training after three months, showed no gains in either area. The authors proposed that children's improvement in verbal working memory following continued music training was related to the reorganization of the temporal lobe (Ho et al., 2003).

A related question has been examined in another longitudinal study, where the focus was on training induced structural changes in the brain that could not be attributed to pre-existing biological traits (Habibi et al., 2018). For two years, these authors studied the effects of music training on six-year-old children's brain structures and compared the data to those from two control groups: children involved in physical training activities and children who did not participate in any extracurricular activities. The baseline measures showed no structural differences among the children in the different groups. Following two years of music training, they found a different rate of cortical thickness maturation in temporal areas of the brain, specifically an asymmetric reduction of cortical thickness and volume of the posterior segment of the superior temporal gyrus and higher fractional anisotropy in the corpus callosum. The implication is that music training resulted in both macro- and microstructural changes in the brain.

These findings have been supported by further neurophysiological outcomes suggesting a link between music training and brain structures that are also involved in language processing at both subcortical and cortical levels of the brain (Jentschke & Koelsch, 2009; Wong et al., 2007). For example, music to language neural transfer was found in four–six-year-old children, who benefited from music training in an electrophysiological study using an oddball paradigm with musical notes (piano tones) and French vowels (Carpentier et al., 2016). These outcomes are consistent with previous results that have suggested increased brain signal complexity in temporal regions which are involved in perceptual processing of both music and language following music training (Koelsch, 2009; Moreno, 2009). Moreover, the music training-related changes in auditory discrimination seem to be modulated by individual differences in cognitive control. In a mismatch negativity study examining event-related potentials induced by sound changes, Saarikivi and colleagues (2016) found larger mismatch negativity, indicating advanced sound discrimination, following music training in children with high cognitive flexibility scores, regardless of their age. In contrast, children with low cognitive flexibility scores showed increases in mismatch negativity amplitude as they aged. Thus, children with lower cognitive flexibility scores were less advanced in sound discrimination, despite their participation in music training. In the control group (no music training), children with high cognitive flexibility scores showed increases in mismatch negativity amplitude with age, similar to the children who received music training but exhibited low cognitive scores. Children with no music training and low cognitive flexibility scores showed small mismatch negativity amplitude, and that did not increase with age. Hence, these data suggest that cognitive flexibility may influence both age-related and training-related plasticity of neural sound discrimination in children (Saarikivi et al., 2016). This is another example of the interaction among multiple factors that influence training outcomes.

In contrast to the findings of these studies (i.e., Ho et al., 2003; Roden et al., 2014), Degé and colleagues (2011) reported improvement in both auditory and visual short-term memory in nine–eleven-year-old children following music training. Their study differed from the others in methods: specifically in the age distribution of the participants; in the tasks administered to measure the memory functions; as well as in the length of training. The results from the study by Degé and colleagues showed more consistencies with the adult literature than with other studies on children. The literature on adults suggests that music training may contribute to the enhancement of general cognitive abilities that are reflected in improved verbal and visual memory performance. A critical issue in the literature is that most of the data come from correlational studies which do not allow any analysis of causal relationships (Swaminathan & Schellenberg, 2021). On the one hand, there are findings suggesting that children's cognitive control skills may modulate the effect of music training (Saarikivi et al., 2016); on the other hand, it has been proposed that music training may exaggerate individual differences in cognitive control and language (Swaminathan & Schellenberg, 2021). It is important for future research to use designs and analyses that enable us to explore the direction of the relationship between music training and different cognitive-linguistic functions.

9.3 Training Effects in Children with Different Language Skills

Studies focusing on far transfer have frequently asked the question whether the benefits from working memory or music training could transfer to different spoken or written language skills. It has been well established in the literature that working memory plays an important role in various aspects of language development, such as vocabulary acquisition (de Abreu et al., 2013; Gathercole, 2006), sentence processing (Marton et al., 2006; Montgomery et al., 2008), reading comprehension (Loosli et al., 2012; Swanson & Jerman, 2007), and second language proficiency (Van Den Noort et al., 2006). The relationship between music and language processing has also received notable attention. At the neurophysiological level, Patel's overlap, precision, emotion, repetition, attention (OPERA) hypothesis proposed overlapping networks for music and language (2011); a link has been suggested between auditory rapid spectrotemporal and language processing (Tallal & Gaab, 2006); common underlying processes have been found between linguistic stress and musical meter (Gordon et al., 2011); and interactive effects have been identified between a musical chord's tonal function and syntactic processing (Hoch et al., 2011). At the behavioral level, phonological and pitch awareness have been associated with the development of pre-literacy skills in children (Degé & Schwarzer, 2011; Flaugnacco et al., 2015), and music experience has been linked to vocabulary acquisition (DeHaan et al., 2010).

9.3.1 Training Effects in Second Language (L2) Learners

A direct approach to examining the effects of working memory or music training on language can be employed by studying L2 acquisition and proficiency in children. A series of studies within this line of research have focused on the relationship between working memory and L2 vocabulary acquisition. Interestingly, distinct working memory approaches have been used, from phonological working memory training to visual, nonverbal working memory training. For example, phonological working memory training has been employed to study the recognition, short-term retention, and recall of single words and nonwords in English-learning Greek children. The experimental group received phonological working memory training for thirty-three sessions over twelve weeks, while the control group received regular language instructions for the same amount of time. Unlike the control group, the experimental group showed significant gains in both nonword repetition accuracy and productive vocabulary. There was no transfer to receptive vocabulary though, a finding which was associated with the fact that the mapping process is different for productive and receptive vocabularies. While in comprehension, a given phonological form has to be mapped onto its meaning, in production, a concept and related semantic meaning has to be linked to a specific phonological form. It has been proposed that the latter process places higher cognitive demands on the system (Karousou & Nerantzaki, 2022).

9.3 Training Effects and Different Language Skills

Unlike most working memory and L2 studies, Opitz and colleagues (2014) focused on the effects of visual working memory training using the N-back paradigm with abstract shapes on Chinese vocabulary character learning in German students. Outcomes from visual working memory training had been compared to the results of two control groups. One group participated in an auditory working memory training using bird sounds, while the other control group was passive and received no training. To examine changes at the neurophysiological level, functional magnetic resonance imaging (fMRI) was used pre- and post-training. Only the visual working memory training group showed positive transfer effects on visual Chinese vocabulary learning, while the two control groups showed none. Furthermore, the fMRI data revealed sustained activation in the left infero-temporal cortex following the visual working memory training only, and this activation was associated with behavioral transfer. As a result of visual working memory training, higher order visual regions, specifically the left mid-fusiform gyrus and the precuneus were recruited for Chinese vocabulary learning. The findings from the study by Opitz and colleagues (2014), from Karousou and Nerantzaki (2022), and from our Cognition and Language laboratory (Wadhera, 2020), all provide support to the notion that real transfer occurs when overlapping processes and brain regions are engaged by the working memory training tasks and the untrained tasks. In Karousou's study, phonological working memory training transferred to productive but not to receptive vocabulary, because the training enhanced phonological awareness, a key component underlying vocabulary production. In Wadhera's study, working memory training with a focus on interference control in English-language learners transferred to sentence processing with ambiguous words but not to regular reading comprehension. Sentences including ambiguous words require the suppression of interference among competing meanings. Thus, it is important for researchers to determine the underlying mechanisms that are activated during working memory training and by the post-training tasks themselves. Unless there is an overlap between the relevant mechanisms underlying those different activities, no real transfer can be expected.

Similar concepts have been suggested by studies exploring the relationship between music training and L2 acquisition. A stronger relationship has been found between music training and auditory perception during dictation than between music training and grammatical knowledge in Italian children learning English as their L2 (Talamini et al., 2018). Participants in the music training group outperformed the controls in dictation. Both music learning and dictation require auditory analysis with a transformation between auditory sounds and written symbols. Delogu and colleagues (2010) also reported selective transfer effects in children and adults. Melodic proficiency and music experience predicted participants' tonal but not phonological identification (in Mandarin Chinese). Work from the same laboratory a year later, however, showed that musical experience positively affected both phoneme processing and overall language segmentation (Marie et al., 2011). The electrophysiological data indicated that lexical pitch perception and discrimination were faster for participants with prior music experience. Moreover, those participants made fewer errors in lexical categorization and showed higher levels of confidence in their categorization decisions than those without music training. This finding indicates differences in cognitive processes between the two groups, in addition to perceptual differences.

A number of studies have also suggested that attention and memory drive perception of acoustic features (Strait et al., 2010). Although most of these studies focused on adults, outcomes from preschool-age children also revealed that the combination of phonological and music training was particularly effective in facilitating the development of pre-literacy skills, such as phonological awareness in L2 learning (Herrera et al., 2011). Although there is evidence in the literature about the relationship between working memory and language, specifically vocabulary, listening abilities, and reading in L2 (Kormos & Sáfár, 2008), as well as between music training and L2 listening and reading (Zeromskaite, 2014), most music training studies have not taken the role of working memory in L2 acquisition into account. Given these preliminary findings, we may assume that studying the role of working memory on the relationship between music training and L2 acquisition may lead to a better understanding of the interactions between lower- and higher-level processes (e.g., perception, attention, and memory for acoustic features), as well as of specific training effects.

9.3.2 Training Effects in Children with Developmental Language Disorder (DLD)

Cognitive training has been more effective in children with developmental challenges (e.g., low socioeconomic status, ADHD) than in typically developing children (Scionti et al., 2020). Based on these findings, we could assume that children with DLD might benefit from training programs as well, yet there are only scarce data on this population in the literature. There are at least two major issues that contribute to these limitations. First, the terms training and intervention are often used interchangeably,

9.3 Training Effects and Different Language Skills 149

even though the overall structure and timeline of these two procedures are distinct. Further, based on their meta-analysis, Gillam and colleagues (2018) suggested that clinicians should choose more traditional intervention methods with children with DLD until there is a better understanding of the mechanisms underlying the more recent working memory training programs. Second, a critical component of training is transfer. The weakness in generalization/transfer is well documented in children with DLD (Schwartz & Marton, 2011). Despite these challenges, there are a few promising reports about working memory and music training in children with language impairment.

Working memory training has been employed to achieve both near and far transfer in children with DLD. It is well established in the literature that children with DLD exhibit weaknesses in working memory (Marton & Eichorn, 2014; Marton & Schwartz, 2003; Montgomery et al., 2010), therefore direct improvement of working memory itself (near transfer) is an important goal. Far transfer to language was also expected, based on the relationship between working memory and specific language skills. Stanford and colleagues (2019) developed a training program that was specifically designed to train particular working memory components which had previously been associated with the development of syntax. Following twenty-four sessions of working memory training (over 8 weeks), children with DLD in the experimental group performed better on both trained and untrained working memory tasks than the control children, who participated in a scholastic training program (general cognitive stimulation) but showed no improvement in performance on the same working memory tasks. Furthermore, the children with DLD in the working memory training group improved their production of accusative clitics pronouns, which is a construct that was not targeted during training but has been associated with working memory capacity (far transfer). Children in the scholastic training group did not improve in clitics production (Stanford et al., 2019). In more recent research from the same laboratory, Delage and colleagues (2021) employed the same working memory training program as in the 2019 study to examine its effect on sentence repetition. The sentence repetition task included both syntactically simple and complex sentences with a focus on relative clauses. The control group participated in a scholastic training program again. In addition to showing improvement in untrained working memory tasks, children with DLD in the working memory training group also improved in sentence repetition, whereas the children in the scholastic training program did not show any changes in this area. Moreover, in the working memory training group, the changes were greater with the more difficult (object-relative) complex sentences than with the easier (subject-relative) sentences. In a follow-up study three months later with a subgroup of participants, the same effects were observed, indicating persistence of improved skills.

While Stanford and colleagues targeted verbal working memory in children with DLD, Vugs and colleagues (2017) trained for visuospatial working memory and other cognitive skills. In addition to the immediate effects, these authors also examined persistence (performance six months later). Although this was only a pilot study with a small sample size, children with DLD showed improved performance in visuospatial storage and cognitive flexibility following training. There was no transfer to verbal working memory though. At the follow-up study six months later, children still exhibited increased attention control. These findings from Stanford and colleagues as well as from Vugs and colleagues further support the notion that successful training programs target underlying mechanisms that overlap with specific processes that are needed to perform the untrained tasks.

A music training method specifically targeting the development of cognitive-linguistic skills in children with DLD and other groups with neurodevelopmental disorders is the "Developmental speech and language training through music" program (Thaut & Hoemberg, 2014). The overall idea is that training should be based on goal-oriented music with age-appropriate creative elements. Rhythm may be used as the primary facilitator of speech-language production, while melody may promote the development of prosody. Key components are motivation, the creation of multiple opportunities to practice the desired behavior, and the balance between novelty and repetition. This music program is a clinically oriented method that has been recommended to facilitate language comprehension in children with DLD (LaGasse, 2014); however, there are no systematic studies examining its effectiveness in this population.

The SALTMusic training approach was developed for preschool-age children within an action research framework with the active involvement of all participants, including children with communication disorders and their families (Pitt, 2020). This method incorporated a number of qualitative research elements, such as the use of reflective journals, focus groups, and interviews. SALTMusic has been used by teams of early intervention specialists, speech therapists, music practitioners, and researchers. The musically playful, child-led, improvisatory approach has resulted in an increase in social interactions and spoken word production, as well as in enhanced self-confidence.

Although these few examples suggest positive outcomes in children with DLD, future research is needed to study the effects of training in this population with a particular focus on real transfer and persistence. Research with typically developing children has shown strong associations between cognitive flexibility and training outcomes. It is well known from the literature that children with DLD are less flexible than their peers (Marton, 2008; Roello et al., 2015), but the relationship between cognitive flexibility and working memory or music training has not been explored in these children.

9.4 Conclusions

We have seen a rise in the creation and use of different training methods during the past few decades. This increase in popularity has had both positive and negative consequences. On the one hand, we have gained a great deal of knowledge about the complexity of training methodologies and their effectiveness and about the multitude of variables that affect the outcomes. We have been able to identify multiple populations that could benefit from various types of cognitive training, and we have seen some very beneficial short- and long-term effects. On the other hand, we have also seen many inconsistencies and contradictions in findings because of the lack of well-controlled study designs. It is essential that researchers determine those specific cognitive and linguistic skills that they aim to target prior to the beginning of the training process. The selected pre- and

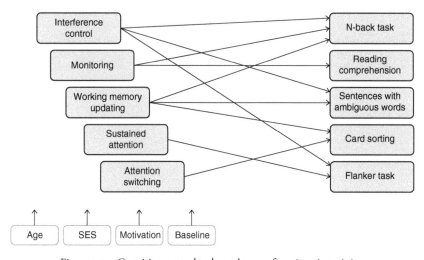

Figure 9.2   Cognitive control tasks and target functions in training

post-training tasks, as well as the training methods must be able to assess and train specific aspects of these predetermined skills. Thus, it is imperative to identify the underlying mechanisms that are targeted by the training tasks and the post-training measures, even if the post-training tasks are in a different modality or domain than the training tasks themselves (see Figure 9.2). Many conflicting data in the literature reveal mismatches between the targeted underlying mechanisms and the training tasks and the post-training measures.

In addition to the overlapping processing components, the involvement of similar neural regions is also important in order to achieve transfer to untrained tasks (Jonides, 2004). Given the complexity of most cognitive tasks and the multifaceted nature of nearly all cognitive functions, it is highly likely that theoretical debates about the path to real, not just superficial improvements in behavior will continue in future training literature.

CHAPTER 10

Conclusions

10.1 Current Issues

The aim of this book has been to provide a systematic review and analysis of the relationship between cognitive control and language in speakers with various language skills. Language skill variations have been examined along two dimensions: language ability and bilingual proficiency. The goal in this chapter is to highlight both general and specific associations between children's cognitive control and language skills within an integrative framework. Although the cognitive control literature has shown extensive growth over the past decade, many theories and conceptual constructs still focus on adults, and there is less information about the development of the cognitive control processes in children. Furthermore, most developmental research has been conducted with typically developing (preschool to school-age) children, providing little information about those at the two ends of the language ability continuum (i.e., children with language talent and children with language impairment) or concerning children who speak minority languages or nonstandard dialects.

As discussed in various chapters of this book, cognitive control performance is influenced by a number of age- and language-related factors, such as children's language input/intake, frequency of use, and age of acquisition, among others. These contributing factors further interact in complex ways with culture and socioeconomic status (SES). Unfortunately, very few studies on cognitive control in children have taken these interactions into consideration. There are many reasons for these limitations in the literature; therefore, the following sections provide examples of major issues and offer solutions to selected problems by identifying and describing patterns of the relationship between various cognitive control components and language.

153

10.1.1 Critical Questions

The heterogeneity of the participants and the shortage of sufficiently sensitive, valid tasks are among the most challenging issues for research on cognitive control in children with various language skills. Moreover, these two sets of problems are closely linked because on the one hand, the low level of conceptually driven, well-controlled tasks is a major factor for inadequate selection of participants and the vast heterogeneity of the groups; on the other hand, this diversity hinders the development of sensitive and specific tasks. Even though the following suggestions may seem counterintuitive, we need to extend our research to include children who speak nonmainstream languages; come from various social and cultural backgrounds; and exhibit a range of language skills, in order to identify developmental patterns of domain-general and language-specific cognitive skills. Cross-linguistic studies of grammar in children with DLD have shown us the effectiveness of this approach. Data from a number of languages support distinct theoretical accounts, but there has been no conceptual model that could explain all the performance patterns and error types of children with DLD across languages. The vulnerability of specific linguistic structures differs across languages, and there is an association between general cognitive-linguistic functions and language-specific features (Leonard, 2014; Marton & Yoon, 2014).

In order to create comprehensive models that describe and interpret the relationship between cognitive control and language and develop efficient intervention methods that target both language and cognitive control skills together, we must understand why certain language structures are more vulnerable in one language than in others and determine how those particular structures are linked to different cognitive control components. To achieve these goals, seemingly opposing processes have to be integrated. We must broaden the language spectrum to include young speakers of various languages at a variety of proficiency and ability levels. We also have to design more child-friendly and culturally sensitive tasks, while resolving the issues related to task impurity to enhance our diagnostic and classification accuracy and to decrease the inconsistencies in findings across studies. It is critical to develop new tasks that can assist us in disentangling children's language abilities and levels of proficiency to enhance our identification and classification of children with language talent, particularly in groups that speak minority languages, and to increase the diagnostic accuracy for bilingual children with DLD and children who are emerging bilingual speakers (e.g., English Language Learners [ELL]).

The initial steps toward the integration of cognitive and linguistic approaches in language learning aptitude tasks are in the right direction, but more research is needed with children who come from various language backgrounds. Our preliminary findings suggest that nonverbal or minimally verbal cognitive control tasks could significantly increase the classification power for bilingual children with DLD and children with language differences, such as ELL. Thus, we should integrate experimental research with individual-differences approaches, even though these two have traditionally been viewed as fundamentally different in the literature (see more details further on).

Simultaneously, task impurity can be decreased by developing tasks through empirical studies that are designed to explore how the control processes are affected in different language groups by the manipulations of conditions, trials, and item types. These manipulations, however, have to correspond to conceptually predetermined control processes and components. A clear match between the targeted cognitive control components and the measures provided by the experimental task must be established. Thus, the boost in diversity has to occur concurrently to the increase in specificity in identifying the underlying mechanisms that are targeted by particular tasks.

10.1.2 Interactions between Cognitive Control and Language

Analysis of the relationship between cognitive control and language has revealed both general and specific patterns. The data on language input and exposure indicate that children's intake of speech-language is highly influenced by their lower- as well as higher-level cognitive functions, such as perception, attention, and memory, in addition to their overall language knowledge and linguistic experience (Badger, 2018; Rowe, 2015). These interactions, however, are also linked to children's cultural background, SES, and other social factors, such as immigration or minority group status (see Figure 4.2 in Chapter 6).

As described in Chapter 7, independent cultures are characterized by analytic cognition and field independent attention, whereas interdependent cultures show more holistic cognition and field dependent attention, as indicated by both behavioral and neurophysiological findings (Chua et al., 2005; Kafetsios, 2019). These differences must be considered when examining the learning styles and strategies of children with different language skills. For example, ELL students are often viewed as students who only need to learn English, so teachers and policy-makers may not consider these children's social-cultural background or life experiences. The conceptual framework of intersectionality (language, class, ethnicity, etc.) and policy emphasizes the relevance of the multiple dimensions in ELL students' sociolinguistic background (Jiménez-Castellanos & García, 2017). Thus, the interaction between cognitive control and language is part of a dynamic system that is highly influenced by variations in local and global contexts, such as the social environment and cultural background, as well as by children's previous sociolinguistic-economic experiences. Therefore, it is critical for these influential factors to be considered along with language ability in the evaluation of children's cognitive control skills and the procedures for selecting participants in cognitive control studies.

Moreover, control processes also interact with motivation and emotions, particularly in social situations. These processes have received less attention in the cognitive control literature in children than the core cognitive control components, even though they play critical roles in goal-directed behaviors and in solving conflicts (Inzlicht et al., 2015). As discussed in previous chapters, behavioral regulation involves both emotional and cognitive control. For instance, while negative experiences lead to reduced memory performance, the increase in cognitive control may neutralize negative emotions without impairing memory functions (Gross, 2002; Ochsner & Gross, 2005). Considering that children's ability to regulate emotion is closely linked to their social relationships with peers and positive peer relations are critical during childhood, we need to pay more attention to the interactions between cognitive control and emotions in the future. This is even more critical for children with DLD, who show weaknesses in initiating and maintaining peer relationships and friendships (Conti-Ramsden & Botting, 2004; Marton et al., 2005). Their social problems are certainly related to their language impairment but are further influenced by their difficulties in cognitive control, such as perspective taking, resisting distraction, and poor working memory. While negative social and emotional experiences may contribute to low-level motivation (e.g., "learned helplessness"), positive emotional experiences and friendships could result in increased motivation. An in-depth discussion of the relationship between cognitive control and motivation was beyond the scope of this work, but we know that intrinsic motivation determines quality of learning, the selection of learning strategies, and overall academic achievement (Di Domenico & Ryan, 2017; Singh, 2011).

Another universal feature of the relationship between cognitive control and language can be captured by the reversed pattern of cognitive control performance between children with DLD and their typically developing peers or children with a language talent and by significant differences along the language proficiency continuum from emerging bilingual speakers to balanced highly proficient individuals. Despite some inconsistencies in the literature, the overall picture shows that better language abilities and higher levels of language proficiency are associated with more advanced cognitive control skills, especially in attention, memory, monitoring, and resistance to interference (e.g., Abutalebi et al., 2013; Iluz-Cohen & Armon-Lotem, 2013; Marton et al., 2012; 2019). Particular aspects of language, such as vocabulary, show notably strong relationships with certain cognitive control components, especially with working memory and interference control (Gathercole, 2006; Marton et al., 2014). There is converging evidence on the close link between working memory and interference control, as demonstrated by one of the latest accounts explaining the capacity limitations in working memory within an interference model (Lewandowski et al., 2008; Oberauer, 2009). Interference control and vocabulary scores were linked in children who differed in their language abilities (i.e., children with DLD and their typically developing peers) and in their level of bilingual proficiency (Bialystok & Feng, 2009; Marton et al., 2014). Children with larger vocabularies produced fewer interference errors than their peers with smaller vocabularies. Bilingual children showed superior performance compared to their monolingual peers in a conflict paradigm when the difference in expressive vocabulary was included in the analysis (Carlson & Meltzoff, 2008). In addition to vocabulary, language comprehension has also shown strong relationships with working memory and interference control in adults (Van Dyke & Johnson, 2012).

One cognitive control component that appears to be more independent from children's language status, especially after the preschool years, is response inhibition. A number of studies have demonstrated that children with different language abilities and levels of bilingual proficiency perform similarly on tasks of response inhibition (Bonifacci et al., 2011; Laloi et al., 2017; Marton et al., 2012). This contrasting pattern between response inhibition and resistance to interference along the language continuum is particularly interesting in light of the outcomes from the latent variable analysis by Friedman and Miyake (2004). That study suggested a close link between prepotent response inhibition and resistance to distractor interference but no strong association with proactive interference. In contrast, the findings on the relationship between working memory and interference control typically reveal a link to proactive interference.

158 Conclusions

Age may be a reason for these dissociations between the findings by Freidman and Miyake and studies on response inhibition and interference control along the language continuum. The latent variable analysis included data from 220 adults (Friedman & Miyake, 2004), whereas the studies that showed no difference in response inhibition but indicated a strong effect in both resistance to distractor and proactive interference involved children (e.g., Laloi et al., 2017; Marton et al., 2012; 2014). Moreover, these childhood studies included participants with sundry language skills (monolingual and bilingual children, children with DLD and with typical language development), whereas no data on adult participants' language abilities or levels of bilingual proficiency were presented in the study by Friedman and Miyake (2004). Therefore, it is crucial for future research to examine the unity and diversity of these inhibitory functions from a developmental perspective along the language continuum.

10.2 Future Research

10.2.1 Using an Individual-Differences Approach

To reduce the inconsistencies in findings related to the substantial heterogeneity of participant groups in both the bilingualism and the language impairment literatures, we must use an individual-differences approach more frequently. Research over the past decades has provided us with a large amount of data showing the critical contribution of heterogeneity to the inconsistent findings in group studies. Procedures for matching and counterbalancing specific participant characteristics have their own limits. Therefore, applying an individual-differences approach to our designs and examining more variables along various continua, rather than within categories, may allow us to more efficiently explore the interactions among the different language and cognitive components as well as the contributions of culture and children's life experiences (Kaushanskaya & Prior, 2015; Marton, 2019). Dynamic and flexible, the individual-differences approach has the potential to capture the cultural and linguistic richness in children's speech-language. Language scientists have already suggested that the examination of associations and dissociations across the language subsystems (vocabulary, grammar, etc.) and their relationship with different cognitive processes from an individual-differences perspective may reveal important information about the underlying architecture of the language system (Kidd et al., 2018).

10.2 *Future Research*

Taking an individual-differences approach need not mean giving up on the application of experimental methods, as suggested by some scholars in the literature; conversely, it may encourage researchers to create and study novel and innovative research questions. This approach is not tied to specific measurement types, as previously thought (Sackett et al., 2017). As recommended by Goodhew and Edwards (2019), we can modify experimental tasks to fit into individual-differences designs in order to examine variations among participants along particular dimensions and to test individual-level reliability. This can be achieved by applying continuous measures whenever possible, to capture the spectrum of essential components and processes related to diversity. This approach requires a different mindset because unlike in traditional studies, researchers have to view variability in performance as key information. For example, cognitive control skills may be measured using continuous variables across multiple contexts to capture individual differences, and then statistical models may be used to identify specific patterns (Friedman & Robbins, 2022).

Adapting an individual-differences approach is particularly important for studies on language and cognition across populations because the group-designs (i.e., the comparison of bilingual children to monolingual peers or children with DLD to typically developing groups) strengthen the deficit-model thinking among scholars – a perspective that often leads to the stigmatization of minority, diverse, or so-called atypical groups (Garivaldo & Fabiano-Smith, 2023). Variations in error patterns, learning potentials and strategies, and trade-offs in performance (e.g., trade-off between speed and accuracy), all provide researchers with critical details about human goal-directed behavior. The application of an individual-differences approach and the weakening of deficit-model thinking may lead the bilingualism literature toward diminishment of the "native speaker" bias as well, which is a specific form of the monolingual bias (De Houwer, 2023). This old view idealized monolingualism and contributed to many negative attitudes toward people with diverse language skills (e.g., emerging bilingual speakers and speakers of nonstandard dialects).

Moreover, an individual-differences approach may also dilute the negativity bias among scholars. There is evidence at the behavioral as well as the neural level that negative stimuli have stronger effects on both lower- and higher-level processing than does equally strong positive information (Norris, 2021). A more dynamic and flexible approach that uses diversity as a rich resource may help us to develop a more nuanced and tolerant view and an inclusive attitude towards language variations. To that end, significant changes in mentality toward diversity among researchers, teachers,

160   Conclusions

clinicians, and policy-makers should be encouraged through the practice of interprofessional collaborations.

10.2.2 Interprofessional Collaborations

The term "interprofessional collaboration" is used in this section with a broad meaning including interdisciplinary collaborations, multidisciplinary coordination, and transprofessional teamwork (Reeves et al., 2017). Interprofessional collaborations are based on regular discussions and interactions among professionals from different disciplines who value each other's knowledge, expertise, and contributions to the populations with whom they are working. To better understand the dynamic relationship between language and cognitive control, scholars must continue synthesizing behavioral and neural approaches. For instance, as described in Chapter 2, findings from behavioral studies suggest a gradual separation of cognitive control functions throughout childhood and adolescence. Concurrently, at the neural level, both segregation and integration of brain connectivity are apparent. Interprofessional collaboration is needed to identify the specific processes in brain networks that affect and shape the developmental course of differentiation across cognitive control components. An individual-differences approach using a variety of tasks could help an interprofessional team to better explore how brain networks become more task-specific with development.

Collaborations, however, may be adversely affected by differences in training, perspectives, attitudes, and misunderstandings about the roles of each professional within the team, especially in hierarchically structured settings where unequal power relations might exist (Baker et al., 2011). Interprofessional education may be needed to highlight that in teams, particularly in interdisciplinary ones, all professions have their own and equally important roles. As demonstrated in Chapter 9, the lack of interprofessional collaborations led to the widespread use by educators and clinicians of certain cognitive training strategies and techniques without verified effectiveness. Thus, clients have paid for products and interventions that had questionable outcomes. Seeing these negative examples, researchers from both fields, neuroscience and education, have started collaborations to link basic research findings to educational practice (Hruby, 2012). These interprofessional collaborations inspired the development of numerous neuroscience-based approaches for educational and clinical practices.

Finally, the dissemination of results across disciplines is critical. Publishing interdisciplinary work requires, not only the presentation of each discipline's perspective, but the integration and synthesis of ideas and methods. The research community has to make every effort to overcome publication biases. Researchers and practitioners must have confidence that their work can be published, even if they report unexpected or contradictory results, particularly if the research involved disadvantaged communities, speakers of minority languages, and participants from ethnically and culturally diverse backgrounds.

References

Absher, J. R., & Cummings, J. L. (1995). Neurobehavioural examination of frontal lobe functions. *Aphasiology*, *9*(2), 181–192. https://doi.org/10.1080/02687039508248705

Abutalebi, J. (2008). Neural aspects of second language representation and language control. *Acta Psychologica*, *128*(3), 466–478. https://doi.org/10.1016/j.actpsy.2008.03.014

Abutalebi, J., Della Rosa, P. A., Ding, G., Weekes, B., Costa, A., & Green, D. W. (2013). Language proficiency modulates the engagement of cognitive control areas in multilinguals. *Cortex*, *49*(3), 905–911. http://dx.doi.org/10.1016/j.cortex.2012.08.018

Abutalebi, J., & Green, D. (2007). Bilingual language production: The neurocognition of language representation and control. *Journal of Neurolinguistics*, *20*(3), 242–275. https://doi.org/10.1016/j.jneuroling.2006.10.003

Alferink, L. A., & Farmer-Dougan, V. (2010). Brain-(not) based education: Dangers of misunderstanding and misapplication of neuroscience research. *Exceptionality*, *18*(1), 42–52. https://doi.org/10.1080/09362830903462573

Ambrosi, S., Śmigasiewicz, K., Burle, B., & Blaye, A. (2020). The dynamics of interference control across childhood and adolescence: Distribution analyses in three conflict tasks and ten age groups. *Developmental Psychology*, *56*(12), 2262–2280. https://doi.org/10.1037/dev0001122

Amrhein, V., & Greenland, S. (2022). Discuss practical importance of results based on interval estimates and p-value functions, not only on point estimates and null p-values. *Journal of Information Technology*, *37*(3), 316–320. https://doi.org/10.1177/02683962221105904

Anderson, N. J., Graham, S. A., Prime, H., Jenkins, J. M., & Madigan, S. (2021). Linking quality and quantity of parental linguistic input to child language skills: A meta-analysis. *Child Development*, *92*(2), 484–501. https://doi.org/10.1111/cdev.13508

Andrés-Roqueta, C., Adrian, J. E., Clemente, R. A., & Villanueva, L. (2016). Social cognition makes an independent contribution to peer relations in children with Specific Language Impairment. *Research in Developmental Disabilities*, *49*, 277–290. https://doi.org/10.1016/j.ridd.2015.12.015

Antonova Ünlü, E., & Wei, L. (2018). Examining the effect of reduced input on language development: The case of gender acquisition in Russian as a non-dominant and dispreferred language by a bilingual Turkish–Russian child. *International Journal of Bilingualism*, *22*(2), 215–233. https://doi.org/10.1177/1367006916666390

Arain, M., Haque, M., Johal, L., Mathur, P., Nel, W., Rais, A., …, & Sharma, S. (2013). Maturation of the adolescent brain. *Neuropsychiatric Disease and Treatment*, *9*, 449–461. https://doi.org/10.2147/NDT.S39776

Archibald, L. M. (2017). Working memory and language learning: A review. *Child Language Teaching and Therapy*, *33*(1), 5–17. https://doi.org/10.1177/0265659016654206

Archibald, L. M., & Gathercole, S. E. (2006a). Short-term and working memory in specific language impairment. *International Journal of Language & Communication Disorders*, *41*(6), 675–693. https://doi.org/10.1080/13682820500442602

Archibald, L., & Gathercole, S. E. (2006b). Visuospatial immediate memory in specific language impairment. *Journal of Speech, Language, and Hearing Research*, *49*(2), 265–277. https://doi.org/10.1044/1092-4388(2006/022)

Armon-Lotem, S., de Jong, J., & Meir, N. (Eds.). (2015). *Assessing multilingual children: Disentangling bilingualism from language impairment* (Vol. 13). Multilingual Matters.

Armon-Lotem, S., & Meir, N. (2019). The nature of exposure and input in early bilingualism. In A. De Houwer & L. Ortega (Eds.), *The Cambridge handbook of bilingualism* (pp. 193–212). Cambridge University Press.

Armstrong, R., Scott, J. G., Whitehouse, A. J., Copland, D. A., Mcmahon, K. L., & Arnott, W. (2017). Late talkers and later language outcomes: Predicting the different language trajectories. *International Journal of Speech-Language Pathology*, *19*(3), 237–250. https://doi.org/10.1080/17549507.2017.1296191

Ashby, F. G., Turner, B. O., & Horvitz, J. C. (2010). Cortical and basal ganglia contributions to habit learning and automaticity. *Trends in Cognitive Sciences*, *14*(5), 208–215. https://doi.org/10.1016/j.tics.2010.02.001

Ågren, M., Granfeldt, J., & Thomas, A. (2014). Combined effects of age of onset and input on the development of different grammatical structures: A study of simultaneous and successive bilingual acquisition of French. *Linguistic Approaches to Bilingualism*, *4*(4), 462–493. https://doi.org/10.1075/lab.4.4.03agr

Baddeley, A. (2003). Working memory and language: An overview. *Journal of Communication Disorders*, *36*(3), 189–208. https://doi.org/10.1016/S0021-9924(03)00019-4

Baddeley, A., Gathercole, S., & Papagno, C. (1998). The phonological loop as a language learning device. *Psychological Review*, *105*(1), 158–173. https://doi.org/10.1037/0033-295X.105.1.158.

Baddeley, A. D., & Hitch, G. J. (1974). Working memory. In G. H. Bower (Ed.), *The psychology of learning and motivation* (Vol. 8, pp. 47–89). Academic Press. https://doi.org/10.1016/S0079-7421(08)60452-1

Baddeley, A. D., Papagno, C., & Vallar, G. (1988). When long term learning depends on short-term storage. *Journal of Memory and Language*, *27*, 586–595. https://doi.org/10.1016/0749-596X(88)90028-9

Baddeley, A. D., Thomson, N., & Buchanan, M. (1975). Word length and the structure of short-term memory. *Journal of Verbal Learning and Verbal Behavior*, *14*, 575–589. http://dx.doi.org/10.1016/S0022-5371(75)80045-4

References

Badger, R. (2018). From input to intake: Researching learner cognition. *TESOL Quarterly*, *52*(4), 1073–1084. ISSN 0039-8322

Badre, D. (2011). Defining an ontology of cognitive control requires attention to component interactions. *Topics in Cognitive Science*, *3*(2), 217–221. https://doi.org/10.1111/j.1756-8765.2011.01141.x

Badre, D., & Wagner, A. D. (2007). Left ventrolateral prefrontal cortex and the cognitive control of memory. *Neuropsychologia*, *45*, 2883–2901. https://doi.org/10.1016/j.neuropsychologia.2007.06.015

Baggetta, P., & Alexander, P. A. (2016). Conceptualization and operationalization of executive function. *Mind, Brain, and Education*, *10*(1), 10–33. https://doi.org/10.1111/mbe.12100

Baker, L., Egan-Lee, E., Martimianakis, M. A., & Reeves, S. (2011). Relationships of power: Implications for interprofessional education. *Journal of Interprofessional Care*, *25*(2), 98–104. https://doi.org/10.3109/13561820.2010.505350

Baker, M. (2016). Reproducibility crisis. *Nature*, *533*(26), 353–566. https://doi.org/10.1038/533452a

Barbu, S., Nardy, A., Chevrot, J. P., Guellaï, B., Glas, L., Juhel, J., & Lemasson, A. (2015). Sex differences in language across early childhood: Family socioeconomic status does not impact boys and girls equally. *Frontiers in Psychology*, *6*, 1874. https://doi.org/10.3389/fpsyg.2015.01874

Barrouillet, P., & Camos, V. (2001). Developmental increase in working memory span: Resource sharing or temporal decay? *Journal of Memory and Language*, *45*(1), 1–20. https://doi.org/10.1006/jmla.2001.2767

Bates, E., Dale, P. S., & Thal, D. (2017). Individual differences and their implications for theories of language development. In P. Fletcher & B. MacWhinney (Eds.), *The handbook of child language* (pp. 95–151). Blackwell Publishing Ltd. https://doi.org/10.1111/b.9780631203124.1996.x

Bates, E., Marchman, V., Thal, D., Fenson, L., Dale, P., Reznick, J. S., …, & Hartung, J. (1994). Developmental and stylistic variation in the composition of early vocabulary. *Journal of Child Language*, *21*(1), 85–123. https://doi.org/10.1017/S0305000900008680

Bauer, D. J., Goldfield, B. A., & Reznick, J. S. (2002). Alternative approaches to analyzing individual differences in the rate of early vocabulary development. *Applied Psycholinguistics*, *23*(3), 313–335. https://doi.org/10.1017/S0142716402003016

Bavelier, D., Green, C. S., Pouget, A., & Schrater, P. (2012). Brain plasticity through the life span: Learning to learn and action video games. *Annual Review of Neuroscience*, *35*, 391–416. https://doi.org/10.1146/annurev-neuro-060909-152832

Bazzanella, C. (2004). Emotions, language and context. *Emotion in Dialogic Interaction: Advances in the Complex*, 55–72.

Bedore, L. M., Peña, E. D., García, M., & Cortez, C. (2005). Conceptual versus monolingual scoring. *Language, Speech, and Hearing Services in Schools*, *36*, 188–200. https://doi.org/10.1044/0161-1461(2005/020)

Bedore, L. M., Peña, E. D., Griffin, Z. M., & Hixon, J. G. (2016). Effects of age of English exposure, current input/output, and grade on bilingual language performance. *Journal of Child Language*, *43*(3), 687–706. https://doi.org/10.1017/S0305000915000811

References

Bedore, L. M., Peña, E. D., Summers, C. L., Boerger, K. M., Resendiz, M. D., Greene, K., ..., & Gillam, R. B. (2012). The measure matters: Language dominance profiles across measures in Spanish–English bilingual children. *Bilingualism: Language and Cognition, 15*(3), 616–629. https://doi.org/10.1017/S1366728912000090

Benasich, A. A., Thomas, J. J., Choudhury, N., & Leppänen, P. H. (2002). The importance of rapid auditory processing abilities to early language development: Evidence from converging methodologies. *Developmental Psychobiology: The Journal of the International Society for Developmental Psychobiology, 40*(3), 278–292. https://doi.org/10.1002/dev.10032

Benitez, V. L., Vales, C., Hanania, R., & Smith, L. B. (2017). Sustained selective attention predicts flexible switching in preschoolers. *Journal of Experimental Child Psychology, 156*, 29–42. https://doi.org/10.1016/j.jecp.2016.11.004

Berent, G. P. (1996). Learnability constraints on deaf learners' acquisition of English wh-questions. *Journal of Speech, Language, and Hearing Research, 39*(3), 625–642. https://doi.org/10.1044/jshr.3903.625

Bialystok, E. (2010). Global–local and trail-making tasks by monolingual and bilingual children: Beyond inhibition. *Developmental Psychology, 46*(1), 93–105. https://doi.org/10.1037/a0015466

Bialystok, E., & Feng, X. (2009). Language proficiency and executive control in proactive interference: Evidence from monolingual and bilingual children and adults. *Brain and Language, 109*(2–3), 93–100. https://doi.org/10.1016/j.bandl.2008.09.001

Bialystok, E., Luk, G., Peets, K. F., & Sujin, Y. A. N. G. (2010). Receptive vocabulary differences in monolingual and bilingual children. *Bilingualism: Language and Cognition, 13*(4), 525–531. https://doi.org/10.1017/S1366728909990423

Bialystok, E., & Viswanathan, M. (2009). Components of executive control with advantages for bilingual children in two cultures. *Cognition, 112*(3), 494–500. https://doi.org/10.1016/j.cognition.2009.06.014

Birdsong, D. (2014). Dominance and age in bilingualism. *Applied Linguistics, 35*(4), 374–392. https://doi.org/10.1093/applin/amu031

Bishop, D. V., Snowling, M. J., Thompson, P. A., Greenhalgh, T., & Catalise Consortium. (2016). CATALISE: A multinational and multidisciplinary Delphi consensus study. Identifying language impairments in children. *PLOS One, 11*(7), e0158753. https://doi.org/10.1371/journal.pone.0158753

Bishop, D. V., Snowling, M. J., Thompson, P. A., Greenhalgh, T., Catalise-2 Consortium, Adams, C., ..., & house, A. (2017). Phase 2 of CATALISE: A multinational and multidisciplinary Delphi consensus study of problems with language development: Terminology. *Journal of Child Psychology and Psychiatry, 58*(10), 1068–1080. https://doi.org/10.1111/jcpp.12721

Bjorklund, D. F., & Harnishfeger, K. K. (1990). The resources construct in cognitive development: Diverse sources of evidence and a theory of inefficient inhibition. *Developmental Review, 10*(1), 48–71. https://doi.org/10.1016/0273-2297(90)90004-N

Blacker, K. J., Negoita, S., Ewen, J. B., & Courtney, S. M. (2017). N-back versus complex span working memory training. *Journal of Cognitive Enhancement, 1*(4), 434–454.

Blackwell, K. A., Chatham, C. H., Wiseheart, M., & Munakata, Y. (2014). A developmental window into trade-offs in executive function: The case of task switching versus response inhibition in 6-year-olds. *Neuropsychologia, 62,* 356–364. https://doi.org/10.1016/j.neuropsychologia.2014.04.016

Blackwell, K. A., & Munakata, Y. (2014). Costs and benefits linked to developments in cognitive control. *Developmental Science, 17*(2), 203–211. https://doi.org/10.1111/desc.12113

Blanton, R. E., Levitt, J. G., Peterson, J. R., Fadale, D., Sporty, M. L., Lee, M., …, & Toga, A. W. (2004). Gender differences in the left inferior frontal gyrus in normal children. *Neuroimage, 22*(2), 626–636. https://doi.org/10.1016/j.neuroimage.2004.01.010

Blumenfeld, H. K., Bobb, S. C., & Marian, V. (2016). The role of language proficiency, cognate status and word frequency in the assessment of Spanish–English bilinguals' verbal fluency. *International Journal of Speech-Language Pathology, 18*(2), 190–201. https://doi.org/10.3109/17549507.2015.1081288

Blythe LaGasse, A. (2016). Developmental speech and language training through music (DSLM). In Thaut, M., & Hoemberg, V. (Eds.), *Handbook of neurologic music therapy* (pp. 196–216). Oxford University Press.

Bocanegra, B. R., & Hommel, B. (2014). When cognitive control is not adaptive. *Psychological Science, 25*(6), 1249–1255. https://doi.org/10.1177/0956797614528522

Boerma, T., Leseman, P., Wijnen, F., & Blom, E. (2017). Language proficiency and sustained attention in monolingual and bilingual children with and without language impairment. *Frontiers in Psychology, 8,* 1241. https://doi.org/10.3389/fpsyg.2017.01241

Bonifacci, P., Giombini, L., Bellocchi, S., & Contento, S. (2011). Speed of processing, anticipation, inhibition and working memory in bilinguals. *Developmental Science, 14*(2), 256–269. https://doi.org/10.1111/j.1467-7687.2010.00974.x

Bonnin, C. A., Gaonac'h, D., & Bouquet, C. A. (2011). Adjustments of task-set control processes: Effect of task switch frequency on task-mixing and task-switching costs. *Journal of Cognitive Psychology, 23*(8), 985–997. https://doi.org/10.1080/20445911.2011.594435

Botting, N., Jones, A., Marshall, C., Denmark, T., Atkinson, J., & Morgan, G. (2017). Nonverbal executive function is mediated by language: A study of deaf and hearing children. *Child Development, 88*(5), 1689–1700. https://doi.org/10.1111/cdev.12659

Botvinick, M. M., & Braver, T. (2015). Motivation and cognitive control: From behavior to neural mechanism. *Annual Review of Psychology, 66,* 83–113. https://doi.org/10.1146/annurev-psych-010814-015044

Botvinick, M. M., Braver, T. S., Barch, D. M., Carter, C. S., & Cohen, J. D. (2001). Conflict monitoring and cognitive control. *Psychological Review, 108*(3), 624–652. https://doi.org/10.1037/0033-295X.108.3.624

Botvinick, M., & Cohen, J. (2014). The computational and neural basis of cognitive control: Charted territory and new frontiers. *Cognitive Science, 38*(6), 1249–1285. https://doi.org/10.1111/cogs.12126

References

Botvinick, M. M., Cohen, J. D., & Carter, C. S. (2004). Conflict monitoring and anterior cingulate cortex: An update. *Trends in Cognitive Science, 8*, 539–546. https://doi.org/10.1016/j.tics.2004.10.003

Braver, T. S. (2012). The variable nature of cognitive control: A dual mechanisms framework. *Trends in Cognitive Sciences, 16*(2), 106–113. https://doi.org/10.1016/j.tics.2011.12.010

Braver, T. S., & Cohen, J. D. (1999). Dopamine, cognitive control, and schizophrenia: The gating model. *Progress in Brain Research, 121*, 327–349. https://doi.org/10.1016/S0079-6123(08)63082-4

Braver, T. S., Reynolds, J. R., & Donaldson, D. I. (2003). Neural mechanisms of transient and sustained cognitive control during task switching. *Neuron, 39*(4), 713–726. https://doi.org/10.1016/S0896-6273(03)00466-5

Brenhouse, H. C., & Andersen, S. L. (2011). Developmental trajectories during adolescence in males and females: A cross-species understanding of underlying brain changes. *Neuroscience & Biobehavioral Reviews, 35*(8), 1687–1703. https://doi.org/10.1016/j.neubiorev.2011.04.013

Brinton, B., Fujiki, M., & McKee, L. (1998). Negotiation skills of children with specific language impairment. *Journal of Speech, Language and Hearing Research, 41*, 927–940. https://doi.org/10.1044/jslhr.4104.927

Brody, G. H., Yu, T., Nusslock, R., Barton, A. W., Miller, G. E., Chen, E., …, & Sweet, L. H. (2019). The protective effects of supportive parenting on the relationship between adolescent poverty and resting-state functional brain connectivity during adulthood. *Psychological Science, 30*(7), 1040–1049. https://doi.org/10.1177/0956797619847989

Brydges, C. R., Fox, A. M., Reid, C. L., & Anderson, M. (2014). The differentiation of executive functions in middle and late childhood: A longitudinal latent-variable analysis. *Intelligence, 47*, 34–43. https://doi.org/10.1016/j.intell.2014.08.010

Bugos, J. A., DeMarie, D., Stokes, C., & Power, L. P. (2022). Multimodal music training enhances executive functions in children: Results of a randomized controlled trial. *Annals of the New York Academy of Sciences, 1516*(1), 95–105. https://doi.org/10.1111/nyas.14857

Cagiltay, N. E., Ozcelik, E., & Ozcelik, N. S. (2015). The effect of competition on learning in games. *Computers & Education, 87*, 35–41. https://doi.org/10.1016/j.compedu.2015.04.001

Cameron, J., & Pierce, W. D. (2002). *Rewards and intrinsic motivation: Resolving the controversy* (p. 255). Bergin & Garvey.

Camos, V., & Barrouillet, P. (2011). Developmental change in working memory strategies: From passive maintenance to active refreshing. *Developmental Psychology, 47*(3), 898–904. https://doi.org/10.1037/a0023193.

Campbell, D. J. (1988). Task complexity: A review and analysis. *Academy of Management Review, 13*(1), 40–52. https://doi.org/10.5465/amr.1988.4306775

Cardin, V., Rudner, M., De Oliveira, R. F., Andin, J., Su, M. T., Beese, L., …, & Rönnberg, J. (2018). The organization of working memory networks is shaped by early sensory experience. *Cerebral Cortex, 28*(10), 3540–3554. https://doi.org/10.1093/cercor/bhx222

References

Carlson, S. M., & Meltzoff, A. N. (2008). Bilingual experience and executive functioning in young children. *Developmental Science, 11*(2), 282–298. https://doi.org10.1111/j.1467-7687.2008.00675.x

Carp, J., & Compton, R. J. (2009). Alpha power is influenced by performance errors. *Psychophysiology, 46,* 336–343. https://doi.org/10.1111/j.1469-8986.2008.00773.x

Carpentier, S. M., Moreno, S., & McIntosh, A. R. (2016). Short-term music training enhances complex, distributed neural communication during music and linguistic tasks. *Journal of Cognitive Neuroscience, 28*(10), 1603–1612. https://doi.org/10.1162/jocn_a_00988

Carroll, S. E. (2017). Exposure and input in bilingual development. *Bilingualism: Language and Cognition, 20*(1), 3–16. https://doi.org/10.1017/S1366728915000863

Carter, C. S., & Van Veen, V. (2007). Anterior cingulate cortex and conflict detection: An update of theory and data. *Cognitive, Affective, & Behavioral Neuroscience, 7*(4), 367–379. https://doi.org/10.3758/CABN.7.4.367

Case, R., Kurland, D. M., & Goldberg, J. (1982). Operational efficiency and the growth of short-term memory span. *Journal of Experimental Child Psychology, 33,* 386–404. https://doi.org/10.1016/0022-0965(82)90054-6

Casey, B. J., Getz, S., & Galvan, A. (2008). The adolescent brain. *Developmental Review, 28*(1), 62–77. https://doi.org/10.1016/j.dr.2007.08.003

Cenoz, J., Hufeisen, B., & Jessner, U. (2003b). Why investigate the multilingual lexicon? In J. Cenoz, B. Hufeisen, & U. Jessner (Eds.), *The multilingual lexicon* (pp. 1–9). Kluwer Academic. https://doi.org/10.1007/978-0-306-48367-7_1

Cepeda, N. J., Blackwell, K. A., & Munakata, Y. (2013). Speed isn't everything: Complex processing speed measures mask individual differences and developmental changes in executive control. *Developmental Science, 16*(2), 269–286. https://doi.org/10.1111/desc.12024

Cepeda, N. J., Pashler, H., Vul, E., Wixted, J. T., & Rohrer, D. (2006). Distributed practice in verbal recall tasks: A review and quantitative synthesis. *Psychological Bulletin, 132*(3), 354–380. https://doi.org/10.1037/0033-2909.132.3.354

Chaddock-Heyman, L., Hillman, C. H., Cohen, N. J., & Kramer, A. F. (2014). The importance of physical activity and aerobic fitness for cognitive control and memory in children. *Monographs of the Society for Research in Child Development, 79*(4), 25–50. https://doi.org/10.1111/mono.12129

Chan, R. C., Shum, D., Toulopoulou, T., & Chen, E. Y. (2008). Assessment of executive functions: Review of instruments and identification of critical issues. *Archives of Clinical Neuropsychology, 23*(2), 201–216. https://doi.org/10.1016/j.acn.2007.08.010

Chang, M., Park, B., & Kim, S. (2009). Parenting classes, parenting behavior, and child cognitive development in Early Head Start: A longitudinal model. *School Community Journal, 19*(1), 155–174. https://doi.org/10.1111/sode.12069

Chapelle, C. A. (2006). DIALANG: A diagnostic language test in 14 European languages. *Language Testing, 23*(4), 544–550. https://doi.org/10.1191/0265532206lt341xx

Chatham, C. H., Frank, M. J., & Munakata, Y. (2009). Pupillometric and behavioral markers of a developmental shift in the temporal dynamics of cognitive control. *Proceedings of the National Academy of Sciences, U.S.A., 106*(14), 5529–5533. https://doi.org/10.1073/pnas.0810002106.

Chen, X., & Padilla, A. M. (2019). Role of bilingualism and biculturalism as assets in positive psychology: Conceptual dynamic gear model. *Frontiers in Psychology*, 2122. https://doi.org/10.3389/fpsyg.2019.02122

Chevalier, N., Jackson, J., Roux, A. R., Moriguchi, Y., & Auyeung, B. (2019). Differentiation in prefrontal cortex recruitment during childhood: Evidence from cognitive control demands and social contexts. *Developmental Cognitive Neuroscience, 36*, 100629, 1–10. https://doi.org/10.1016/j.dcn.2019.100629

Chiaravalloti, N. D., Christodoulou, C., Demaree, H. A., & DeLuca, J. (2003). Differentiating simple versus complex processing speed: Influence on new learning and memory performance. *Journal of Clinical and Experimental Neuropsychology, 25*(4), 489–501. https://doi.org/10.1076/jcen.25.4.489.13878

Chikazoe, J., Jimura, K., Hirose, S., Yamashita, K. I., Miyashita, Y., & Konishi, S. (2009). Preparation to inhibit a response complements response inhibition during performance of a stop-signal task. *Journal of Neuroscience, 29*(50), 15870–15877. https://doi.org/10.1523/JNEUROSCI.3645-09.2009

Chondrogianni, V., & Marinis, T. (2011). Differential effects of internal and external factors on the development of vocabulary, tense morphology and morphosyntax in successive bilingual children. *Linguistic Approaches to Bilingualism, 1*(3), 318–345. https://doi.org/10.1075/lab.1.3.05cho

Chrysikou, E. G., Weber, M. J., & Thompson-Schill, S. L. (2014). A matched filter hypothesis for cognitive control. *Neuropsychologia, 62*, 341–355. https://doi.org/10.1016/j.neuropsychologia.2013.10.021

Chua, H. F., Boland, J. E., & Nisbett, R. E. (2005). Cultural variation in eye movements during scene perception. *Proceedings of the National Academy of Sciences, 102*(35), 12629–12633. https://doi.org/10.1073/pnas.0506162102

Clahsen, H., Bartke, S., & Göllner, S. (1997). Formal features in impaired grammars: A comparison of English and German SLI children. *Journal of Neurolinguistics, 10*(2–3), 151–171. https://doi.org/10.1016/S0911-6044(97)00006-7

Clearfield, M. W., & Niman, L. C. (2012). SES affects infant cognitive flexibility. *Infant Behavior and Development, 35*(1), 29–35. https://doi.org/10.1016/j.infbeh.2011.09.007

Cleary, M., & Pisoni, D. B. (2002). Talker discrimination by prelingually-deaf children with cochlear implants: Preliminary results. *Annals of Otology, Rhinology, & Laryngology Supplement-Proceedings of the 8th Symposium on Cochlear Implants in Children, 111*, 113–118.

Cohen, J. D. (2017). Cognitive control: Core constructs and current considerations. In T. Egner (Ed.), *The Wiley handbook of cognitive control*, 1–28, John Wiley & Sons. https://doi.org/10.1002/9781118920497.ch1

Cohen, J. D., & Servan-Schreiber, D. (1992). Context, cortex, and dopamine: A connectionist approach to behavior and biology in schizophrenia. *Psychological Review, 99*(1), 45–77. https://doi.org/10.1037/0033-295X.99.1.45

CohenMiller, A. S., & Pate, E. (2019). A model for developing interdisciplinary research theoretical frameworks. *The Qualitative Report, 24*(6), 1211–1226. ISSN 10520147

Colunga, E., & Sims, C. E. (2017). Not only size matters: Early-talker and late-talker vocabularies support different word-learning biases in babies and networks. *Cognitive Science, 41,* 73–95. https://doi.org/10.1111/cogs.12409

Colzato, L. S., van den Wildenberg, W. P., Zmigrod, S., & Hommel, B. (2013). Action video gaming and cognitive control: Playing first person shooter games is associated with improvement in working memory but not action inhibition. *Psychological Research, 77,* 234–239. https://doi.org/10.1007/s00426-012-0415-2

Conklin, H. M., Luciana, M., Hooper, C. J., & Yarger, R. S. (2007). Working memory performance in typically developing children and adolescents: Behavioral evidence of protracted frontal lobe development. *Developmental Neuropsychology, 31*(1), 103–128. https://doi.org/10.1080/87565640709336889

Conti, R., Collins, M. A., & Picariello, M. L. (2001). The impact of competition on intrinsic motivation and creativity: Considering gender, gender segregation and gender role orientation. *Personality and Individual Differences, 31*(8), 1273–1289. https://doi.org/10.1016/S0191-8869(00)00217-8

Conti-Ramsden, G., & Botting, N. (2004). Social difficulties and victimization in children with SLI at 11 years of age. *Journal of Speech, Language, & Hearing Research, 47,* 145–161. https://doi.org/10.1044/1092-4388(2004/013)

Conti-Ramsden, G., & Botting, N. (2008). Emotional health in adolescents with and without a history of specific language impairment (SLI). *Journal of Child Psychology and Psychiatry, 49*(5), 516–525. https://doi.org/10.1111/j.1469-7610.2007.01858.x

Costa, A., Hernández, M., & Sebastián-Gallés, N. (2008). Bilingualism aids conflict resolution: Evidence from the ANT task. *Cognition, 106,* 59–86. https://doi.org/10.1016/j.cognition.2006.12.013

Council of Europe. Council for Cultural Co-operation. Education Committee. Modern Languages Division. (2001). *Common European framework of reference for languages: Learning, teaching, assessment.* Cambridge University Press.

Cowan, N. (2005). Working memory capacity limits in a theoretical context. In C. Izawa & N. Ohta (Eds.), *Human learning and memory: Advances in theory and application. The 4th Tsukuba international conference on memory* (pp. 155–175). Erlbaum.

Cowan, N. (2016). Working memory maturation: Can we get at the essence of cognitive growth? *Perspectives on Psychological Science, 11*(2), 239–264. https://doi.org/10.1177/1745691615621279.

Cragg, L. (2016). The development of stimulus and response interference control in midchildhood. *Developmental Psychology, 52*(2), 242–252. https://doi.org/10.1037/dev0000074

Crespo, K., Gross, M., & Kaushanskaya, M. (2019). The effects of dual language exposure on executive function in Spanish–English bilingual children with different language abilities. *Journal of Experimental Child Psychology, 188,* 104663. https://doi.org/10.1016/j.jecp.2019.104663

Dahnlin, E., Neely, A., Larsson, A., Backman, L., & Nyberg, L. (2008). Transfer of learning after updating training mediated by the striatum. *Science, 320,* 1510–1512. https://doi.org/10.1126/science.1155466

References

Dale, P. S., Price, T. S., Bishop, D. V., & Plomin, R. (2003). Outcomes of early language delay. *Journal of Speech, Language, and Hearing Research*, *46*, 544–560. https://doi.org/10.1044/1092-4388(2003/044)

Dale, P. S., Tosto, M. G., Hayiou-Thomas, M. E., & Plomin, R. (2015). Why does parental language input style predict child language development? A twin study of gene–environment correlation. *Journal of Communication Disorders*, *57*, 106–117. https://doi.org/10.1016/j.jcomdis.2015.07.004

Daneman, M., & Carpenter, P. A. (1980). Individual differences in working memory and reading. *Journal of Verbal Learning and Verbal Behavior*, *19*(4), 450–466. https://doi.org/10.1016/S0022-5371(80)90312-6.

Danielmeier, C., & Ullsperger, M. (2011). Post-error adjustments. *Frontiers in Psychology*, *2*. https://doi.org/10.3389/fpsyg.2011.00233

Daselaar, S. M., Iyengar, V., Davis, S. W., Eklund, K., Hayes, S. M., & Cabeza, R. E. (2015). Less wiring, more firing: Low-performing older adults compensate for impaired white matter with greater neural activity. *Cerebral Cortex*, *25*(4), 983–990. https://doi.org/10.1093/cercor/bht289

Davidson, M. C., Amso, D., Anderson, L. C., & Diamond, A. (2006). Development of cognitive control and executive functions from 4 to 13 years: Evidence from manipulations of memory, inhibition, and task switching. *Neuropsychologia*, *44*(11), 2037–2078. https://doi.org/10.1016/j.neuropsychologia.2006.02.006

Davies, P. L., Segalowitz, S. J., & Gavin, W. J. (2004). Development of response-monitoring ERPs in 7-to 25-year-olds. *Developmental Neuropsychology*, *25*(3), 355–376. https://doi.org/10.1207/s15326942dn2503_6

de Abreu, P. M. E., Baldassi, M., Puglisi, M. L., & Befi-Lopes, D. M. (2013). Cross-linguistic and cross-cultural effects on verbal working memory and vocabulary: Testing language-minority children with an immigrant background. *Journal of Speech, Language, and Hearing Research*, *56*(2), 630–642. https://doi.org/10.1044/1092-4388.2012/12-0079

De Bruin, A. (2019). Not all bilinguals are the same: A call for more detailed assessments and descriptions of bilingual experiences. *Behavioral Sciences*, *9*(3), 33. https://doi.org/10.3390/bs9030033

De Bruin, A., Carreiras, M., & Duñabeitia, J. A. (2017). The BEST dataset of language proficiency. *Frontiers in Psychology*, *8*, 522. https://doi.org/10.3389/fpsyg.2017.00522.

De Bruin, A., Treccani, B., & Della Sala, S. (2015). Cognitive advantage in bilingualism: An example of publication bias? *Psychological Science*, *26*(1), 99–107. https://doi.org/10.1177/0956797614557866

de Bruyn, E. H., Cillessen, A. H., & Wissink, I. B. (2010). Associations of peer acceptance and perceived popularity with bullying and victimization in early adolescence. *The Journal of Early Adolescence*, *30*(4), 543–566. https://doi.org/10.1177/0272431609340517

Deci, E. L., Koestner, R., & Ryan, R. M. (2001). Extrinsic rewards and intrinsic motivation in education: Reconsidered once again. *Review of Educational Research*, *71*(1), 1–27. https://doi.org/10.3102/00346543071001001

De Dreu, C. K., Nijstad, B. A., Baas, M., Wolsink, I., & Roskes, M. (2012). Working memory benefits creative insight, musical improvisation, and original ideation through maintained task-focused attention. *Personality and Social Psychology Bulletin, 38*(5), 656–669. https://doi.org/10.1177/0146167211435795

Degé, F., & Schwarzer, G. (2011). The effect of a music program on phonological awareness in preschoolers. *Frontiers in Psychology, 2*, 124. https://doi.org/10.3389/fpsyg.2011.00124

Degé, F., Wehrum, S., Stark, R., & Schwarzer, G. (2011). The influence of two years of school music training in secondary school on visual and auditory memory. *European Journal of Developmental Psychology, 8*(5), 608–623. https://doi.org/10.1080/17405629.2011.590668

DeHaan, J., Reed, W. M., & Kuwanda, K. (2010). The effect of interactivity with a music video game on second language vocabulary recall. *Language Learning & Technology, 14*(2), 74–94. ISSN 1094-3501

De Houwer, A. (2009). *Bilingual first language acquisition*. Multilingual Matters. https://doi.org/10.21832/9781847691507

De Houwer, A. (2011). The speech of fluent child bilinguals. In P. Howell & J. Van Borsel (Eds.), *Multilingual aspects of fluency disorders* (pp. 3–23). Multilingual Matters. https://doi.org/10.21832/9781847693570-003

De Houwer, A. (2014). The absolute frequency of maternal input to bilingual and monolingual children: A first comparison. In T. Grüter & J. Paradis (Eds.), *Input and experience in bilingual development* (pp. 163–186). John Benjamins.

De Houwer, A. (2017). Bilingual language input environments, intake, maturity and practice. *Bilingualism: Language and Cognition, 20*(1), 19–20. http://dx.doi.org/10.1017/S1366728916000298

De Houwer, A. (2023). The danger of bilingual–monolingual comparisons in applied psycholinguistic research. *Applied Psycholinguistics, 44*(3), 343–357. https://doi.org/10.1017/S014271642200042X

Delage, H., Stanford, E., & Durrleman, S. (2021). Working memory training enhances complex syntax in children with Developmental Language Disorder. *Applied Psycholinguistics, 42*(5), 1341–1375. https://doi.org/10.1017/S0142716421000369

Della Rosa, P. A., Videsott, G., Borsa, V. M., Canini, M., Weekes, B. S., Franceschini, R., & Abutalebi, J. (2013). A neural interactive location for multilingual talent. *Cortex, 49*(2), 605–608. https://doi.org/10.1016/j.cortex.2012.12.001

Delogu, F., Lampis, G., & Belardinelli, M. O. (2010). From melody to lexical tone: Musical ability enhances specific aspects of foreign language perception. *European Journal of Cognitive Psychology, 22*(1), 46–61. https://doi.org/10.1080/09541440802708136

Demetriou, A., Spanoudis, G., Shayer, M., Mouyi, A., Kazi, S., & Platsidou, M. (2013). Cycles in speed-working memory-G relations: Towards a developmental–differential theory of the mind. *Intelligence, 41*(1), 34–50. https://doi.org/10.1016/j.intell.2012.10.010

Dempster, F. N., & Corkill, A. J. (1999). Interference and inhibition in cognition and behavior: Unifying themes for educational psychology. *Educational Psychology Review, 11*, 1–88. https://doi.org/10.1023/A:1021992632168

References 173

Derakshan, N., Smyth, S. & Eysenck, M. W. (2009). Effects of state anxiety on performance using a task-switching paradigm: An investigation of attentional control theory. *Psychonomic Bulletin & Review, 16*, 1112–1117. https://doi.org/10.3758/PBR.16.6.1112

Deveau, J., Jaeggi, S. M., Zordan, V., Phung, C., & Seitz, A. R. (2015). How to build better memory training games. *Frontiers in Systems Neuroscience, 8*, 243–248. https://doi.org/10.3389/fnsys.2014.00243

De Villiers, J., De Villiers, P., & Hoban, E. (1994). The central problem of functional categories in the English syntax of oral deaf children. In H. Tager Flusberg (Ed.), *Constraints on language acquisition: Studies of atypical children* (pp. 9–47). Erlbaum.

Di Domenico, S. I., & Ryan, R. M. (2017). The emerging neuroscience of intrinsic motivation: A new frontier in self-determination research. *Frontiers in Human Neuroscience, 11*, 145. https://doi.org/10.3389/fnhum.2017.00145

Diamond, A. (2013). Executive functions. *Annual Review of Psychology, 64*, 135–168. https://doi.org/10.1146/annurev-psych-113011-143750

Diamond, A. (2016). Why improving and assessing executive functions early in life is critical. In *Executive function in preschool-age children: Integrating measurement, neurodevelopment, and translational research* (pp. 11–43). American Psychological Association. https://doi.org/10.13140/RG.2.1.2644.6483

Diamond, A., & Lee, K. (2011). Interventions shown to aid executive function development in children 4 to 12 years old. *Science, 333*(6045), 959–964. https://doi.org/10.1126/science.1204529

Diamond, A., & Ling, D. S. (2020). Review of the evidence on, and fundamental questions about, efforts to improve executive functions, including working memory. In J. M. Novick, M. F. Bunting, M. R. Dougherty, & R. W. Engle (Eds.), *Cognitive and working memory training: Perspectives from psychology, neuroscience, and human development* (pp. 143–431). Oxford University Press. https://doi.org/10.1093/oso/9780199974467.001.0001

Dibbets, P., Bakker, K., & Jolles, J. (2006). Functional MRI of task switching in children with specific language impairment (SLI). *Neurocase, 12*(1), 71–79. https://doi.org/10.1080/13554790500507032

Dodd, B. (2011). Differentiating speech delay from disorder: Does it matter? *Topics in Language Disorders, 31*(2), 96–111. https://doi.org/10.1097/TLD.0b013e318217b66a

Dodge, K. A., Lansford, J. E., Salzer Burks, V., Bates, J. E., Pettit, G. S., Fontaine, R., & Price, J. M. (2003). Peer rejection and social information-processing factors in the development of aggressive behavior problems in children. *Child Development, 74*(2), 374–393. https://doi.org/10.1111/1467-8624.7402004.

Dosenbach, N. U., Fair, D. A., Miezin, F. M., Cohen, A. L., Wenger, K. K., Dosenbach, R. A., …, & Petersen, S. E. (2007). Distinct brain networks for adaptive and stable task control in humans. *Proceedings of the National Academy of Sciences, 104*(26), 11073–11078. https://doi.org/10.1073/pnas.0704320104

Dowsett, S. M., & Livesey, D. J. (2000). The development of inhibitory control in preschool children: Effects of "executive skills" training.

Developmental Psychobiology: The Journal of the International Society for Developmental Psychobiology, 36(2), 161–174. https://doi.org/10.1002/(SICI)1098-2302(200003)36:2<161::AID-DEV7>3.0.CO;2-0

Dörnyei, Z., & Skehan, P. (2003). 18 individual differences in second language learning. In C. J. Doughty, & M. H. Long (Eds.), *The handbook of second language acquisition* (pp. 589–630). Blackwell Publishing Ltd. https://doi.org/10.1002/9780470756492

Dreisbach, G. (2012). Mechanisms of cognitive control: The functional role of task rules. *Current Directions in Psychological Science, 21*(4), 227–231. https://doi.org/10.1177/0963721412449830

Dreisbach, G., & Fröber, K. (2019). On how to be flexible (or not): Modulation of the stability-flexibility balance. *Current Directions in Psychological Science, 28*(1), 3–9. https://doi.org/10.1177/0963721418800030

Dreisbach, G., & Haider, H. (2006). Preparatory adjustment of cognitive control in the task switching paradigm. *Psychonomic Bulletin & Review, 13*, 334–338. https://doi.org/10.3758/BF03193853

Driemeyer, J., Boyke, J., Gaser, C., Büchel, C., & May, A. (2008). Changes in gray matter induced by learning – Revisited. *PLoS ONE, 3*(7): e2669. https://doi.org/10.1371/journal.pone.0002669

Dromi, E., Leonard, L. B., Adam, G., & Zadunaisky-Ehrlich, S. (1999). Verb agreement morphology in Hebrew-speaking children with specific language impairment. *Journal of Speech, Language, and Hearing Research, 42*(6), 1414–1431. https://doi.org/10.1044/jslhr.4206.1414

Dumont, É., Castellanos-Ryan, N., Parent, S., Jacques, S., Séguin, J. R., & Zelazo, P. D. (2022). Transactional longitudinal relations between accuracy and reaction time on a measure of cognitive flexibility at 5, 6, and 7 years of age. *Developmental Science, 25*(5), e13254. https://doi.org/10.1111/desc.13254

Dutilh, G., Van Ravenzwaaij, D., Nieuwenhuis, S., Van der Maas, H. L., Forstmann, B. U., & Wagenmakers, E. J. (2012). How to measure post-error slowing: A confound and a simple solution. *Journal of Mathematical Psychology, 56*(3), 208–216. https://doi.org/10.1016/j.jmp.2012.04.001

Dye, M. W., Baril, D. E., & Bavelier, D. (2007). Which aspects of visual attention are changed by deafness? The case of the Attentional Network Test. *Neuropsychologia, 45*(8), 1801–1811. https://doi.org/10.1016/j.neuropsychologia.2006.12.019

Ebert, K. D. (2021). Revisiting the influences of bilingualism and developmental language disorder on children's nonverbal processing speed. *Journal of Speech, Language, and Hearing Research, 64*(9), 3564–3570. https://doi.org/10.1044/2021_JSLHR-21-00156

Egner, T. (2017). Past, present, and future of the congruency sequence effect as an index of cognitive control. In T Egner (Ed.), *The Wiley handbook of cognitive control,* 64–78. John Wiley & Sons.

Eichorn, N., & Marton, K. (2015). When less can be more: Dual task effects on speech fluency. In D. C. Noelle, R. Dale, A. S. Warlaumont, J. Yoshimi, T. Matlock, C. D. Jennings, & P. P. Maglio (Eds.), *Proceedings of the 37th Annual*

Conference of the Cognitive Science Society (pp.). Cognitive Science Society https://mindmodeling.org/cogsci2015/papers/0116/paper0116.pdf

Eichorn, N., Marton, K., Schwartz, R. G., Melara, R. D., & Pirutinsky, S. (2016). Does working memory enhance or interfere with speech fluency in adults who do and do not stutter? Evidence from a dual-task paradigm. *Journal of Speech, Language, and Hearing Research, 59*(3), 415–429. https://doi.org/10.1044/2015_JSLHR-S-15-0249

Eling, P., Derckx, K., & Maes, R. (2008). On the historical and conceptual background of the Wisconsin Card Sorting Test. *Brain and Cognition, 67*(3), 247–253. https://doi.org/10.1016/j.bandc.2008.01.006

Engel de Abreu, P. M. J., Cruz-Santos, A., & Puglisi, M. L. (2014). Specific language impairment in language-minority children from low-income families. *International Journal of Language and Communication Disorders, 49*(06), 736–747. https://doi.org/10.1111/1460-6984.12107

Engel de Abreu, P. M., Cruz-Santos, A., Tourinho, C. J., Martin, R., & Bialystok, E. (2012). Bilingualism enriches the poor: Enhanced cognitive control in low-income minority children. *Psychological Science, 23*(11), 1364–1371. https://doi.org/10.1177/0956797612443836

Engle R. W. (2002). Working memory capacity as executive attention. *Current Directions in Psychological Science, 11*(1), 19–23. https://doi.org/10.1111/1467-8721.00160

Engle, R. W., & Kane, M. J. (2004). Executive attention, working memory capacity, and a two-factor theory of cognitive control. In B. H. Ross (Ed.), *The psychology of learning and motivation: Advances in research and theory* (Vol. 44, pp. 145–199). Elsevier Science.

Epstein, B., Shafer, V. L., Melara, R. D., & Schwartz, R. G. (2014). Can children with SLI detect cognitive conflict? Behavioral and electrophysiological evidence. *Journal of Speech, Language, and Hearing Research, 57*(4), 1453–1467. https://doi.org/10.1044/2014_JSLHR-L-13-0234

Erdodi, L. A., Sagar, S., Seke, K., Zuccato, B. G., Schwartz, E. S., & Roth, R. M. (2018). The Stroop test as a measure of performance validity in adults clinically referred for neuropsychological assessment. *Psychological Assessment, 30*(6), 755–766. https://doi.org/10.1037/pas0000525

Erickson, K. I., Gildengers, A. G., & Butters, M. A. (2013). Physical activity and brain plasticity in late adulthood. *Dialogues in Clinical Neuroscience, 15*(1), 99–108. https://doi.org/10.31887/DCNS.2013.15.1/kerickson

Evans, C. B., Smokowski, P. R., & Cotter, K. L. (2014). Cumulative bullying victimization: An investigation of the dose–response relationship between victimization and the associated mental health outcomes, social supports, and school experiences of rural adolescents. *Children and Youth Services Review, 44,* 256–264. https://doi.org/10.1016/j.childyouth.2014.06.021

Evans, J. L. (2001). An emergent account of language impairments in children with SLI: Implications for assessment and intervention. *Journal of Communication Disorders, 34*(1–2), 39–54. https://doi.org/10.1016/S0021-9924(00)00040-X

Eysenck, M. W., Derakshan, N., Santos, R., and Calvo, M. G. (2007). Anxiety and cognitive performance: Attentional control theory. *Emotion, 7,* 336–353. https://doi.org/10.1037/1528-3542.7.2.336

Fair, D. A., Dosenbach, N. U., Church, J. A., Cohen, A. L., Brahmbhatt, S., Miezin, F. M., ..., & Schlaggar, B. L. (2007). Development of distinct control networks through segregation and integration. *Proceedings of the National Academy of Sciences*, *104*(33), 13507–13512. https://doi.org/10.1073/pnas.0705843104

Farah, M. J., Shera, D. M., Savage, J. H., Betancourt, L., Giannetta, J. M., Brodsky, N. L., Malmud, E. K., & Hurt, H. (2006). Childhood poverty: Specific associations with neurocognitive development. *Brain Research*, *1110*(1), 166–174. https://doi.org/10.1016/j.brainres.2006.06.072

Farrant, B. M., Maybery, M. T., & Fletcher, J. (2012). Language, cognitive flexibility, and explicit false belief understanding: Longitudinal analysis in typical development and specific language impairment. *Child Development*, *83*(1), 223–235. https://doi.org/10.1111/j.1467-8624.2011.01681.x

Fenson, L., Dale, P. S., Reznick, J. S., Bates, E., Thal, D. J., Pethick, S. J., ..., & Stiles, J. (1994). Variability in early communicative development. *Monographs of the Society for Research in Child Development*, i-185. www.jstor.org/stable/1166093

Fernald, A., & Marchman, V. A. (2012). Individual differences in lexical processing at 18 months predict vocabulary growth in typically developing and late-talking toddlers. *Child Development*, *83*(1), 203–222. https://doi.org/10.1111/j.1467-8624.2011.01692.x

Fine, I., Finney, E. M., Boynton, G. M., & Dobkins, K. R. (2005). Comparing the effects of auditory deprivation and sign language within the auditory and visual cortex. *Journal of Cognitive Neuroscience*, *17*(10), 1621–1637. https://doi.org/10.1162/089892905774597173

Finn, A. S., Minas, J. E., Leonard, J. A., Mackey, A. P., Salvatore, J., Goetz, C., West, M. R., Gabrieli, C. F. O., & Gabrieli, J. D. E. (2017). Functional brain organization of working memory in adolescents varies in relation to family income and academic achievement. *Developmental Science*, *20*(5). https://doi-org.ezproxy.gc.cuny.edu/10.1111/desc.12450

Finneran, D. A., Francis, A. L., & Leonard, L. B. (2009). Sustained attention in children with specific language impairment (SLI). *Journal of Speech, Language, & Hearing Research*, *52*(4), 915–929. https://doi.org/10.1044/1092-4388(2009/07-0053)

Fischer, P., Camba, L., Ooi, S. H., & Chevalier, N. (2018). Supporting cognitive control through competition and cooperation in childhood. *Journal of Experimental Child Psychology*, *173*, 28–40. https://doi.org/10.1016/j.jecp.2018.03.011

Fisher, E. L. (2017). A systematic review and meta-analysis of predictors of expressive-language outcomes among late talkers. *Journal of Speech, Language, and Hearing Research*, *60*(10), 2935–2948. https://doi.org/10.1044/2017_JSLHR-L-16-0310

Flaugnacco, E., Lopez, L., Terribili, C., Montico, M., Zoia, S., & Schön, D. (2015). Music training increases phonological awareness and reading skills in developmental dyslexia: A randomized control trial. *PloS One*, *10*(9), e0138715. https://doi.org/10.1371/journal.pone.0138715

Friedman, N. P., & Miyake, A. (2004). The relations among inhibition and interference control functions: A latent-variable analysis. *Journal of Experimental Psychology: General*, *133*, 101–135. https://doi.org/10.1037/0096-3445.133.1.101

Friedman, N. P., & Miyake, A. (2017). Unity and diversity of executive functions: Individual differences as a window on cognitive structure. *Cortex, 86*, 186–204. https://doi.org/10.1016/j.cortex.2016.04.023

Friedman, N. P., Miyake, A., Young, S. E., DeFries, J. C., Corley, R. P., & Hewitt, J. K. (2008). Individual differences in executive functions are almost entirely genetic in origin. *Journal of Experimental Psychology: General, 137*(2), 201–225. https://doi.org/10.1037/0096-3445.137.2.201

Friedman, N. P., & Robbins, T. W. (2022). The role of prefrontal cortex in cognitive control and executive function. *Neuropsychopharmacology, 47*(1), 72–89. https://doi.org/10.1016/j.nlm.2011.07.002

Friedmann, N., & Haddad-Hanna, M. (2014). The comprehension of sentences derived by syntactic movement in Palestinian Arabic speakers with hearing impairment. *Applied Psycholinguistics, 35*(3), 473–513. https://doi.org/10.1017/S0142716412000483

Friedmann, N., & Rusou, D. (2015). Critical period for first language: The crucial role of language input during the first year of life. *Current Opinion in Neurobiology, 35*, 27–34. https://doi.org/10.1016/j.conb.2015.06.003

Fröber, K., Raith, L., & Dreisbach, G. (2018). The dynamic balance between cognitive flexibility and stability: The influence of local changes in reward expectation and global task context on voluntary switch rate. *Psychological Research, 82*, 65–77. https://doi.org/10.1007/s00426-017-0922-2

Fry, A. F., & Hale, S. (1996). Processing speed, working memory, and fluid intelligence: Evidence for a developmental cascade. *Psychological Science, 7*, 237–241. https://doi.org/10.1111/j.1467-9280.1996.tb00366.x

Fry, A. F., & Hale, S. (2000). Relationships among processing speed, working memory, and fluid intelligence in children. *Biological Psychology, 54*(1–3), 1–34. https://doi.org/10.1016/S0301-0511(00)00051-X

Gagne, F. (2000). Understanding the complete choreography of talent development through DMGT-analysis. In K. A. Heller, F. J. Mönks, R. Subotnik, & R. J. Sternberg (Eds.), *International handbook of giftedness and talent*. Elsevier Science.

García, O., Flores, N., & Chu, H. (2011). Extending bilingualism in US secondary education: New variations. *International Multilingual Research Journal, 5*(1), 1–18. https://doi.org/10.1080/19313152.2011.539486

Garivaldo, B., & Fabiano-Smith, L. (2023). Reframing Bilingual Acquisition and Theory: An insider perspective through a translanguaging lens. *Language, Speech, and Hearing Services in Schools*, 1–16. https://doi.org/10.1044/2023_LSHSS-22-00136

Gathercole, S. E. (2006). Nonword repetition and word learning: The nature of the relationship. *Applied Psycholinguistics, 27*(4), 513–543. https://doi.org/10.1017/S0142716406060383

Gathercole, S. E., & Baddeley, A. D. (1993). *Working memory and language*. Psychology Press.

Gathercole, S. E., Dunning, D. L., Holmes, J., & Norris, D. (2019). Working memory training involves learning new skills. *Journal of Memory and Language, 105*, 19–42. https://doi.org/10.1016/j.jml.2018.10.003

Gathercole, S. E., Pickering, S. J., Ambridge, B., & Wearing, H. (2004). The structure of working memory from 4 to 15 years of age. *Developmental Psychology*, *40*(2), 177–190. https://doi.org/10.1037/0012-1649.40.2.177

Gazman, Z., Pazuelo, L., Scheuer, J., Campanelli, L., Ouchikh, Y., & Marton, K. (2019). Best practices in assessing language proficiency in bilingual children with and without DLD. *12th International Symposium on Bilingualism, The Next Generation*, pp. 194–195.

Gehebe, T., Wadhera, D., & Marton, K. (2023). Interactions between bilingual language proficiency and exposure: Comparing subjective and objective measures across modalities in bilingual young adults. *International Journal of Bilingual Education and Bilingualism*, *26*(7), 845–860. https://doi.org/10.1080/13670050.2022.2125285

Geier, C., & Luna, B. (2009). The maturation of incentive processing and cognitive control. *Pharmacology Biochemistry and Behavior*, *93*(3), 212–221. https://doi.org/10.1016/j.pbb.2009.01.021

Genesee, F. (2019). Language development in simultaneous bilinguals: The early years. In N. Akhtar, J. Tolins, J. E. F. Tree, J. S. Horst, & J. von Koss Torkildsen (Eds.), *International handbook of language acquisition* (pp. 300–320). Routledge.

Genesee, F., & Nicoladis, E. (2007). Bilingual first language acquisition. In E. Hoff & M., Shatz. *Blackwell handbook of language development* (pp. 324–342). Blackwell Publishing Ltd. https://doi.org/10.1002/9780470757833

Gentner, D., Özyürek, A., Gürcanli, Ö., & Goldin-Meadow, S. (2013). Spatial language facilitates spatial cognition: Evidence from children who lack language input. *Cognition*, *127*(3), 318–330. https://doi.org/10.1016/j.cognition.2013.01.003

Gerardi-Caulton, G. (2000). Sensitivity to spatial conflict and the development of self-regulation in children 24–36 months of age. *Developmental Science*, *3*(4), 397–404. https://doi.org/10.1111/1467-7687.00134

Gertner, B. L., Rice, M. L., & Hadley, P. A. (1994). Influence of communicative competence on peer preferences in a preschool classroom. *Journal of Speech, Language, and Hearing Research*, *37*(4), 913–923. https://doi.org/10.1044/jshr.3704.913

Giedd, J. N., Blumenthal, J., Jeffries, N. O., Castellanos, F. X., Liu, H., Zijdenbos, A., …, & Rapoport, J. L. (1999). Brain development during childhood and adolescence: A longitudinal MRI study. *Nature Neuroscience*, *2*(10), 861–863. https://doi.org/10.1038/13158

Gilger, J. W., & Wise, S. E. (2004). Genetic correlates of language and literacy impairments. In C. A. Stone, E. R. Silliman, B. J. Ehren, & K. Apel (Eds.), *Handbook of language and literacy. Development and disorders* (pp. 25–48). The Guilford Press.

Gillam, R. B., Cowan, N., & Day, L. S. (1995). Sequential memory in children with and without language impairment. *Journal of Speech, Language, and Hearing Research*, *38*(2), 393–402. https://doi.org/10.1044/jshr.3802.393

Gillam, S., Holbrook, S., Mecham, J., & Weller, D. (2018). Pull the Andon rope on working memory capacity interventions until we know more. *Language, Speech, and Hearing Services in Schools*, *49*(3), 434–448. https://doi.org/10.1044/2018_LSHSS-17-0121

References

Glass, G. V., Willson, V. L., & Gottman, J. M. (Eds.). (2008). *Design and analysis of time-series experiments*. IAP.

Goodhew, S. C., & Edwards, M. (2019). Translating experimental paradigms into individual-differences research: Contributions, challenges, and practical recommendations. *Consciousness and Cognition, 69*, 14–25. https://doi.org/10.1016/j.concog.2019.01.008

Gordon, P. C., Hendrick, R., & Levine, W. H. (2002). Memory-load interference in syntactic processing. *Psychological Science, 13*(5), 425–430. https://doi.org/10.1111/1467-9280.00475

Gordon, R. L., Magne, C. L., & Large, E. W. (2011). EEG correlates of song prosody: A new look at the relationship between linguistic and musical rhythm. *Frontiers in Psychology, 2*, 352. https://doi.org/10.3389/fpsyg.2011.00352

Gotlib, I. H., & Joormann, J. (2010). Cognition and depression: Current status and future directions. *Annual Review of Clinical Psychology, 6*, 285–312. https://doi.org/10.1146/annurev.clinpsy.121208.131305

Grahek, I., Shenhav, A., Musslick, S., Krebs, R. M., & Koster, E. H. (2019). Motivation and cognitive control in depression. *Neuroscience & Biobehavioral Reviews, 102*, 371–381. https://doi.org/10.1016/j.neubiorev.2019.04.011

Gratton, G., Cooper, P., Fabiani, M., Carter, C. S., & Karayanidis, F. (2018). Dynamics of cognitive control: Theoretical bases, paradigms, and a view for the future. *Psychophysiology, 55*(3), e13016. https://doi.org/10.1111/psyp.13016

Grayson, D. S., Ray, S., Carpenter, S., Iyer, S., Dias, T. G. C., Stevens, C., …, & Fair, D. A. (2014). Structural and functional rich club organization of the brain in children and adults. *PLoS One, 9*(2), e88297. https://doi.org/10.1371/journal.pone.0088297

Green, C. S. (2020). Interventions to do real-world good: Generalization and persistence. *Psychological Science in the Public Interest, 21*(2), 43–49. https://doi.org/10.1177/1529100620933847

Green, D. W. (1998). Mental control of the bilingual lexico-semantic system. *Bilingualism: Language and Cognition, 1*(2), 67–81. https://doi.org/10.1017/S1366728998000133

Green, D. W., & Abutalebi, J. (2013). Language control in bilinguals: The adaptive control hypothesis. *Journal of Cognitive Psychology, 25*(5), 515–530. https://doi.org/10.1177/1529100620933847

Greenland, S. (2017). Invited commentary: The need for cognitive science in methodology. *American Journal of Epidemiology, 186*(6), 639–645. https://doi.org/10.1093/aje/kwx259

Grela, B. G., & Leonard, L. B. (2000). The influence of argument-structure complexity on the use of auxiliary verbs by children with SLI. *Journal of Speech, Language, and Hearing Research, 43*(5), 1115–1125. https://doi.org/10.1044/jslhr.4305.1115

Grinstead, J., Baron, A., Vega-Mendoza, M., De la Mora, J., Cantú-Sánchez, M., & Flores, B. (2013). Tense marking and spontaneous speech measures in Spanish specific language impairment: A discriminant function analysis. *Journal of Speech, Language, and Hearing Research, 56*(1), 352–363. https://doi.org/10.1044/1092-4388(2012/11-0289)

Grogan, A., Jones, O. P., Ali, N., Crinion, J., Orabona, S., Mechias, M. L., et al. (2012). Structural correlates for lexical efficiency and number of languages in non-native speakers of English. *Neuropsychologia, 50*(7), 1347–1352. https://doi .org/10.1016/j.neuropsychologia.2012.02.019

Grosjean, F. (1989). Neurolinguists, beware! The bilingual is not two mono-linguals in one person. *Brain and Language, 36*(1), 3–15. https://doi .org/10.1016/0093-934X(89)90048-5

Gross, J. J. (2002). Emotion regulation: Affective, cognitive, and social consequences. *Psychophysiology, 39*(3), 281–291. https://doi.org/10.1017/S0048577201393198

Grossmann, I., & Varnum, M. E. (2011). Social class, culture, and cognition. *Social Psychological and Personality Science, 2*(1), 81–89. https://doi .org/10.1177/1948550610377119

Grüter, T., & Paradis, J. (Eds.), *Input and experience in bilingual development* (pp. 119–140). Benjamins.

Gupta, R., Kar, B. R., & Srinivasan, N. (2009). Development of task switching and post-error-slowing in children. *Behavioral and Brain Functions, 5*(1), 1–13. https://doi.org/10.1186/1744-9081-5-38

Gutiérrez-Clellen, V. F., Simon-Cereijido, G., & Leone, A. E. (2009). Code-switching in bilingual children with specific language impairment. *International Journal of Bilingualism, 13*(1), 91–109. https://doi.org/10.1177/1367006909103530

Habibi, A., Damasio, A., Ilari, B., Veiga, R., Joshi, A. A., Leahy, R. M., ..., & Damasio, H. (2018). Childhood music training induces change in micro and macroscopic brain structure: Results from a longitudinal study. *Cerebral Cortex, 28*(12), 4336–4347. https://doi.org/10.1093/cercor/bhx286

Hackman, D. A., & Farah, M. J. (2009). Socioeconomic status and the develop-ing brain. *Trends in Cognitive Sciences, 13*(2), 65–73. https://doi.org/10.1016/j .tics.2008.11.003

Hadley, P. A., & Holt, J. K. (2006). Individual differences in the onset of tense marking: A growth-curve analysis. *Journal of Speech, Language, and Hearing Research, 49*(5), 984–1000. https://doi.org/10.1044/1092-4388(2006/071)

Hajcak, G. (2012). What we've learned from mistakes: Insights from error-related brain activity. *Current Directions in Psychological Science, 21*(2), 101–106. https:// doi.org/10.1177/0963721412436809

Hajcak, G., Moser, J. S., Yeung, N., & Simons, R. F. (2005). On the ERN and the significance of errors. *Psychophysiology, 42*(2), 151–160. https://doi .org/10.1111/j.1469-8986.2005.00270.x

Hakuta, K. (1986). *Mirror of language.* Basic Books.

Hallquist, M. N., Hwang, K., & Luna, B. (2013). The nuisance of nuisance regression: Spectral misspecification in a common approach to resting-state fMRI preprocessing reintroduces noise and obscures functional connectivity. *Neuroimage, 82,* 208–225. https://doi.org/10.1016/j.neuroimage.2013.05.116

Hamzei, F., Glauche, V., Schwarzwald, R., & May, A. (2012). Dynamic gray matter changes within cortex and striatum after short motor skill training are associated with their increased functional interaction. *Neuroimage, 59*(4), 3364–3372. https://doi.org/10.1016/j.neuroimage.2011.10.089

Hansson, K. (1997). Patterns of verb usage in Swedish children with SLI: An application of recent theories. *First Language, 17*(51), 195–217. https://doi.org/10.1177/014272379701705109

Hansson, K., & Nettelbladt, U. (1995). Grammatical characteristics of Swedish children with SLI. *Journal of Speech, Language, and Hearing Research, 38*(3), 589–598. https://doi.org/10.1044/jshr.3803.589

Hansson, K., Nettelbladt, U., & Leonard, L. B. (2000). Specific language impairment in Swedish: The status of verb morphology and word order. *Journal of Speech, Language, and Hearing Research, 43*(4), 848–864. https://doi.org/10.1044/jslhr.4304.848

Harnishfeger, K. K., & Bjorklund, D. F. (1993). The ontogeny of inhibition mechanisms: A renewed approach to cognitive development. In *Emerging themes in cognitive development* (pp. 28–49). Springer.

Hart, B., & Risley T. R. (1995). *Meaningful differences in the everyday experience of young American children.* Brookes.

Hartanto, A., & Yang, H. (2020). The role of bilingual interactional contexts in predicting interindividual variability in executive functions: A latent variable analysis. *Journal of Experimental Psychology: General, 149*(4), 609. https://doi.org/10.1037/xge0000672

Hasher, L., Lustig, C., & Zacks, R. T. (2007). Inhibitory mechanisms and the control of attention. In A. R. A. Conway, C. E. Jarrold, M. J. Kane, A. Miyake, & J. N. Towse (Eds.), *Variation in working memory* (pp. 227–249). Oxford University Press.

Hasson, N., & Joffe, V. (2007). The case for dynamic assessment in speech and language therapy. *Child Language Teaching and Therapy, 23*(1), 9–25. https://doi.org/10.1177/0265659007072142

He, S. U. N., Yussof, N., Vijayakumar, P., Gabrielle, L. A. I., O'Brien, B. A., & Ong, Q. H. (2020). Teacher's code-switching and bilingual children's heritage language learning and cognitive switching flexibility. *Journal of Child Language, 47*(2), 309–336. https://doi.org/10.1017/S030500091900059X

Henrichs, J., Rescorla, L., Schenk, J. J., Schmidt, H. G., Jaddoe, V. W., Hofman, A., …, & Tiemeier, H. (2011). Examining continuity of early expressive vocabulary development: The Generation R study. *Journal of Speech, Language, and Hearing Research, 54*, 854–869. https://doi.org/10.1044/1092-4388(2010/09-0255)

Henry, L. A., Messer, D. J., & Nash, G. (2012). Executive functioning in children with specific language impairment. *Journal of Child Psychology and Psychiatry, 53*(1), 37–45. https://doi.org/10.1111/j.1469-7610.2011.02430.x

Hernandez, A. E., Hofmann, J., & Kotz, S. A. (2007). Age of acquisition modulates neural activity for both regular and irregular syntactic functions. *NeuroImage, 36*(3), 912–923. https://doi.org/10.1016/j.neuroimage.2007.02.055

Herrera, L., Lorenzo, O., Defior, S., Fernandez-Smith, G., & Costa-Giomi, E. (2011). Effects of phonological and musical training on the reading readiness of native-and foreign-Spanish-speaking children. *Psychology of Music, 39*(1), 68–81. https://doi.org/10.1177/0305735610361995

Hick, R., Botting, N., & Conti-Ramsden, G. (2005). Cognitive abilities in children with specific language impairment: Consideration of visuo-spatial skills. *International Journal of Language & Communication Disorders*, *40*(2), 137–149. https://doi.org/10.1080/13682820400011507

Hicks, K., & Engle, R. W. (2020). Cognitive perspectives of working memory training. In *Cognitive and working memory training: Perspectives from psychology, neuroscience, and human development* (pp. 3–13). Oxford University Press.

Higby, E., Kim, J., & Obler, L. K. (2013). Multilingualism and the brain. *Annual Review of Applied Linguistics*, *33*, 68–101. https://doi.org/10.1017/S0267190513000081

Hilchey, M. D., & Klein, M. (2011). Are there bilingual advantages on nonlinguistic interference tasks? Implications for the plasticity of executive control processes. *Psychonomic Bulletin & Review*, *18*, 625–658. https://doi.org/10.3389/fpsyg.2011.00309

Hinnant, J. B., & O'Brien, M. (2007). Cognitive and emotional control and perspective taking and their relations to empathy in 5-year-old children. *The Journal of Genetic Psychology*, *168*(3), 301–322. https://doi.org/10.3200/GNTP.168.3.301-322

Hintermair, M. (2013). Executive functions and behavioral problems in deaf and hard-of-hearing students at general and special schools. *Journal of Deaf Studies and Deaf Education*, *18*(3), 344–359. https://doi.org/10.1093/deafed/ent003

Hitch, G. J., Towse, J. N., & Hutton, U. (2001). What limits children's working memory span? Theoretical accounts and applications for scholastic development. *Journal of Experimental Psychology: General*, *130*(2), 184–198. https://doi.org/10.1037/0096-3445.130.2.184

Ho, Y. C., Cheung, M. C., & Chan, A. S. (2003). Music training improves verbal but not visual memory: Cross-sectional and longitudinal explorations in children. *Neuropsychology*, *17*(3), 439–450. https://doi.org/10.1037/0894-4105.17.3.439

Hoch, L., Poulin-Charronnat, B., & Tillmann, B. (2011). The influence of task-irrelevant music on language processing: Syntactic and semantic structures. *Frontiers in Psychology*, *2*, 112. https://doi.org/10.3389/fpsyg.2011.00112

Hoff, E. (2003). The specificity of environmental influence: Socioeconomic status affects early vocabulary development via maternal speech. *Child Development*, *74*(5), 1368–1378. https://doi.org/10.1111/1467-8624.00612

Hoff, E. (2013). *Language development* (p. 490). Cengage Learning.

Hoff, E., Core, C., Place, S., Rumiche, R., Señor, M., & Parra, M. (2012). Dual language exposure and early bilingual development. *Journal of Child Language*, *39*(1), 1–27. https://doi.org/10.1017/S0305000910000759

Hoff, E., Welsh, S., Place, S., Ribot, K., Grüter, T., & Paradis, J. (2014). Properties of dual language input that shape bilingual development and properties of environments that shape dual language input. *Input and Experience in Bilingual Development*, *13*, 119–140.

Homack, S., & Riccio, C. A. (2004). A meta-analysis of the sensitivity and specificity of the Stroop Color and Word Test with children. *Archives of Clinical Neuropsychology*, *19*(6), 725–743. https://doi.org/10.1016/j.acn.2003.09.003

Houben, K., & Wiers, W. (2009). Response inhibition moderates the relationship between implicit associations and drinking behavior. *Alcoholism Clinical and Experimental Research, 33*(4), 626–633. https://doi.org/10.1111/j.1530-0277.2008.00877.x

Hölzel, B. K., Carmody, J., Vangel, M., Congleton, C., Yerramsetti, S. M., Gard, T., & Lazar, S. W. (2011). Mindfulness practice leads to increases in regional brain gray matter density. *Psychiatry Research: Neuroimaging, 191*(1), 36–43. https://doi.org/10.1016/j.pscychresns.2010.08.006

Hruby, G. G. (2012). Three requirements for justifying an educational neuroscience. *British Journal of Educational Psychology, 82*(1), 1–23. https://doi.org/10.1111/j.2044-8279.2012.02068.x

Hsin, L., Legendre, G., & Omaki, A. (2013). Priming cross-linguistic interference in Spanish–English bilingual children. In *Proceedings of the 37th Annual Boston University Conference on Language Development* (pp. 165–177). Cascadilla Press.

Hsu, H. J., & Bishop, D. V. (2010). Grammatical difficulties in children with specific language impairment: Is learning deficient? *Human Development, 53*(5), 264–277. https://doi.org/10.1159/000321289

Hudson Kam, C. L. (2014). Age of acquisition effects. In P. J. Brooks, & V. Kempe (Eds.), *Encyclopedia of language development* (pp. 9–13). Sage Publications.

Huizinga, M, Dolan, C. V., & van der Molen, M. W. (2006). Age-related change in executive function: Developmental trends and a latent variable analysis. *Neuropsychologia, 44*, 2017–2036. https://doi.org/10.1016/j.neuropsychologia.2006.01.01

Hund, A. M., & Foster, E. K. (2008). Understanding developmental changes in the stability and flexibility of spatial categories based on object relatedness. *Developmental Psychology, 44*(1), 218–232. https://doi.org/10.1037/0012-1649.44.1.218

Hurtado, N., Grüter, T., Marchman, V. A., & Fernald, A. (2014). Relative language exposure, processing efficiency and vocabulary in Spanish–English bilingual toddlers. *Bilingualism: Language and Cognition, 17*(1), 189–202. https://doi.org/10.1017/S136672891300014X

Hulstijn, J. H. (2012). The construct of language proficiency in the study of bilingualism from a cognitive perspective. *Bilingualism: Language and Cognition, 15*(2), 422–433. https://doi.org/10.1017/S1366728911000678

Hübner, R., & Töbel, L. (2019). Conflict resolution in the Eriksen flanker task: Similarities and differences to the Simon task. *PloS One, 14*(3), e0214203. https://doi.org/10.1371/journal.pone.0214203

Ibrahim, R., Shoshani, R., Prior, A., & Share, D. (2013). Bilingualism and measures of spontaneous and reactive cognitive flexibility. *Psychology, 4*(7), 1–10. http://dx.doi.org/10.4236/psych.2013.47A00

Iluz-Cohen, P., & Armon-Lotem, S. (2013). Language proficiency and executive control in bilingual children. *Bilingualism: Language and Cognition, 16*(4), 884–899. https://doi.org/10.1017/S1366728912000788

Im-Bolter, N., Johnson, J., & Pascual-Leone, J. (2006). Processing limitations in children with specific language impairment: The role of executive function. *Child Development, 77*(6), 1822–1841. https://doi.org/10.1111/j.1467-8624.2006.00976.x

184 *References*

Inzlicht, M., Bartholow, B. D., & Hirsh, J. B. (2015). *Trends in Cognitive Sciences*, *19*(3), 126–132. https://doi.org/10.1016/j.tics.2015.01.004

Iuculano, T., Rosenberg-Lee, M., Richardson, J., Tenison, C., Fuchs, L., Supekar, K., & Menon, V. (2015). Cognitive tutoring induces widespread neuroplasticity and remediates brain function in children with mathematical learning disabilities. *Nature Communications*, *6*(1), 1–10. https://doi.org/10.1038/ncomms9453

Jacobson, P. F., & Schwartz, R. G. (2002). Morphology in incipient bilingual Spanish-speaking preschool children with specific language impairment. *Applied Psycholinguistics*, *23*(1), 23–41. https://doi.org/10.1017/S0142716402000024

Jacobson, P. F., & Schwartz, R. G. (2005). English past tense use in bilingual children with language impairment. *American Journal of Speech-Language Pathology*, *14*(4), 313–323. https://doi.org/10.1044/1058-0360(2005/030)

Jaeggi, S. M., Buschkuehl, M., Jonides, J., & Shah, P. (2011). Short-and long-term benefits of cognitive training. *Proceedings of the National Academy of Sciences*, *108*(25), 10081–10086. https://doi.org/10.1073/pnas.1103228108

Jensen, A. R. (2005). Mental chronometry and the unification of differential psychology. In R. J. Sternberg, & J. E. Pretz (Eds.), *Cognition and intelligence: Identifying the mechanisms of the mind* (pp. 26–50). Cambridge University Press.

Jensen, A. R. (2006). *Clocking the mind: Mental chronometry and individual differences*. Elsevier.

Jentschke, S., & Koelsch, S. (2009). Musical training modulates the development of syntax processing in children. *Neuroimage*, *47*(2), 735–744. https://doi.org/10.1016/j.neuroimage.2009.04.090

Jeon, H. A., & Friederici, A. D. (2015). Degree of automaticity and the prefrontal cortex. *Trends in Cognitive Sciences*, *19*(5), 244–250. https://doi.org/10.1016/j.tics.2015.03.003

Jilka, M. (2009). Talent and proficiency in language. In G. Dogil, & S. M. Reiterer (Eds.), *Language talent and brain activity* (pp. 1–16). Mouton de Gruyter,.

Jiménez-Castellanos, O., & García, E. (2017). Intersection of language, class, ethnicity, and policy: Toward disrupting inequality for English language learners. *Review of Research in Education*, *41*(1), 428–452. https://doi.org/10.3102/0091732X16688623

Johann, V. E., & Karbach, J. (2021). Educational application of cognitive training. In *Cognitive training* (pp. 333–350). Springer, Cham. https://doi.org/10.1007/978-3-030-39292-5_23

John, L. K., Loewenstein, G., & Prelec, D. (2012). Measuring the prevalence of questionable research practices with incentives for truth telling. *Psychological Science*, *23*(5), 524–532. https://doi.org/10.1177/0956797611430953

Jokihaka, S., Laasonen, M., Lahti-Nuuttila, P., Smolander, S., Kunnari, S., Arkkila, E., ..., & Heinonen, K. (2022). Cross-sectional and longitudinal associations between quality of parent–child interaction and language ability in preschool-age children with developmental language disorder. *Journal of Speech, Language, and Hearing Research*, 1–14. https://doi.org/10.1044/2022_JSLHR-21-00479

Jonides, J. (2004). How does practice makes perfect? *Nature Neuroscience*, *7*(1), 10–11. https://doi.org/10.1038/nn0104-10

References

Just, M. A. & Carpenter, P. A. (1992). A capacity theory of comprehension: Individual differences in working memory. *Psychological Review, 99*, 122–49. https://doi.org/10.1037/0033-295X.99.1.122

Kafetsios, K. G. (2019). Interdependent self-construal moderates relationships between positive emotion and quality in social interactions: A case of person to culture fit. *Frontiers in Psychology, 10*, 914. https://doi.org/10.3389/fpsyg.2019.00914

Kail, R. (1991). Development of processing speed in childhood and adolescence. *Advances in Child Development and Behavior, 23*, 151–185. https://doi.org/10.1016/S0065-2407(08)60025-7

Kail, R. (1994). A method for studying the generalized slowing hypothesis in children with specific language impairment. *Journal of Speech, Language, and Hearing Research, 37*(2), 418–421. https://doi.org/10.1044/jshr.3702.418

Kail, R. (2002). Developmental change in proactive interference. *Child Development, 73*(6), 1703–1714. https://doi.org/10.1111/1467-8624.00500

Kail, R. V. (2008). Speed of processing in childhood and adolescence: Nature, consequences, and implications for understanding atypical development. In J. DeLuca, & J. H. Kalmar (Eds.), *Information processing speed in clinical populations* (pp. 101–123). Taylor & Francis.

Kail, R. V., & Miller, C. A. (2006). Developmental change in processing speed: Domain specificity and stability during childhood and adolescence. *Journal of Cognition and Development, 7*(1), 119–137. https://doi.org/10.1207/s15327647jcd0701_6

Kail, R., & Park, Y. S. (1990). Impact of practice on speed of mental rotation. *Journal of Experimental Child Psychology, 49*(2), 227–244. https://doi.org/10.1016/0022-0965(90)90056-E

Kail, R., & Salthouse, T. A. (1994). Processing speed as a mental capacity. *Acta Psychologica, 86*(2–3), 199–225. https://doi.org/10.1016/0001-6918(94)90003-5

Kalia, V., Wilbourn, M. P., & Ghio, K. (2014). Better early or late? Examining the influence of age of exposure and language proficiency on executive function in early and late bilinguals. *Journal of Cognitive Psychology, 26*(7), 699–713. https://doi.org/10.1080/20445911.2014.956748

Kalnak, N., Peyrard-Janvid, M., Forssberg, H., & Sahlén, B. (2014). Nonword repetition–a clinical marker for specific language impairment in Swedish associated with parents' language-related problems. *PloS One, 9*(2), e89544. https://doi.org/10.1371/journal.pone.0089544

Kang, K., Alexander, N., Wessel, J. R., Wimberger, P., Nitzsche, K., Kirschbaum, C., & Li, S. C. (2021). Neurocognitive development of novelty and error monitoring in children and adolescents. *Scientific Reports, 11*(1), 19844. https://doi.org/10.1038/s41598-021-99043-z

Kapa, L. L., & Colombo, J. (2013). Attentional control in early and later bilingual children. *Cognitive Development, 28*(3), 233–246. https://doi.org/10.1016/j.cogdev.2013.01.011

Kapa, L. L., & Plante, E. (2015). Executive function in SLI: Recent advances and future directions. *Current Developmental Disorders Reports, 2*, 245–252. https://doi.org/10.1007/s40474-015-0050-x

Karbach, J., & Kray, J. (2009). How useful is executive control training? Age differences in near and far transfer of task-switching training. *Developmental Science, 12*(6), 978–990. https://doi.org/10.1111/j.1467-7687.2009.00846.x

Karousou, A., & Nerantzaki, T. (2022). Phonological memory training and its effect on second language vocabulary development. *Second Language Research, 38*(1), 31–54. https://doi.org/10.1177/0267658319898514

Karr, J. E., Areshenkoff, C. N., Rast, P., Hofer, S. M., Iverson, G. L., & Garcia-Barrera, M. A. (2018). The unity and diversity of executive functions: A systematic review and re-analysis of latent variable studies. *Psychological Bulletin, 144*(11), 1147–1185. https://doi.org/10.1037/bul0000160

Kašćelan, D., & De Cat, C. (2022). A constellation of continua: Reconceptualising bilingualism, autism and language research. *Linguistic Approaches to Bilingualism*, 59–64. https://doi.org/10.1075/lab.21069.kas

Katz, B., Jones, M. R., Shah, P., Buschkuehl, M., & Jaeggi, S. M. (2021). Individual differences in cognitive training research. In *Cognitive training* (pp. 107–123). Springer, Cham. https://doi.org/10.1007/978-3-030-39292-5_8

Katz, B., & Shah, P. (2020). Logical and methodological considerations in cognitive training research. In J. M. Novick, M. F. Bunting, M. R. Dougherty, & R. W. Engle (Eds.), *Cognitive and working memory training: Perspectives from psychology, neuroscience, and human development* (pp. 455–486). Oxford University Press. https://doi.org/10.1093/oso/9780199974467.001.0001

Kaushanskaya, M., & Marian, V. (2007). Bilingual language processing and interference in bilinguals: Evidence from eye tracking and picture naming. *Language Learning, 57*(1), 119–163. https://doi.org/10.1111/j.1467-9922.2007.00401.x

Kaushanskaya, M., & Prior, A. (2015). Variability in the effects of bilingualism on cognition: It is not just about cognition, it is also about bilingualism. *Bilingualism: Language and Cognition, 18*(1), 27–28. https://doi.org/10.1017/S1366728914000510

Kautto, A., Jansson-Verkasalo, E., & Mainela-Arnold, E. (2021). Generalized slowing rather than inhibition is associated with language outcomes in both late talkers and children with typical early development. *Journal of Speech, Language, and Hearing Research, 64*(4), 1222–1234. https://doi.org/10.1044/2020_JSLHR-20-00523

Kerns, J. G., Cohen, J. D., MacDonald III, A. W., Cho, R. Y., Stenger, V. A., & Carter, C. S. (2004). Anterior cingulate conflict monitoring and adjustments in control. *Science, 303*(5660), 1023–1026. https://doi.org/10.1126/science.1089910.

Kheder, S., & Kaan, E. (2021). Cognitive control in bilinguals: Proficiency and code-switching both matter. *Cognition, 209*, 104575. https://doi.org/10.1016/j.cognition .2020.104575

Kidd, E., Donnelly, S., & Christiansen, M. H. (2018). Individual differences in language acquisition and processing. *Trends in Cognitive Sciences, 22*(2), 154–169. https://doi.org/10.1016/j.tics.2017.11.00

Kim, J. Marton, K., & Obler, L. K. (2019). Interference control in bilingual auditory sentence processing in noise. In I. A. Sekerina, L. Spradlin, & V. Valian (Eds.), *Bilingualism, executive function, and beyond. Questions and insights*. John Benjamins Publishing Company, 103–116.

References 187

Kim-Spoon, J., Maciejewski, D., Lee, J., Deater-Deckard, K., & King-Casas, B. (2017). Longitudinal associations among family environment, neural cognitive control, and social competence among adolescents. *Developmental Cognitive Neuroscience, 26,* 69–76. https://doi.org/10.1016/j.dcn.2017.04.009

King, J., & Just, M. A. (1991). Individual differences in syntactic processing: The role of working memory. *Journal of Memory and Language, 30*(5), 580–602. https://doi.org/10.1016/0749-596X(91)90027-H

Kirkham, N. Z., Cruess, L., & Diamond, A. (2003). Helping children apply their knowledge to their behavior on a dimension-switching task. *Developmental Science, 6*(5), 449–467. https://doi.org/10.1111/1467-7687.00300

Klahr, D., & Chen, Z. (2011). Finding one's place in transfer space. *Child Development Perspectives, 5*(3), 196–204. https://doi.org/10.1111/j.1750-8606.2011.00171.x

Klauer, K. C., Herfordt, J., & Voss, A. (2008). Social presence effects on the Stroop task: Boundary conditions and an alternative account. *Journal of Experimental Social Psychology, 44,* 469–476. https://doi.org/10.1016/j.jesp.2007.02.009

Knoll, L. J., Fuhrmann, D., Sakhardande, A. L., Stamp, F., Speekenbrink, M., & Blakemore, S. J. (2016). A window of opportunity for cognitive training in adolescence. *Psychological Science, 27*(12), 1620–1631. https://doi.org/10.1177/0956797616671327

Koelsch, S. (2009). Neural substrates of processing syntax and semantics in music. In R. Haas, & V. Brandes (Eds.), *Music that works* (pp 143–153). Springer, Vienna. https://doi.org/10.1007/978-3-211-75121-3_9

Kohnert, K., Windsor, J., & Yim, D. (2006). Do language-based processing tasks separate children with language impairment from typical bilinguals? *Learning Disabilities Research & Practice, 21*(1), 19–29. https://doi.org/10.1111/j.1540-5826.2006.00204.x

Kolb, B., Gibb, R., & Robinson, T. E. (2003). Brain plasticity and behavior. *Current Directions in Psychological Science, 12*(1), 1–5. https://doi.org/10.1111/1467-8721.01210

Kolb, A. Y., & Kolb, D. A. (2005b). *The Kolb Learning Style Inventory – Version 3.1 2005 technical specifications* (pp. 1–72). Hay Group.

Kool, W., & Botvinick, M. (2014). A labor/leisure tradeoff in cognitive control. *Journal of Experimental Psychology: General, 143*(1), 131–141. https://doi.org/10.1037/a0031048.

Kormos, J., & Sáfár, A. (2008). Phonological short-term memory, working memory and foreign language performance in intensive language learning. *Bilingualism: Language and Cognition, 11*(2), 261–271. https://doi.org/10.1017/S1366728908003416

Kovács, Á. M. (2015). Cognitive adaptations induced by a multi-language input in early development. *Current Opinion in Neurobiology, 35,* 80–86. https://doi.org/10.1016/j.conb.2015.07.003

Kovács, Á. M., & Mehler, J. (2009). Cognitive gains in 7-month-old bilingual infants. *Proceedings of the National Academy of Sciences, 106*(16), 6556–6560. https://doi.org/10.1073/pnas.0811323106

Könen, T., Strobach, T., & Karbach, J. (2021). Working memory training. In *Cognitive training* (pp. 155–167). Springer, Cham. https://doi.org/10.1007/978-3-030-39292-5_11

Kray, J., Karbach, J., Haenig, S., & Freitag, C. (2012). Can task-switching training enhance executive control functioning in children with attention deficit/hyperactivity disorder? *Frontiers in Human Neuroscience, 5*, 180. https://doi.org/10.3389/fnhum.2011.00180

Kroll, J. F., & Bialystok, E. (2013). Understanding the consequences of bilingualism for language processing and cognition. *Journal of Cognitive Psychology, 25*(5), 497–514. https://doi.org/10.1080/20445911.2013.799170

Kroll, J. F., Dussias, P. E., Bice, K., & Perrotti, L. (2015). Bilingualism, mind, and brain. *Annual Review of Linguistics, 1*(1), 377–394. https://doi.org/10.1146/annurev-linguist-030514-124937

Krueger, C. E., Bird, A. C., Growdon, M. E., Jang, J. Y., Miller, B. L., & Kramer, J. H. (2009). Conflict monitoring in early frontotemporal dementia. *Neurology, 73*(5), 349–355. https://doi.org/10.1212/WNL.0b013e3181b04b24

Kuchinsky, S. E., & Haarmann, H. J. (2020). Neuroscience perspectives on cognitive training. In J. M. Novick, M. F. Bunting, M. R. Dougherty, & R. W. Engle (Eds.), *Cognitive and working memory training: Perspectives from psychology, neuroscience, and human development* (pp. 79–104). Oxford University Press. https://doi.org/10.1093/oso/9780199974467.001.0001

Kühn, S., Gleich, T., Lorenz, R. C., Lindenberger, U., & Gallinat, J. (2014). Playing Super Mario induces structural brain plasticity: Gray matter changes resulting from training with a commercial video game. *Molecular Psychiatry, 19*(2), 265–271. https://doi.org/10.1038/mp.2013.120

Ladányi, E., & Lukács, Á. (2019). Word retrieval difficulties and cognitive control in specific language impairment. *Journal of Speech, Language, and Hearing Research, 62*(4), 918–931. https://doi.org/10.1044/2018_JSLHR-L-17-0446

LaGasse, A. B. (2014). Developmental speech and language training through music (DSLM). In M. Thaut, & V. Hoemberg (Eds.), *Handbook of neurologic music therapy* (pp.196–216). Oxford University Press.

Lahey, M., Edwards, J., & Munson, B. (2001). Is processing speed related to severity of language impairment? *Journal of Speech, Language, & Hearing Research, 44*(6), 1354–1361. https://doi.org/10.1044/1092-4388(2001/105)

Laloi, A., de Jong, J., & Baker, A. (2017). Can executive functioning contribute to the diagnosis of SLI in bilingual children?: A study on response inhibition. *Linguistic Approaches to Bilingualism, 7*(3–4), 431–459. https://doi.org/10.1075/lab.15020.lal

Laureys, F., De Waelle, S., Barendse, M. T., Lenoir, M., & Deconinck, F. J. (2022). The factor structure of executive function in childhood and adolescence. *Intelligence, 90*, 101600. https://doi.org/10.1016/j.intell.2021.101600

Leeser, M. J., Sunderman, G. L., Granena, G., Jackson, D. O., & Yilmaz, Y. (2016). Methodological implications of working memory tasks for L2 processing research. In G. Granena, D. O. Jackson, & Y. Yilmaz (Eds.), *Cognitive individual differences in second language processing and acquisition* (pp. 89–104). John Benjamins Publishing Company. https://doi.org/10.1075/bpa.3

Leonard, L. B. (2014). *Children with specific language impairment.* Massachusetts Institute of Technology.

Leonard, L. B., Eyer, J. A., Bedore, L. M., & Grela, B. G. (1997). Three accounts of the grammatical morpheme difficulties of English-speaking children with specific language impairment. *Journal of Speech, Language, and Hearing Research, 40*(4), 741–753. https://doi.org/10.1044/jslhr.4004.741

Leonard, L. B., Weismer, S. E., Miller, C. A., Francis, D. J., Tomblin, J. B., & Kail, R. V. (2007). Speed of processing, working memory, and language impairment in children. *Journal of Speech, Language, and Hearing Research, 50*, 408–428. https://doi.org/10.1044/1092-4388(2007/029)

Lepper, M. R., Greene, D., & Nisbett, R. E. (1973). Undermining children's intrinsic interest with extrinsic reward: A test of the "overjustification" hypothesis. *Journal of Personality and Social Psychology, 28*(1), 129–137. https://doi.org/10.1037/h0035519

Lewandowsky, S., Geiger, S. M., & Oberauer, K. (2008). Interference-based forgetting in verbal short-term memory. *Journal of Memory and Language, 59*(2), 200–222. https://doi.org/10.1016/j.jml.2008.04.004

Lewandowsky, S., Oberauer, K., & Brown, G. D. (2009). No temporal decay in verbal short-term memory. *Trends in Cognitive Sciences, 13*(3), 120–126. https://doi.org/10.1016/j.tics.2008.12.003

Lewis, F. C., Reeve, R. A., Kelly, S. P., & Johnson, K. A. (2017). Evidence of substantial development of inhibitory control and sustained attention between 6 and 8 years of age on an unpredictable Go/No-Go task. *Journal of Experimental Child Psychology, 157*, 66–80. https://doi.org/10.1016/j.ecp.2016.12.08

Li, M., Lindenmuth, M., Tarnai, K., Lee, J., KingCasas, B., Kim-Spoon, J., & Deater-Deckard, K. (2022). Development of cognitive control during adolescence: The integrative effects of family socioeconomic status and parenting behaviors. *Developmental Cognitive Neuroscience*, 101139. https://doi.org/10.1016/j.dcn.2022.101139

Li, P., Legault, J., & Litcofsky, K. A. (2014). Neuroplasticity as a function of second language learning: Anatomical changes in the human brain. *Cortex, 58*, 301–324. https://doi.org/10.1016/j.cortex.2014.05.001

Li, Y., Yang, J., Suzanne Scherf, K., & Li, P. (2013). Two faces, two languages: An fMRI study of bilingual picture naming. *Brain and Language, 127*, 452–462. https://doi.org/10.1016/j.bandl.2013.09.005

Lidz, C. S., & Macrine, S. L. (2001). An alternative approach to the identification of gifted culturally and linguistically diverse learners: The contribution of dynamic assessment. *School Psychology International, 22*(1), 74–96. https://doi.org/10.1177/0143034301022001006

Lieven, E. (2014). First language development: A usage-based perspective on past and current research. *Journal of Child Language, 41*(S1), 48–63. https://doi.org/10.1017/S0305000914000282

Little, T. D. (2013). *Longitudinal structural equation modeling.* The Guilford Press.

Liu, C., Timmer, K., Jiao, L., Yuan, Y., & Wang, R. (2019). The influence of contextual faces on bilingual language control. *Quarterly Journal of Experimental Psychology, 72*(9), 2313–2327. https://doi.org/10.1177/1747021819836713

Liu, L., & Kager, R. (2017). Is mommy talking to daddy or to me? Exploring parental estimates of child language exposure using the Multilingual Infant Language Questionnaire. *International Journal of Multilingualism, 14*(4), 366–377. https://doi.org/10.1080/14790718.2016.1216120

Loehlin, J. C. (2004). *Latent variable models: An introduction to factor, path, and structural equation analysis.* Psychology Press.

Loosli, S. V., Buschkuehl, M., Perrig, W. J., & Jaeggi, S. M. (2012). Working memory training improves reading processes in typically developing children. *Child Neuropsychology, 18*(1), 62–78. https://doi.org/10.1080/09297049.2011.575772

López-Crespo, G., Daza, M. T., & Méndez-López, M. (2012). Visual working memory in deaf children with diverse communication modes: Improvement by differential outcomes. *Research in Developmental Disabilities, 33*(2), 362–368. https://doi.org/10.1016/j.ridd.2011.10.022

Lövdén, M., Bäckman, L., Lindenberger, U., Schaefer, S., & Schmiedek, F. (2010). A theoretical framework for the study of adult cognitive plasticity. *Psychological Bulletin, 136*(4), 659–676. https://doi.org/10.1037/a0020080

Lövdén, M., Brehmer, Y., Li, S. C., & Lindenberger, U. (2012). Training-induced compensation versus magnification of individual differences in memory performance. *Frontiers in Human Neuroscience, 6,* 141. https://doi.org/10.3389/fnhum.2012.00141

Luckner, J. L., & McNeill, J. H. (1994). Performance of a group of deaf and hard-of-hearing students and a comparison group of hearing students on a series of problem-solving tasks. *American Annals of the Deaf,* 371–377.

Luk, G., & Bialystok, E. (2013). Bilingualism is not a categorical variable: Interaction between language proficiency and usage. *Journal of Cognitive Psychology, 25*(5), 605–621. https://doi.org/10.1080/20445911.2013.795574

Luk, G., De Sa, E. R. I. C., & Bialystok, E. (2011). Is there a relation between onset age of bilingualism and enhancement of cognitive control? *Bilingualism: Language and Cognition, 14*(4), 588–595. https://doi.org/10.1017/S1366728911000010

Lukács, Á., Leonard, L. B., Kas, B., & Pléh, C. (2009). The use of tense and agreement by Hungarian-speaking children with language impairment. *Journal of Speech, Language, and Hearing Research, 52*(1), 98–117. https://doi.org/10.1044/1092-4388(2008/07-0183)

Luna, B., Marek, S., Larsen, B., Tervo-Clemmens, B., & Chahal, R. (2015). An integrative model of the maturation of cognitive control. *Annual Review of Neuroscience, 38,* 151–170. https://doi.org/10.1146/annurev-neuro-071714-034054

MacDonald, M. C., & Christiansen, M. H. (2002). Reassessing working memory: Comment on Just and Carpenter (1992) and Waters and Caplan (1996). *Psychological Review, 109*(1), 35–54. https://doi.org/10.1037/0033-295X.109.1.35

References

Mackey, A. P., Hill, S. S., Stone, S. I., & Bunge, S. A. (2011). Differential effects of reasoning and speed training in children. *Developmental Science, 14*(3), 582–590. https://doi.org/10.1111/j.1467-7687.2010.01005.x

Mackin, R. S., Ayalon, L., Feliciano, L., & Areán, P. A. (2010). The sensitivity and specificity of cognitive screening instruments to detect cognitive impairment in older adults with severe psychiatric illness. *Journal of Geriatric Psychiatry and Neurology, 23*(2), 94–99. https://doi.org/10.1177/0891988709358589

MacLeod, C. M. (1991). Half a century of research on the stroop effect: An integrative review. *Psychological Bulletin, 109*(2), 163–203. https://doi.org/10.1037/0033-2909.109.2.163

MacRoy-Higgins, M., Schwartz, R. G., Shafer, V. L., & Marton, K. (2013). Influence of phonotactic probability/neighbourhood density on lexical learning in late talkers. *International Journal of Language & Communication Disorders, 48*(2), 188–199. https://doi.org/10.1111/j.1460-6984.2012.00198.x

Mahncke, H. W., Bronstone, A., & Merzenich, M. M. (2006). Brain plasticity and functional losses in the aged: Scientific bases for a novel intervention. *Progress in Brain Research, 157*, 81–109. https://doi.org/10.1016/S0079-6123(06)57006-2

Mainela-Arnold, E., & Evans, J. L. (2005). Beyond capacity limitations: Determinants of word recall performance on verbal working memory span tasks in children with SLI. *Journal of Speech, Language and Hearing Research, 48*(4), 897–909. https://10.1044/1092-4388(2005/062)

Marian, V., H. Blumenfeld, & Kaushanskaya, M. (2007). The Language Experience and Proficiency Questionnaire (LEAPQ): Assessing Language profiles in bilinguals and multilinguals. *Journal of Speech, Language, and Hearing Research, 50*(4), 940–967. https://doi.org/10.1044/1092-4388(2007/067)

Marie, C., Delogu, F., Lampis, G., Belardinelli, M. O., & Besson, M. (2011). Influence of musical expertise on segmental and tonal processing in Mandarin Chinese. *Journal of Cognitive Neuroscience, 23*(10), 2701–2715. https://doi.org/10.1162/jocn.2010.21585

Marinis, T., & Armon-Lotem, S. (2015). Sentence repetition. In S. Armon-Lotem, J. de Jong, & N. Meir (Eds.), *Assessing multilingual children: Disentangling bilingualism from language impairment* (pp. 95–124). Multilingual Matters.

Martin, K. I., & Ellis, N. C. (2012). The roles of phonological short-term memory and working memory in L2 grammar and vocabulary learning. *Studies in Second Language Acquisition, 34*(3), 379–413. https://doi.org/10.1017/S0272263112000125

Martin, J. D., Tsukahara, J. S., Draheim, C., Shipstead, Z., Mashburn, C. A., Vogel, E. K., & Engle, R. W. (2021). The visual arrays task: Visual storage capacity or attention control? *Journal of Experimental Psychology: General, 150*(12), 2525–2551. https://doi.org/10.1037/xge0001048

Marton, K. (2006). Do nonword repetition errors in children with specific language impairment (SLI) reflect a weakness in an unidentified skill specific to nonword repetition or a deficit in simultaneous processing? *Applied Psycholinguistics, 27*(4), 569–573. https://doi.org/10.1017.S0142716406060450

Marton, K. (2008). Visuo-spatial processing and executive functions in children with specific language impairment. *International Journal of Language & Communication Disorders, 43*(2), 181–200. https://doi.org/10.1080/16066350701340719

Marton, K. (2009). Imitation of body postures and hand movements in children with specific language impairment. *Journal of Experimental Child Psychology, 102*(1), 1–13. https://doi.org/10.1016/j.jecp.2008.07.007

Marton, K. (2015). Do bilingual children perform more efficiently in experimental tasks than their monolingual peers? Paper presented at the Workshop on Bilingualism and Executive functions. An interdisciplinary approach. New York, NY.

Marton, K. (2019). Executive control in bilingual children: Factors that influence the outcomes. In I. A. Sekerina, L. Spradlin, & V. Valian (Eds.), *Bilingualism, Executive Function, and Beyond. Questions and insights* (pp. 265–279). John Benjamins Publishing Company. https://doi.org/10.1075/sibil.57.17mar

Marton, K., Abramoff, B., & Rosenzweig, S. (2005). Social cognition and language in children with specific language impairment (SLI). *Journal of Communication Disorders, 38*(2), 143–162. https://doi.org/10.1016/j.jcomdis.2004.06.003

Marton, K., Campanelli, L., Eichorn, N., Scheuer, J., & Yoon, J. (2014). Information processing and proactive interference in children with and without specific language impairment (SLI). *Journal of Speech, Language, and Hearing Research, 57*, 106–119. https://doi.org/10.1044/1092-4388(2013/12-0306)

Marton, K., Campanelli, L., Scheuer, J., Yoon, J., & Eichorn, N. (2012). Executive function profiles in children with and without specific language impairment. *Rivista di Psycolinguistica Applicata /Journal of Applied Psycholinguistics, 12*(3), 9–25.

Marton, K., & Eichorn, N. (2014). Interaction between working memory and long-term memory. *Zeitschrift für Psychologie, 222*(2), 90–99. https://doi.org/10.1027/2151-2604/a000170

Marton, K., Eichorn, N., Campanelli, L., & Zakarias, L. (2016). Working memory and interference control in children with specific language impairment. *Language and Linguistics Compass, 10*(5), 211–224. https://doi.org/10.1111/lnc3.12189

Marton, K., Gehebe, T. & Pazuelo, L. (2019). Cognitive control along the language spectrum: From the typical bilingual child to language impairment. *Seminars in Speech & Language, 40*(4), 256–271. DOI: https://doi.org/10.1055/s-0039-1692962

Marton, K., Kelmenson, L., & Pinkhasova, M. (2007). Inhibition control and working memory capacity in children with SLI. *Psychologia, 50*, 110–121. https://doi.org/10.2117/psysoc.2007.110

Marton, K., Kövi, Zs., & Egri, T. (2018). Is interference control in children with specific language impairment similar to that of children with autistic spectrum disorder? *Research in Developmental Disabilities, 72*, 179–190. https://doi.org/10.1016/j.ridd.2017.11.007

Marton, K., & Scheuer, J. (2020). The relationship between proceduralization and cognitive control. *Journal of Communication Disorders, 83*, 105941. https://doi.org/10.1016/j.jcomdis.2019.105941

Marton, K., & Schwartz, R. G. (2003). Working memory capacity and language processes in children with specific language impairment. *Journal of Speech, Language, and Hearing Research, 46*, 1138–1153. https://doi.org/1092-4388/03/4605-1138

Marton, K., Schwartz, R. G., & Braun, A. (2006). The effect of age and language structure in working memory performance. In Bara, B. G., Barsalou, L., & Bucciarelli, M. (Eds.), *Proceedings of the XXVII. Annual Meeting of the Cognitive Science Society* (pp. 1413–1418). Lawrence Erlbaum Associates, Inc.

Marton, K., Schwartz, R. G., Farkas, L., & Katsnelson, V. (2006). Effect of sentence length and complexity on working memory performance in Hungarian children with specific language impairment (SLI): A cross-linguistic comparison. *International Journal of Language & Communication Disorders, 41*(6), 653–673. https://doi.org/10.1080/13682820500420418

Marton, K., & Wellerstein, M. (2008). What can social psychology gain from and offer to children with specific language impairment: Social perception of the self and others. In Jenifer B. Teiford (Ed.), *Social perception: 21st century issues and challenges* (pp. 103–125). Nova Science Publishers.

Marton, K., & Yoon, J. (2014). Cross-linguistic investigations of language impairments. In P. Brooks, & V. Kempe (Eds.), *Encyclopedia of language development* (pp. 123–127). Sage Reference.

Matte-Landry, A., Boivin, M., Tanguay-Garneau, L., Mimeau, C., Brendgen, M., Vitaro, F., …, & Dionne, G. (2020). Children with persistent versus transient early language delay: Language, academic, and psychosocial outcomes in elementary school. *Journal of Speech, Language, and Hearing Research, 63*(11), 3760–3774. https://doi.org/10.1044/2020_JSLHR-20-00230

Mayes, S. D., & Calhoun, S. L. (2007). Learning, attention, writing, and processing speed in typical children and children with ADHD, autism, anxiety, depression, and oppositional-defiant disorder. *Child Neuropsychology, 13*(6), 469–493. https://doi.org/10.1080/09297040601112773

Mazuka, R., Jincho, N., & Oishi, H. (2009). Development of executive control and language processing. *Language and Linguistics Compass, 3*(1), 59–89. https://doi.org/10.1111/j.1749-818X.2008.00102.x

McCabe, P. C., & Meller, P. J. (2004). The relationship between language and social competence: How language impairment affects social growth. *Psychology in the Schools, 41*(3), 313–321. https://doi.org/10.1002/pits.10161

McCormick, E. M., Qu, Y., & Telzer, E. H. (2016). Adolescent neurodevelopment of cognitive control and risk-taking in negative family contexts. *NeuroImage, 124*, 989–996. https://doi.org/10.1016/j.neuroimage.2015.09.063

McGregor, K. K., Goffman, L., Van Horne, A. O., Hogan, T. P., & Finestack, L. H. (2020). Developmental language disorder: Applications for advocacy, research, and clinical service. *Perspectives of the ASHA Special Interest Groups, 5*(1), 38–46. https://doi.org/10.1044/2019_PERSP-19-00083

McIntyre, D. (2005). Bridging the gap between research and practice. *Cambridge Journal of Education, 35*(3), 357–382. https://doi.org/10.1080/03057640500319065

McVay, J. C., & Kane, M. J. (2012b). Why does working memory capacity predict variation in reading comprehension? On the influence of mind wandering and executive attention. *Journal of Experimental Psychology: General, 141*(2), 302–320. https://doi.org/10.1037/a0025250

Mechelli, A., Crinion, J. T., Noppeney, U., O'Doherty, J. P., Ashburner, J., Frackowiak, R. S., et al. (2004). Structural plasticity in the bilingual brain: Proficiency in a second language and age at acquisition affect grey-matter density. *Nature, 431*(7010), 757. https://doi.org/10.1038/431757a

Meier, M. E., & Kane, M. J. (2017). Attentional control and working memory capacity. In Egner, T. (Ed.), *The Wiley handbook of cognitive control*. John Wiley & Sons. https://doi.org/10.1002/9781118920497

Meiran, N., Pereg, M., Kessler, Y., Cole, M. W., & Braver, T. S. (2015). The power of instructions: Proactive configuration of stimulus–response translation. *Journal of Experimental Psychology: Learning, Memory, and Cognition, 41*(3), 768–786. https://doi.org/10.1037/xlm0000063

Meisel, J. M. (2011). *First and second language acquisition: Parallels and differences.* Cambridge University Press.

Melby-Lervåg, M., & Hulme, C. (2013). Is working memory training effective? A meta-analytic review. *Developmental Psychology, 49*(2), 270–291. https://doi.org/10.1037/a0028228

Mercer, S., & Ryan, S. (2010). A mindset for EFL: Learners' beliefs about the role of natural talent. *ELT Journal, 64*(4), 436–444. https://doi.org/10.1093/elt/ccp083.

Merz, E. C., Wiltshire, C. A., & Noble, K. G. (2019). Socioeconomic inequality and the developing brain: Spotlight on language and executive function. *Child Development Perspectives, 13*(1), 15–20. https://doi.org/10.1111/cdep.12305

Meyer, A., Nelson, B., Perlman, G., Klein, D. N., & Kotov, R. (2018). A neural biomarker, the error-related negativity, predicts the first onset of generalized anxiety disorder in a large sample of adolescent females. *Journal of Child Psychology and Psychiatry, 59*(11), 1162–1170. https://doi.org/10.1111/jcpp.12922

Mezzacappa, E. (2004). Alerting, orienting, and executive attention: Developmental properties and sociodemographic correlates in an epidemiological sample of young, urban children. *Child Development, 75*(5), 1373–1386. https://doi.org/10.1111/j.1467-8624.2004.00746.x

Miller, C. A., Kail, R., Leonard, L. B., & Tomblin, J. B. (2001). Speed of processing in children with specific language impairment. *Journal of Speech, Language, and Hearing Research, 44*(2), 416–433. https://doi.org/10.1044/1092-4388(2001/034)

Milner, B. (1963). Effects of different brain lesions on card sorting: The role of the frontal lobes. *Archives of Neurology, 9*(1), 90–100. https://doi.org/10.1001/archneur.1963.00460070100010

Miltner, W. H., Lemke, U., Weiss, T., Holroyd, C., Scheffers, M. K., & Coles, M. G. (2003). Implementation of error-processing in the human anterior cingulate cortex: A source analysis of the magnetic equivalent of the error-related negativity. *Biological Psychology*, *64*(1–2), 157–166. https://doi.org/10.1016/S0301-0511(03)00107-8

Mistry, J., Li, J., Yoshikawa, H., Tseng, V., Tirrell, J., Kiang, L., ..., & Wang, Y. (2016). An integrated conceptual framework for the development of Asian American children and youth. *Child Development*, *87*(4), 1014–1032. https://doi.org/10.1111/cdev.12577

Mitchell, T. V., & Quittner, A. L. (1996). Multimethod study of attention and behavior problems in hearing-impaired children. *Journal of Clinical Child Psychology*, *25*(1), 83–96. https://doi.org/10.1207/s15374424jccp2501_10

Miyake, A., Friedman, N. P., Emerson, M. J., Witzki, A. H., Howerter, A., & Wager, T. D. (2000). The unity and diversity of executive functions and their contributions to complex "frontal lobe" tasks: A latent variable analysis. *Cognitive Psychology*, *41*(1), 49–100. https://doi.org/10.1006/cogp.1999.0734

Monsrud, M. B., Rydland, V., Geva, E., Thurmann-Moe, A. C., & Halaas Lyster, S. A. (2019). The advantages of jointly considering first and second language vocabulary skills among emergent bilingual children. *International Journal of Bilingual Education and Bilingualism*, 1–17. https://doi.org/10.1080/13670050.2019.1624685

Montgomery, J. W. (2003). Working memory and comprehension in children with specific language impairment: What we know so far. *Journal of Communication Disorders*, *36*(3), 221–231. https://doi.org/10.1016/S0021-9924(03)00021-2

Montgomery, J. W. (2005). Effects of input rate and age on the real-time language processing of children with specific language impairment. *International Journal of Language & Communication Disorders*, *40*(2), 171–188. https://doi.org/10.1080/13682820400011069

Montgomery, J. W., Magimairaj, B. M., & Finney, M. C. (2010). Working memory and specific language impairment: An update on the relation and perspectives on assessment and treatment. *American Journal of Speech-Language Pathology*, *19*, 78–94. https://doi.org/10.1044/1058-0360(2009/09-0028)

Montgomery, J. W., Magimairaj, B. M., & O'Malley, M. H. (2008). Role of working memory in typically developing children's complex sentence comprehension. *Journal of Psycholinguistic Research*, *37*(5), 331–354. https://doi.org/10.1007/s10936-008-9077-z

Morales, J., Calvo, A., & Bialystok, E. (2013). Working memory development in monolingual and bilingual children. *Journal of Experimental Child Psychology*, *114*(2), 187–202. https://doi.org/10.1016/j.jecp.2012.09.002

Moreno, S. (2009). Can music influence language and cognition? *Contemporary Music Review*, *28*(3), 329–345. https://doi.org/10.1080/07494460903404410

Moreno, S., Bialystok, E., Barac, R., Schellenberg, E. G., Cepeda, N. J., & Chau, T. (2011). Short-term music training enhances verbal intelligence and executive function. *Psychological Science*, *22*(11), 1425–1433. https://doi.org/10.1177/0956797611416999

Morgan, P. L., Farkas, G., Hillemeier, M. M., Li, H., Pun, W. H., & Cook, M. (2017). Cross-cohort evidence of disparities in service receipt for speech or language impairments. *Exceptional Children*, *84*(1), 27–41. https://doi.org/10.1177/0014402917718341

Moriguchi, Y., Evans, A. D., Hiraki, K., Itakura, S., & Lee, K. (2012). Cultural differences in the development of cognitive shifting: East–West comparison. *Journal of Experimental Child Psychology*, *111*(2), 156–163. https://doi.org/10 .1016/j.jecp.2011.09.001

Moriguchi, Y., & Hiraki, K. (2009). Neural origin of cognitive shifting in young children. *Proceedings of the National Academy of Sciences*, *106*(14), 6017–6021. https://doi.org/10.1073/pnas.0809747106

Morton, J., & Munakata, Y. (2002). Active versus latent representations: A neural network model of perseveration, dissociation, and decalage. *Developmental Psychobiology*, *40*, 255–265. https://doi.org/10.1002/dev.10033

Moseley Harris, B. (2021). Exploring parents' experiences: Parent-focused intervention groups for communication needs. *Child Language Teaching and Therapy*, *37*(2), 193–209. https://doi.org/10.1177/02656590211019461

Moyer, A. (2014). Exceptional outcomes in L2 phonology: The critical factors of learner engagement and self-regulation. *Applied Linguistics*, *35*(4), 418–440. https://doi.org/10.1093/applin/amu012

Mulder, H., Pitchford, N. J., & Marlow, N. (2010). Processing speed and working memory underlie academic attainment in very preterm children. *Archives of Disease in Childhood-Fetal and Neonatal Edition*, *95*(4), F267–F272. http:// dx.doi.org/10.1136/adc.2009.167965

Muñoz-Sandoval, A. F., Cummins, J., Alvarado, C. G., & Ruef, M. L. (2005). *Bilingual verbal ability tests. Normative update*. Rolling Meadows, IL: The Riverside Publishing Company.

Murao, A., Ito, T., Fukuda, S. E., & Fukuda, S. (2017). Grammatical case-marking in Japanese children with SLI. *Clinical Linguistics & Phonetics*, *31*(7–9), 711–723. https://doi.org/10.1080/02699206.2017.1310929

Musslick, S., & Cohen, J. D. (2021). Rationalizing constraints on the capacity for cognitive control. *Trends in Cognitive Sciences*, *25*(9), 757–775. https://doi.org/10 .1016/j.tics.2021.06.001

Musslick, S., Shenhav, A., Botvinick, M. M., & Cohen, J. D. (2015). A computational model of control allocation based on the expected value of control. In *Reinforcement learning and decision making conference* (Vol. 2015), Alberta, Canada.

Nelson, J. M., James, T. D., Chevalier, N., Clark, C. A., & Espy, K. A. (2016). Structure, measurement, and development of preschool executive control. In J. A. Griffin, P. McCardle, & L. S. Freund (Eds.), *Executive function in preschool age children: Integrating measurement, neurodevelopment, and translational research* (pp. 65–89). American Psychological Association. https://doi .org/10.1037/14797-004

Nelson, T. D., James, T. D., Nelson, J. M., Tomaso, C. C., & Espy, K. A. (2022). Executive control throughout elementary school: Factor structure and associations with early childhood executive control. *Developmental Psychology*, *58*(4), 730–750. https://doi.org/10.1037/dev0001314

Neville, H. J., Stevens, C., Pakulak, E., Bell, T. A., Fanning, J., Klein, S., & Isbell, E. (2013). Family-based training program improves brain function, cognition, and behavior in lower socioeconomic status preschoolers. *Proceedings of the National Academy of Sciences, 110*(29), 12138–12143. https://doi.org/10.1073/pnas.1304437110

Newbury, J., Klee, T., Stokes, S. F., & Moran, C. (2016). Interrelationships between working memory, processing speed, and language development in the age range 2–4 years. *Journal of Speech, Language, and Hearing Research, 59*(5), 1146–1158. https://doi.org/10.1044/2016_JSLHR-L-15-0322

Nicolay, A. C., & Poncelet, M. (2013). Cognitive advantage in children enrolled in a second-language immersion elementary school program for three years. *Bilingualism: Language and Cognition, 16*(3), 597–607. https://doi.org/10.1017/S1366728912000375

Noble, K. G., Houston, S. M., Brito, N. H., Bartsch, H., Kan, E., Kuperman, J. M., Akshoomoff, N., Amaral, D. G., Bloss, C. S., Libiger, O., Schork, N. J., Murray, S. S., Casey, B. J., Chang, L., Ernst, T. M., Frazier, J. A., Gruen, J. R., Kennedy, D. N., Van Zijl, P., ..., & Sowell, E. R. (2015). Family income, parental education and brain structure in children and adolescents. *Nature Neuroscience, 18(5)*, 773+.

Norbury, C. F. (2005). Barking up the wrong tree? Lexical ambiguity resolution in children with language impairments and autistic spectrum disorders. *Journal of Experimental Child Psychology, 90*(2), 142–171. https://doi.org/10.1016/j.jecp.2004.11.003

Norbury, C. F., Bishop, D. V., & Briscoe, J. (2002). Does impaired grammatical comprehension provide evidence for an innate grammar module? *Applied Psycholinguistics, 23*(2), 247–268. https://doi.org/10.1017/S0142716402002059

Norbury, C. F., Gooch, D., Wray, C., Baird, G., Charman, T., Simonoff, E., ..., & Pickles, A. (2016). The impact of nonverbal ability on prevalence and clinical presentation of language disorder: Evidence from a population study. *Journal of Child Psychology and Psychiatry, 57*(11), 1247–1257. https://doi.org/10.1111/jcpp.12573

Norris, C. J. (2021). The negativity bias, revisited: Evidence from neuroscience measures and an individual differences approach. *Social Neuroscience, 16*(1), 68–82. https://doi.org/10.1080/17470919.2019.1696225

Notebaert, W., Houtman, F., Van Opstal, F., Gevers, W., Fias, W., & Verguts, T. (2009). Post-error slowing: An orienting account. *Cognition, 111*(2), 275–279. https://doi.org/10.1016/j.cognition.2009.02.002

Nunez Castellar, E., Kuhn, S., Fias, W., and Notebaert, W. (2010). Outcome expectancy and not accuracy determines posterror slowing: ERP support. *Cognitive Affective Behavioral Neuroscience, 10*, 270–278. https://doi.org/10.3758/CABN.10.2.270

Nye, Jr., J. S. (2008). Bridging the gap between theory and policy. *Political Psychology, 29*(4), 593–603. https://doi.org/10.1111/j.1467-9221.2008.00651.x.

Oberauer, K. (2005). Binding and inhibition in working memory: Individual and age differences in short-term recognition. *Journal of Experimental Psychology: General, 134*(3), 368–387. https://doi.org/10.1037/0096-3445.134.3.368

Oberauer, K. (2009). Design for a working memory. *Psychology of Learning and Motivation, 51*, 45–100. https://doi.org/10.1016/S0079-7421(09)51002-X

Oberauer, K., Farrell, S., Jarrold, C., & Lewandowsky, S. (2016). What limits working memory capacity? *Psychological Bulletin, 142*(7), 758–799. https://doi.org/10.1037/bul0000046.

Oberauer, K., & Lange, E. (2009). Activation and binding in verbal working memory: A dual-process model for the recognition of nonwords. *Cognitive Psychology, 58*, 102–136. https://doi.org/10.1016/j.cogpsych.2008.05.003

Oberauer, K., & Lewandowsky, S. (2008). Forgetting in immediate serial recall: Decay, temporal distinctiveness, or interference? *Psychological Review, 115*(3), 544. https://doi.org/10.1037/0033-295X.115.3.544

Oberauer, K., Lewandowsky, S., Farrell, S., Jarrold, C., & Greaves, M. (2012). Modeling working memory: An interference model of complex span. *Psychonomic Bulletin Review, 19*(5), 779–819. https://doi.org/10.3758/s13423-012-0272-4

Ochsner, K. N., & Gross, J. J. (2005). The cognitive control of emotion. *Trends in Cognitive Sciences, 9*(5), 242–249. https://doi.org/10.1016/j.tics.2005.03.010

O'Connor, T. A., & Burns, N. R. (2003). Inspection time and general speed of processing. *Personality and Individual Differences, 35*(3), 713–724. https://doi.org/10.1016/S0191-8869(02)00264-7

Oller, D. K., Pearson, B. Z., & Cobo-Lewis, A. B. (2007). Profile effects in early bilingual language and literacy. *Applied Psycholinguistics, 28*(2), 191–230. https://doi.org/10.1017/S0142716407070117

Opitz, B., Schneiders, J. A., Krick, C. M., & Mecklinger, A. (2014). Selective transfer of visual working memory training on Chinese character learning. *Neuropsychologia, 53*, 1–11. https://doi.org/10.1016/j.neuropsychologia.2013.10.017

Ortiz-Mantilla, S., Choudhury, N., Alvarez, B., & Benasich, A. A. (2010). Involuntary switching of attention mediates differences in event-related responses to complex tones between early and late Spanish–English bilinguals. *Brain Research, 1362*, 78–92. https://doi.org/10.1016/j.brainres.2010.09.031

Owen, A. M., Roberts, A. C., Hodges, J. R., & Robbins, T. W. (1993). Contrasting mechanisms of impaired attentional set-shifting in patients with frontal lobe damage or Parkinson's disease. *Brain, 116*(5), 1159–1175. https://doi.org/10.1093/brain/116.5.1159

Paap, K. R., & Greenberg, Z. I. (2013). There is no coherent evidence for a bilingual advantage in executive processing. *Cognitive Psychology, 66*(2), 232–258. https://doi.org/10.1016/j.cogpsych.2012.12.002

Page, M., Wilhelm, M. S., Gamble, W. C., & Card, N. A. (2010). A comparison of maternal sensitivity and verbal stimulation as unique predictors of infant social–emotional and cognitive development. *Infant Behavior and Development, 33*(1), 101–110. https://doi.org/10.1016/j.infbeh.2009.12.001

Pallesen, K. J., Brattico, E., Bailey, C. J., Korvenoja, A., Koivisto, J., Gjedde, A., & Carlson, S. (2010). Cognitive control in auditory working memory is

enhanced in musicians. *PloS One, 5*(6), e11120. https://doi.org/10.1371/journal
.pone.0011120

Papagno, C., & Vallar, G. (1995). Verbal short-term memory and vocabulary learning in polyglots. *Quarterly Journal of Experimental Psychology, 38A*, 98–107. https://doi.org/10.1080/14640749508401378

Paradis, J., Crago, M., Genesee, F., & Rice, M. (2003). French-English Bilingual Children with SLI. How do they compare with their monolingual peers? *Journal of Speech, Language, and Hearing Research, 46*(1), 113–127. https://doi .org/10.1044/1092-4388(2003/009)

Park, J., Miller, C. A., & Mainela-Arnold, E. (2015). Processing speed measures as clinical markers for children with language impairment. *Journal of Speech, Language, and Hearing Research, 58*(3), 954–960. https://doi .org/10.1044/2015_JSLHR-L-14-0092

Patel, A. D. (2011). Why would musical training benefit the neural encoding of speech? The OPERA hypothesis. *Frontiers in Psychology, 2*, 142. https://doi .org/10.3389/fpsyg.2011.00142

Pauls, L. J., & Archibald, L. M. (2016). Executive functions in children with specific language impairment: A meta-analysis. *Journal of Speech, Language, and Hearing Research, 59*(5), 1074–1086. https://doi.org/10.1044/2016_JSLHR-L-15-0174.

Pearson, B. Z., & Amaral, L. (2014). Interactions between input factors in bilingual language acquisition: Considerations for minority language maintenance. In T. Grüter & J. Paradis (Eds.), *Input and experience in bilingual development* (pp. 99–118). John Benjamins Publishing Company.

Pearson, B. Z., Fernández, S. C., & Oller, D. K. (1993). Lexical development in bilingual infants and toddlers: Comparison to monolingual norms. *Language Learning, 43*(1), 93–120. https://doi.org/10.1111/j.1467-1770.1993.tb00174.x

Pelham, S. D., & Abrams, L. (2014). Cognitive advantages and disadvantages in early and late bilinguals. *Journal of Experimental Psychology: Learning, Memory, and Cognition, 40*(2), 313–325. https://doi.org/10.1037/a0035224

Penke, L., Maniega, S. M., Bastin, M. E., Hernández, M. V., Murray, C., Royle, N. A., …, & Deary, I. J. (2012). Brain white matter tract integrity as a neural foundation for general intelligence. *Molecular Psychiatry, 17*(10), 1026–1030. https://doi.org/10.1038/mp.2012.66

Peña, E., Iglesias, A., & Lidz, C. S. (2001). Reducing test bias through dynamic assessment of children's word learning ability. *American Journal of Speech-Language Pathology, 10*, 138–154. https://doi.org/10.1044/1058-0360(2001/014)

Peterson, C., & Slaughter, V. (2003). Opening windows into the mind: Mothers' preferences for mental state explanations and children's theory of mind. *Cognitive Development, 18*(3), 399–429. https://doi.org/10.1016/S0885-2014(03)00041-8

Peterson, R. L., & McGrath, L. M. (2009). Speech and language disorders. In B. F. Pennington (Ed.), *Diagnosing learning disorders. A neuropsychological framework* (pp. 83–107). The Guilford Press.

Petruccelli, N., Bavin, E. L., & Bretherton, L. (2012). Children with specific language impairment and resolved late talkers: Working memory profiles at

5 years. *Journal of Speech, Language, and Hearing Research*, 55(6), 1690–1703. https://doi.org/10.1044/1092-4388(2012/11-0288)

Piek, J. P., Dyck, M. J., Francis, M., & Conwell, A. (2007). Working memory, processing speed, and set-shifting in children with developmental coordination disorder and attention-deficit–hyperactivity disorder. *Developmental Medicine & Child Neurology*, 49(9), 678–683. https://doi.org/10.1111/j.1469-8749.2007.00678.x

Pierce, L., & Genesee, F. (2014). Language input and language learning. In T. Grüter, & J. Paradis (Eds.), *Input and experience in bilingual development* (pp. 59–76). John Benjamins Publishing Company.

Pisoni, D. B., & Cleary, M. (2003). Measures of working memory span and verbal rehearsal speed in deaf children after cochlear implantation. *Ear and Hearing*, 24(1 Suppl), 106S. https://doi.org/10.1097/01.AUD.0000051692.05140.8E

Pisoni, D. B., Mayberry, R. I., Marschark, M., Anaya, E., Conway, C. M., Spencer, P. E., Kronenberger, W., Rhoten, C., Zupan, M., Sarchet, T., & Henning, S. (2010). Executive function, cognitive control, and sequence learning in deaf children with cochlear implants. In *The Oxford handbook of deaf studies, language, and education, vol. 2* (Vol. 1). Oxford University Press. https://doi.org/10.1093/oxfordhb/9780195390032.013.0029

Pitt, J. (2020). Communicating through musical play: Combining speech and language therapy practices with those of early childhood music education–the SALTMusic approach. *Music Education Research*, 22(1), 68–86. https://doi.org/10.1080/14613808.2019.1703927

Pizzioli, F., & Schelstraete, M. A. (2008). The argument-structure complexity effect in children with specific language impairment: Evidence from the use of grammatical morphemes in French. *Journal of Speech, Language, and Hearing Research*, 51(3), 706–721. https://doi.org/10.1044/1092-4388(2008/050)

Plass, J. L., O'Keefe, P. A., Homer, B. D., Case, J., Hayward, E. O., Stein, M., & Perlin, K. (2013). The impact of individual, competitive, and collaborative mathematics game play on learning, performance, and motivation. *Journal of Educational Psychology*, 105(4), 1050–1066. https://doi.org/10.1037/a0032688

Plebanek, D. J., & Sloutsky, V. M. (2019). Selective attention, filtering, and the development of working memory. *Developmental Science*, 22(1), e12727. https://doi.org/10.1111/desc.12727

Plunkett, K. (1993). Lexical segmentation and vocabulary growth in early language acquisition. *Journal of Child Language*, 20(1), 43–60. https://doi.org/10.1017/S0305000900009119

Pons, F., Sanz-Torrent, M., Ferinu, L., Birulés, J., & Andreu, L. (2018). Children with SLI can exhibit reduced attention to a talker's mouth. *Language Learning*, 68, 180–192. https://doi.org/10.1111/lang.12276

Pourtois, G., Notebaert, W., & Verguts, T. (2012). Cognitive and affective control. *Frontiers in Psychology*, 3, 477. https://doi.org/10.3389/fpsyg.2012.00477

Power, J. D., Barnes, K. A., Snyder, A. Z., Schlaggar, B. L., & Petersen, S. E. (2012). Spurious but systematic correlations in functional connectivity MRI networks arise from subject motion. *Neuroimage, 59*(3), 2142–2154. https://doi.org/10.1016/j.neuroimage.2011.10.018

Power, J. D., Fair, D. A., Schlaggar, B. L., & Petersen, S. E. (2010). The development of human functional brain networks. *Neuron, 67*(5), 735–748. https://doi.org/10.1016/j.neuron.2010.08.017

Preston, J. L., Frost, S. J., Mencl, W. E., Fulbright, R. K., Landi, N., Grigorenko, E., ..., & Pugh, K. R. (2010). Early and late talkers: School-age language, literacy and neurolinguistic differences. *Brain, 133*(8), 2185–2195. https://doi.org/10.1093/brain/awq163

Prior, A., Degani, T., Awawdy, S., Yassin, R., & Korem, N. (2017). Is susceptibility to cross-language interference domain specific? *Cognition, 165*, 10–25. https://doi.org/10.1016/j.cognition.2017.04.006

Purves, D., & Lichtman, J. W. (1980). Elimination of synapses in the developing nervous system. *Science, 210*(4466), 153–157. https://doi.org/10.1126/science.7414326

Qu, L. (2011). Two is better than one, but mine is better than ours: Preschoolers' executive function during co-play. *Journal of Experimental Child Psychology, 108*, 549–566. https://doi.org/10.1016/j.jecp.2010.08.010.

Rapoport, J. L., & Gogtay, N. (2008). Brain neuroplasticity in healthy, hyperactive and psychotic children: Insights from neuroimaging. *Neuropsychopharmacology, 33*(1), 181–197. https://doi.org/10.1038/sj.npp.1301553

Ravitch, S. M. &, Riggan, M. (2017). *Reason & rigor: How conceptual frameworks guide research* (2nd edn., p. 234). Sage Publications.

Redmond, S. M. (2011). Peer victimization among students with specific language impairment, attention-deficit/hyperactivity disorder, and typical development. *Language, Speech, and Hearing Services in Schools, 42*(4), 520–535. https://doi.org/10.1044/0161-1461(2011/10-0078)

Reeves, S., Pelone, F., Harrison, R., Goldman, J., & Zwarenstein, M. (2017). Interprofessional collaboration to improve professional practice and healthcare outcomes. *Cochrane Database of Systematic Reviews*, (6). https://doi.org/10.1002/14651858.CD000072.pub3

Reijntjes, A., Kamphuis, J. H., Prinzie, P., & Telch, M. J. (2010). Peer victimization and internalizing problems in children: A meta-analysis of longitudinal studies. *Child Abuse & Neglect, 34*(4), 244–252. https://doi.org/10.1016/j.chiabu.2009.07.009.

Reilly, S., Bishop, D. V., & Tomblin, B. (2014). Terminological debate over language impairment in children: Forward movement and sticking points. *International Journal of Language & Communication Disorders, 49*(4), 452–462. https://doi.org/10.1111/1460-6984.12111

Reilly, S., Wake, M., Ukoumunne, O. C., Bavin, E., Prior, M., Cini, E., ..., & Bretherton, L. (2010). Predicting language outcomes at 4 years of age: Findings from early language in Victoria study. *Pediatrics, 126*, 1530–1537. https://doi.org/10.1542/peds.2010-0254

Reimers, S., & Maylor, E. A. (2005). Task switching across the life span: Effects of age on general and specific switch costs. *Developmental Psychology, 41*(4), 661–671. https://doi.org/10.1037/0012-1649.41.4.661

Reingold, E. M., Reichle, E. D., Glaholt, M. G., & Sheridan, H. (2012). Direct lexical control of eye movements in reading: Evidence from a survival analysis of fixation durations. *Cognitive Psychology*, *65*, 177–206. https://doi.org/10.1016/j.cogpsych.2012.03.001

Reiterer, S. M., Hu, X., Erb, M., Rota, G., Nardo, D., Grodd, W., …, & Ackermann, H. (2011). Individual differences in audio-vocal speech imitation aptitude in late bilinguals: Functional neuro-imaging and brain morphology. *Frontiers in Psychology*, *2*, 271. https://doi.org/10.3389/fpsyg.2011.00271

Rescorla, L. (2011). Late talkers: Do good predictors of outcome exist? *Developmental Disabilities Research Reviews*, *17*(2), 141–150. https://doi.org/10.1002/ddrr.1108

Ribot, K. M., Hoff, E., & Burridge, A. (2018). Language use contributes to expressive language growth: Evidence from bilingual children. *Child Development*, *89*(3), 929–940. https://doi.org/10.1111/cdev.12770

Rice, D., & Barone Jr, S. (2000). Critical periods of vulnerability for the developing nervous system: Evidence from humans and animal models. *Environmental Health Perspectives*, *108*(suppl 3), 511–533. https://doi.org/10.1289/ehp.00108s3511

Rice, M. L., Taylor, C. L., & Zubrick, S. R. (2008). Language outcomes of 7-year-old children with or without a history of late language emergence at 24 months. *Journal of Speech, Language, and Hearing Research*, *51*, 394–407. https://doi.org/10.1044/1092-4388(2008/029)

Rice, M. L., & Wexler, K. (1996). Toward tense as a clinical marker of specific language impairment in English-speaking children. *Journal of Speech, Language, and Hearing Research*, *39*(6), 1239–1257. https://doi.org/10.1044/jshr.3906.1239

Riches, N. G., Tomasello, M., & Conti-Ramsden, G. (2005). Verb learning in children with SLI. *Journal of Speech, Language, and Hearing Research*, *48*, 1397–1411. https://doi.org/10.1044/1092-4388(2005/097)

Ridderinkhof, K. R., Band, G. P., & Logan, G. D. (1999). A study of adaptive behavior: Effects of age and irrelevant information on the ability to inhibit one's actions. *Acta Psychologica*, *101*(2–3), 315–337. https://doi.org/10.1016/S0001-6918(99)00010-4

Riggs, K. J., McTaggart, J., Simpson, A., & Freeman, R. P. (2006). Changes in the capacity of visual working memory in 5-to 10-year-olds. *Journal of Experimental Child Psychology*, *95*(1), 18–26. https://doi.org/10.1016/j.jecp.2006.03.009

Robinson, P. (2005). Aptitude and second language acquisition. *Annual Review of Applied Linguistics*, *25*, 46-73. https://doi.org/10.1017/S0267190505000036

Roden, I., Grube, D., Bongard, S., & Kreutz, G. (2014). Does music training enhance working memory performance? Findings from a quasi-experimental longitudinal study. *Psychology of Music*, *42*(2), 284–298. 2 https://doi.org/10.1177/0305735612471239

Rodríguez-Fornells, A., Kurzbuch, A. R., & Münte, T. F. (2002). Time course of error detection and correction in humans: Neurophysiological evidence. *Journal of Neuroscience*, *22*(22), 9990–9996. https://doi.org/10.1523/JNEUROSCI.22-22-09990.2002

Roello, M., Ferretti, M. L., Colonnello, V., & Levi, G. (2015). When words lead to solutions: Executive function deficits in preschool children with specific language impairment. *Research in Developmental Disabilities, 37,* 216–222. https://doi.org/10.1016/j.ridd.2014.11.017

Rogers, R. D., & Monsell, S. (1995). Costs of a predictable switch between simple cognitive tasks. *Journal of Experimental Psychology: General, 124*(2), 207–231. https://doi.org/10.1037/0096-3445.124.2.207

Romeo, R. R., Leonard, J. A., Scherer, E., Robinson, S., Takada, M., Mackey, A. P., ..., & Gabrieli, J. D. (2021). Replication and extension of family-based training program to improve cognitive abilities in young children. *Journal of Research on Educational Effectiveness, 14*(4), 792–811. https://doi.org/10.1080/19345747.2 021.1931999

Roncadin, C., Pascual-Leone, J., Rich, J. B., & Dennis, M. (2007). Developmental relations between working memory and inhibitory control. *Journal of the International Neuropsychological Society, 13*(1), 59–67. https://doi.org/10.1017/ S1355617707070099

Rossignoli-Palomeque, T., Perez-Hernandez, E., & Gonzalez-Marques, J. (2018). Brain training in children and adolescents: Is it scientifically valid? *Frontiers in Psychology, 9,* 565. https://doi.org/10.3389/fpsyg.2018.00565

Rothweiler, M., Chilla, S., & Clahsen, H. (2012). Subject–verb agreement in specific language impairment: A study of monolingual and bilingual German-speaking children. *Bilingualism: Language and Cognition, 15*(1), 39–57. http:// dx.doi.org/10.1017/S136672891100037X

Rowe, M. L. (2015). Input versus intake–a commentary on Ambridge, Kidd, Rowland, and Theakson's "The ubiquity of frequency effects in first language acquisition". *Journal of Child Language, 42*(2), 301–305. https://doi.org/10.1017/ S030500091400066X

Rueda, M. R., Fan, J., McCandliss, B. D., Halparin, J. D., Gruber, D. B., Lercari, L. P., & Posner, M. I. (2004). Development of attentional networks in childhood. *Neuropsychologia, 42*(8), 1029–1040. https://doi.org/10.1016/j .neuropsychologia.2003.12.012

Rueda, M. R., & Posner, M. I. (2013). Development of attentional networks. In P. D. Zelazo (Ed.), *The Oxford handbook of developmental psychology* (pp. 683–705). Oxford University Press.

Rueda, M. R., Cómbita, L. M., & Pozuelos, J. P. (2021). Cognitive training in childhood and adolescence. In *Cognitive training: An overview of features and applications* (pp. 127–139). Springer, Cham. https://doi .org/10.1007/978-3-030-39292-5_9

Rutherford, M., Singh-Roy, A., Rush, R., McCartney, D., O'Hare, A., & Forsyth, K. (2019). Parent focused interventions for older children or adults with ASD and parent wellbeing outcomes: A systematic review with meta-analysis. *Research in Autism Spectrum Disorders, 68,* 101450. https://doi.org/10.1016/j .rasd.2019.101450

Saarikivi, K., Putkinen, V., Tervaniemi, M., & Huotilainen, M. (2016). Cognitive flexibility modulates maturation and music-training-related changes in neural sound discrimination. *European Journal of Neuroscience, 44*(2), 1815–1825. https://doi.org/10.1111/ejn.13176

Sackett, P. R., Lievens, F., Van Iddekinge, C. H., & Kuncel, N. R. (2017). Individual differences and their measurement: A review of 100 years of research. *Journal of Applied Psychology, 102*(3), 254–273. https://doi.org/10.1037/apl0000151

Sala, G., Aksayli, N. D., Tatlidil, K. S., Tatsumi, T., Gondo, Y., & Gobet, F. (2019). Near and far transfer in cognitive training: A second-order meta-analysis. *Collabra: Psychology, 5*(1), 18. https://doi.org/10.1525/collabra.203

Salthouse, T. A. (2000). Aging and measures of processing speed. *Biological Psychology, 54*(1–3), 35–54. https://doi.org/10.1016/S0301-0511(00)00052-1

Salvatierra, J. L., & Rosselli, M. (2011). The effect of bilingualism and age on inhibitory control. *International Journal of Bilingualism, 15*, 26–37. http://dx.doi.org/10.1177/1367006910371021

Sandson, J., & Albert, M. L. (1984). Varieties of perseveration. *Neuropsychologia, 22*(6), 715–732. https://doi.org/10.1016/0028-3932(84)90098-8

Schatz, J., Kramer, J. H., Ablin, A., & Matthay, K. K. (2000). Processing speed, working memory, and IQ: A developmental model of cognitive deficits following cranial radiation therapy. *Neuropsychology, 14*(2), 189–200. https://doi.org/10.1037/0894-4105.14.2.189

Scherger, A. L. (2018). German dative case marking in monolingual and simultaneous bilingual children with and without SLI. *Journal of Communication Disorders, 75*, 87–101. https://doi.org/10.1016/j.jcomdis.2018.06.004

Schmidt, R. (1993). Awareness and second language acquisition. *Annual Review of Applied Linguistics, 13*, 206–226. https://doi.org/10.1017/S0267190500002476

Schmidt, R. (2001). Attention. In P. Robinson (Ed.), *Cognition and second language instruction* (pp. 3–32). Cambridge University Press.

Schubert, A. L., Nunez, M. D., Hagemann, D., & Vandekerckhove, J. (2019). Individual differences in cortical processing speed predict cognitive abilities: A model-based cognitive neuroscience account. *Computational Brain & Behavior, 2*(2), 64–84. https://doi.org/10.1007/s42113-018-0021-5

Schul, R., Townsend, J., & Stiles, J. (2003). The development of attentional orienting during the school-age years. *Developmental Science, 6*(3), 262–272. https://doi.org/10.1111/1467-7687.00282

Schwab, J. F., & Lew-Williams, C. (2016). Language learning, socioeconomic status, and child-directed speech. *Wiley Interdisciplinary Reviews: Cognitive Science, 7*(4), 264–275. https://doi.org/10.1002/wcs.1393

Schwartz, D., Gorman, A. H., Dodge, K. A., Pettit, G. S., & Bates, J. E. (2008). Friendships with peers who are low or high in aggression as moderators of the link between peer victimization and declines in academic functioning. *Journal of Abnormal Child Psychology, 36*(5), 719–730. https://doi.org/10.1007/s10802-007-9200-x

Schwartz, R. G., & Marton, K. (2011). Articulatory and phonological disorders. In N. B. Anderson, & G. H. Shames (Eds.), *Human communication disorders: An introduction* (pp. 132–163). Allyn & Bacon Publisher.

Scionti, N., Cavallero, M., Zogmaister, C., & Marzocchi, G. M. (2020). Is cognitive training effective for improving executive functions in preschoolers? A systematic review and meta-analysis. *Frontiers in Psychology*, *10*, 2812. https://doi.org/10.3389/fpsyg.2019.02812

Seiger-Gardner, L., & Schwartz, R. G. (2008). Lexical access in children with and without specific language impairment: A cross-modal picture–word interference study. *International Journal of Language & Communication Disorders*, *43*(5), 528–551. https://doi.org/10.1080/13682820701768581

Senzaki, S., Wiebe, S. A., Masuda, T., & Shimizu, Y. (2018). A cross-cultural examination of selective attention in Canada and Japan: The role of social context. *Cognitive Development*, *48*, 32–41. https://doi.org/10.1016/j.cogdev.2018.06.005

Shaw, P., Greenstein, D., Lerch, J., Clasen, L., Lenroot, R., Gogtay, N. E. E. A., ..., & Giedd, J. (2006). Intellectual ability and cortical development in children and adolescents. *Nature*, *440*(7084), 676–679. https://doi.org/10.1038/nature04513

Shaw, P., Kabani, N. J., Lerch, J. P., Eckstrand, K., Lenroot, R., Gogtay, N., ..., & Wise, S. P. (2008). Neurodevelopmental trajectories of the human cerebral cortex. *Journal of Neuroscience*, *28*(14), 3586–3594. https://doi.org/10.1523/JNEUROSCI.5309-07.2008

Shenhav, A. (2017). The perils of losing control: Why self-control is not just another value-based decision. *Psychological Inquiry*, *28*(2–3), 148–152. https://doi.org/10.1080/1047840X.2017.1337407

Shenhav, A., Botvinick, M. M., & Cohen, J. D. (2013). The expected value of control: An integrative theory of anterior cingulate cortex function. *Neuron*, *79*, 217–240. https://doi.org/10.1016/j.neuron.2013.07.007

Shenhav, A., Musslick, S., Lieder, F., Kool, W., Griffiths, T. L., Cohen, J. D., & Botvinick, M. M. (2017). Toward a rational and mechanistic account of mental effort. *Annual Review of Neuroscience*, *40*, 99–124. https://doi.org/10.1146/annurev-neuro-072116-031526

Sheridan, H., & Reingold, E. M. (2014). Expert vs. novice differences in the detection of relevant information during a chess game: Evidence from eye movements. *Frontiers in Psychology*, *5*, 1–6. https://doi.org/10.3389/fpsyg.2014.00941

Sheridan, M. A., Peverill, M., Finn, A. S., & McLaughlin, K. A. (2017). Dimensions of childhood adversity have distinct associations with neural systems underlying executive functioning. *Development and Psychopathology*, *29*(5), 1777–1794. http://dx.doi.org.ezproxy.gc.cuny.edu/10.1017/S0954579417001390

Shiffrin, R. M., & Schneider, W. (1977). Controlled and automatic information processing, II: Perceptual learning, automatic attending, and a general theory. *Psychological Review*, *84*, 127–190. https://doi.org/10.1037/0033-295X.84.2.127

Shipstead, Z., Redick, T. S., & Engle, R. W. (2012). Is working memory training effective? *Psychological Bulletin*, *138*(4), 628–654. https://doi.org/10.1037/a0027473

Shohamy, D. (2011). Learning and motivation in the human striatum. *Current Opinion in Neurobiology*, *21*(3), 408–414. https://doi.org/10.1016/j.conb.2011.05.009

Singh, K. (2011). Study of achievement motivation in relation to academic achievement of students. *International Journal of Educational Planning & Administration*, *1*(2), 161–171. ISSN 2249-3093

Snyder, H. R., Miyake, A., & Hankin, B. L. (2015). Advancing understanding of executive function impairments and psychopathology: Bridging the gap between clinical and cognitive approaches. *Frontiers in Psychology*, *6*, 328. https://doi.org/10.3389/fpsyg.2015.00328

Soleymani, Z., Amidfar, M., Dadgar, H., & Jalaie, S. (2014). Working memory in Farsi-speaking children with normal development and cochlear implant. *International Journal of Pediatric Otorhinolaryngology*, *78*(4), 674–678. https://doi.org/10.1016/j.ijporl.2014.01.035

Sparks, R. L., Humbach, N., Patton, J. O. N., & Ganschow, L. (2011). Subcomponents of second-language aptitude and second-language proficiency. *The Modern Language Journal*, *95*(2), 253–273. https://doi.org/10.1111/j.1540-4781.2011.01176.x

Spaulding, T. J. (2010). Investigating mechanisms of suppression in preschool children with specific language impairment. *Journal of Speech, Language, & Hearing Research*, *53*(3), 725–738. https://doi.org/10.1044/1092-4388 (2009/09-0041)

Spaulding, T. J., Plante, E., & Vance, R. (2008). Sustained selective attention skills of preschool children with specific language impairment: Evidence for separate attentional capacities. *Journal of Speech, Language, & Hearing Research*, *51*(1), 16–34. https://doi.org/10.1044/1092-4388(2008/002)

Spoelman, M., & Bol, G. W. (2012). The use of subject–verb agreement and verb argument structure in monolingual and bilingual children with specific language impairment. *Clinical Linguistics & Phonetics*, *26*(4), 357–379. https://doi.org/10.3109/02699206.2011.637658

St Clair-Thompson, H. L., & Gathercole, S. E. (2006). Executive functions and achievements in school: Shifting, updating, inhibition, and working memory. *The Quarterly Journal of Experimental Psychology*, *59*(4), 745–759. https://doi.org/10.1080/17470210500162854

Stanford, E., Durrleman, S., & Delage, H. (2019). The effect of working memory training on a clinical marker of French-speaking children with developmental language disorder. *American Journal of Speech-Language Pathology*, *28*(4), 1388–1410. https://doi.org/10.1044/2019_AJSLP-18-0238

Stevens, C., Lauinger, B., & Neville, H. (2009). Differences in the neural mechanisms of selective attention in children from different socioeconomic backgrounds: An event-related brain potential study. *Developmental Science*, *12*(4), 634–646. https://doi.org/10.1111/j.1467-7687.2009.00807.x

Stevens, L. J., & Bliss, L. S. (1995). Conflict resolution abilities of children with specific language impairment and children with normal language. *Journal of Speech and Hearing Research*, 38, 599–611. https://doi.org/10.1044/jshr.3803.599.

Stins, J. F., Polderman, J. C., Boomsma, D. I., & de Geus, E. J. (2005). Response interference and working memory in 12-year-old children. *Child Neuropsychology*, *11*(2), 191–201. https://doi.org/10.1080/09297040590911351.

Stone, A., & Bosworth, R. G. (2019). Exploring infant sensitivity to visual language using eye tracking and the preferential looking paradigm. *JoVE (Journal of Visualized Experiments)*, (147), e59581. https://dx.doi.org/10.3791/59581

References

Strait, D. L., Kraus, N., Parbery-Clark, A., & Ashley, R. (2010). Musical experience shapes top-down auditory mechanisms: Evidence from masking and auditory attention performance. *Hearing Research, 261*(1–2), 22–29. https://doi.org/10.1016/j.heares.2009.12.021

Supekar, K., Musen, M., & Menon, V. (2009). Development of large-scale functional brain networks in children. *PLoS Biology, 7*(7), e1000157. https://doi.org/10.1371/journal.pbio.1000157

Surrain, S., & Luk, G. (2019). Describing bilinguals: A systematic review of labels and descriptions used in the literature between 2005–2015. *Bilingualism: Language and Cognition, 22*(2), 401–415. https://doi.org/10.1017/S1366728917000682

Surrain, S., Rowe, M., & Luk, G. (2021). Dual language learners in transition from home to school: Understanding apparent "delays" in the context of parent input and child usage. Presentation at the IASCL 2021 virtual conference by the International Association for the Study of Child Language, July 15–23, 2021.

Suttora, C., Guarini, A., Zuccarini, M., Aceti, A., Corvaglia, L., & Sansavini, A. (2020). Speech and language skills of low-risk preterm and full-term late talkers: The role of child factors and parent input. *International Journal of Environmental Research and Public Health, 17*(20), 7684. https://doi.org/10.3390/ijerph17207684

Swaminathan, S., & Schellenberg, E. G. (2021). Music training. In *Cognitive training* (pp. 307–318). Springer, Cham. https://doi.org/10.1007/978-3-030-39292-5_21

Swanson, H. L., & Jerman, O. (2007). The influence of working memory on reading growth in subgroups of children with reading disabilities. *Journal of Experimental Child Psychology, 96*(4), 249–283. https://doi.org/10.1016/j.jecp.2006.12.004

Talamini, F., Grassi, M., Toffalini, E., Santoni, R., & Carretti, B. (2018). Learning a second language: Can music aptitude or music training have a role? *Learning and Individual Differences, 64*, 1–7. https://doi.org/10.1016/j.lindif.2018.04.003

Tallal, P., & Gaab, N. (2006). Dynamic auditory processing, musical experience and language development. *Trends in Neurosciences, 29*(7), 382–390. https://doi.org/10.1016/j.tins.2006.06.003

Tamnes, C. K., Walhovd, K. B., Torstveit, M., Sells, V. T., & Fjell, A. M. (2013). Performance monitoring in children and adolescents: A review of developmental changes in the error-related negativity and brain maturation. *Developmental Cognitive Neuroscience, 6*, 1–13. https://doi.org/10.1016/j.dcn.2013.05.001

Tansley, C. (2011). What do we mean by the term "talent" in talent management? *Industrial and Commercial Training, 43*(5), 266–274. https://doi.org/10.1108/00197851111145853

Tao, L., Marzecová, A., Taft, M., Asanowicz, D., & Wodniecka, Z. (2011). The efficiency of attentional networks in early and late bilinguals: The role of age of acquisition. *Frontiers in Psychology, 2*, 123. https://doi.org/10.3389/fpsyg.2011.00123

Thaut, M., & Hoemberg, V. (Eds.). (2014). *Handbook of neurologic music therapy* (p. 383). Oxford University Press.

Thompson, T. W., Waskom, M. L., Garel, K. L. A., Cardenas-Iniguez, C., Reynolds, G. O., Winter, R., ..., & Gabrieli, J. D. (2013). Failure of working memory training to enhance cognition or intelligence. *PloS One*, *8*(5), e63614. https://doi.org/10.1371/journal.pone.0063614

Thordardottir, E. (2011). The relationship between bilingual exposure and vocabulary development. *International Journal of Bilingualism*, *15*(4), 426–445. https://doi.org/10.1177/1367006911403202

Thordardottir, E. (2015). The relationship between bilingual exposure and morphosyntactic development. *International Journal of Speech-Language-Pathology*, *17*(2), 97–114. https://doi.org/10.3109/17549507.2014.923509

Thordardottir, E. T., & Namazi, M. (2007). Specific language impairment in French-speaking children: Beyond grammatical morphology. *Journal of Speech, Language, and Hearing Research*, *50*(3), 698–715. https://doi.org/10.1044/1092-4388(2007/049).

Thorne, K., & Pellant, A. (2007). *The essential guide to managing talent: How top companies recruit, train, & retain the best employees.* Kogan Page Publishers.

Titz, C., & Karbach, J. (2014). Working memory and executive functions: Effects of training on academic achievement. *Psychological Research*, *78*(6), 852–868. https://doi.org/10.1007/s00426-013-0537-1

Timmer, K., Christoffels, I. K., & Costa, A. (2019). On the flexibility of bilingual language control: The effect of language context. *Bilingualism: Language and Cognition*, *22*(3), 555–568. https://doi.org/10.1017/S1366728918000329

Tomasello, M. (2003). *Constructing a language: A usage-based theory of language acquisition.* Harvard University Press.

Tomasello, M., & Farrar, M. J. (1986). Joint attention and early language. *Child Development*, *57*(6), 1454–1463. https://doi.org/10.2307/1130423

Tomblin, J. B., Records, N. L., Buckwalter, P., Zhang, X., Smith, E., & O'Brien, M. (1997). Prevalence of specific language impairment in kindergarten children. *Journal of Speech, Language, and Hearing Research*, *40*(6), 1245–1260. https://doi.org/10.1044/jslhr.4006.1245

Tomoschuk, B., Ferreira, V. S., & Gollan, T. H. (2019). When a seven is not a seven: Self-ratings of bilingual language proficiency differ between and within language populations. *Bilingualism: Language and Cognition*, *22*(3), 516–536. https://doi.org/10.1017/S1366728918000421

Towse, J. N., & Hitch, G. J. (1995). Is there a relationship between task demand and storage space in tests of working memory capacity? *Quarterly Journal of Experimental Psychology: Human Experimental Psychology*, *48A*, 108–124. https://doi.org/10.1080/14640749508401379

Turken, U., Whitfield-Gabrieli, S., Bammer, R., Baldo, J. V., Dronkers, N. F., & Gabrieli, J. D. (2008). Cognitive processing speed and the structure of white matter pathways: Convergent evidence from normal variation and lesion studies. *Neuroimage*, *42*(2), 1032–1044. https://doi.org/10.1016/j.neuroimage.2008.03.057

Tuller, L. (2015). Clinical use of parental questionnaires in multilingual contexts. In S. Armon-Lotem, J. de Jong, & N. Meir (Eds.), *Assessing multilingual children: Disentangling bilingualism from language impairment* (pp. 301–330). Multilingual Matters.

Ulber, J., Hamann, K., & Tomasello, M. (2016). Extrinsic rewards diminish costly sharing in 3-year-olds. *Child Development, 87*(4), 1192–1203. https://doi.org/10.1111/cdev.12534

Umbel, V. M., Pearson, B. Z., Fernández, M. C., & Oller, D. K. (1992). Measuring bilingual children's receptive vocabularies. *Child Development, 63*(4), 1012–1020. https://doi.org/10.1111/j.1467-8624.1992.tb01678.x

Unsworth, N., Brewer, G. A., & Spillers, G. J. (2013). Focusing the search: Proactive and retroactive interference and the dynamics of free recall. *Journal of Experimental Psychology: Learning, Memory, and Cognition, 39*(6), 1742–1756. https://doi.org/10.1037/a0033743

Unsworth, N. & Engle, R. W. (2006). Simple and complex memory spans and their relation to fluid abilities: Evidence from list-length effects. *Journal of Memory and Language, 54*, 68–80. https://doi.org/10.1016/j.jml.2005.06.003

Unsworth, N., Fukuda, K., Awh, E., & Vogel, E. K. (2014). Working memory and fluid intelligence: Capacity, attention control, and secondary memory retrieval. *Cognitive Psychology, 71*, 1–26. https://doi.org/10.1016/j.cogpsych.2014.01.003

Unsworth, N., Miller, A. L., & Robison, M. K. (2021). Are individual differences in attention control related to working memory capacity? A latent variable mega-analysis. *Journal of Experimental Psychology: General, 150*(7), 1332–1357. https://doi.org/10.1037/xge0001000

Ursache, A., & Noble, K. G. (2016). Neurocognitive development in socioeconomic context: Multiple mechanisms and implications for measuring socioeconomic status. *Psychophysiology, 53*(1), 71–82. https://doi.org/10.1111/psyp.12547

Vagh, S. B., Pan, B. A., & Mancilla-Martinez, J. (2009). Measuring growth in bilingual and monolingual children's English productive vocabulary development: The utility of combining parent and teacher report. *Child Development, 80*(5), 1545–1563. https://doi.org/10.1111/j.1467-8624.2009.01350.x

Valian, V. V. (2015). Bilingualism and cognition. *Journal of Bilingualism: Language and Cognition, 18*(1), 3–24. https://doi.org/10.1017/S1366728914000522

van den Berg, R., Awh, E., & Ma, W. J. (2014). Factorial comparison of working memory models. *Psychological Review, 121*, 124–149. http://dx.doi.org/10.1037/a0035234

Van Den Noort, M. W. M. L., P. Bosch & K. Hugdahl (2006). Foreign language proficiency and working memory capacity. *European Psychologist, 11*, 289–296. https://doi.org/10.1027/1016-9040.11.4.289

van der Wilt, F., van der Veen, C., van Kruistum, C., & van Oers, B. (2019). Why do children become rejected by their peers? A review of studies into the relationship between oral communicative competence and sociometric status in childhood. *Educational Psychology Review, 31*(3), 699–724. https://doi.org/10.1007/s10648-019-09479-z

Van der Lely, H. K. (1996). Specifically language impaired and normally developing children: Verbal passive vs. adjectival passive sentence interpretation. *Lingua*, *98*(4), 243–272. https://doi.org/10.1016/0024-3841(95)00044-5

Van Dyke, J. A., & Johns, C. L. (2012). Memory interference as a determinant of language comprehension. *Language and Linguistic Compass*, *6*(4), 193–211. https://doi.org/10.1002/lnc3.330

Van Dyke, J. A., & McElree, B. (2006). Retrieval interference in sentence comprehension. *Journal of Memory and Language*, *55*(2), 157–166. https://doi.org/10.1016/j.jml.2006.03.007

Varnum, M. E., Grossmann, I., Kitayama, S., & Nisbett, R. E. (2010). The origin of cultural differences in cognition: The social orientation hypothesis. *Current Directions in Psychological Science*, *19*(1), 9–13. https://doi.org/10.1177/0963721409359301

Velanova, K., Wheeler, M. E., & Luna, B. (2008). Maturational changes in anterior cingulate and frontoparietal recruitment support the development of error processing and inhibitory control. *Cerebral Cortex*, *18*(11), 2505–2522. https://doi.org/10.1093/cercor/bhn012

Verhoeven, L., Steenge, J., van Weerdenburg, M., & van Balkom, H. (2011). Assessment of second language proficiency in bilingual children with specific language impairment: A clinical perspective. *Research in Developmental Disabilities*, *32*(5), 1798–1807. https://doi.org/10.1016/j.ridd.2011.03.010

Videsott, G., Della Rosa, P. A., Wiater, W., Franceschini, R., & Abutalebi, J. (2012). How does linguistic competence enhance cognitive functions in children? A study in multilingual children with different linguistic competences. *Bilingualism: Language and Cognition*, *15*(4), 884–895. https://doi.org/10.1017/S1366728912000119

Vigil, D. C., Hodges, J., & Klee, T. (2005). Quantity and quality of parental language input to late-talking toddlers during play. *Child Language Teaching and Therapy*, *21*(2), 107–122. https://doi.org/10.1191/0265659005ct284

Vigil, D. C., Tyler, A. A., & Ross, S. (2006). Cultural differences in learning novel words in an attention-following versus attention-directing style. *Journal of Multilingual Communication Disorders*, *4*(1), 59–70. https://doi.org/10.1080/14769670600631016

Vingerhoets, G., Van Borsel, J., Tesink, C., van den Noort, M., Deblaere, K., Seurinck, R., Vandemaele, P., & Achten, E. (2003). Multilingualism: An fMRI study. *NeuroImage*, *20*, 2181–2196. https://doi.org/10.1016/j.neuroimage.2003.07.029

Vissers, C., Koolen, S., Hermans, D., Scheper, A., & Knoors, H. (2015). Executive functioning in preschoolers with specific language impairment. *Frontiers in Psychology*, *6*, 1574. https://doi.org/10.3389/fpsyg.2015.01574

Volkers, N. (2018). Diverging views on language disorders: Researchers debate whether the label "developmental language disorder" should replace "specific language impairment." *The ASHA Leader*, *23*(12), 44–53. https://doi.org/10.1044/leader.FTR1.23122018.44

Von Bastian, C. C., Souza, A. S., & Gade, M. (2016). No evidence for bilingual cognitive advantages: A test of four hypotheses. *Journal of Experimental Psychology: General, 145*(2), 246–258. https://doi.org/10.1037/xge0000120

Vugs, B., Cuperus, J., Hendriks, M., & Verhoeven, L. (2013). Visuospatial working memory in specific language impairment: A meta-analysis. *Research in Developmental Disabilities, 34*(9), 2586–2597. https://doi.org/10.1016/j.ridd.2013.05.014

Vugs, B., Knoors, H., Cuperus, J., Hendriks, M., & Verhoeven, L. (2017). Executive function training in children with SLI: A pilot study. *Child Language Teaching and Therapy, 33*(1), 47–66. https://doi.org/10.1177/0265659016666777

Vukovic, M., & Stojanovik, V. (2011). Characterising developmental language impairment in Serbian-speaking children: A preliminary investigation. *Clinical Linguistics & Phonetics, 25*(3), 187–197. https://doi.org/10.3109/02699206.2010.521611

Wade, M., Browne, D. T., Madigan, S., Plamondon, A., & Jenkins, J. M. (2014). Normal birth weight variation and children's neuropsychological functioning: Links between language, executive functioning, and theory of mind. *Journal of the International Neuropsychological Society, 20*(9), 909–919. https://doi.org/10.1017/S1355617714000745

Wadhera, D. (2020). *Working Memory Training: Cognitive and Linguistic Implications in Adult English Language Learners* (Doctoral dissertation, City University of New York).

Wadhera, D., Campanelli, L., & Marton, K. (2018). The influence of bilingual language experience on working memory updating performance in young adults. In T. T. Rogers, M. Rau, X. Zhu, & C. W. Kalish (Eds.), *Proceedings of the 40th annual conference of the cognitive science society* (pp. 2639–2644), Madison, WI.

Wagner, L., Greene-Havas, M., & Gillespie, R. (2010). Development in children's comprehension of linguistic register. *Child Development, 81*(6), 1678–1686. https://doi.org/10.1111/j.1467-8624.2010.01502.x

Waldman DeLuca, Z., Schwartz, R. G., Marton, K., Houston, D. M., Ying, E., Steinman, S., & Drakopoulou, G. (2023). The effect of sentence length on question comprehension in children with cochlear implants. *Cochlear Implants International, 24*(1), 14–26. https://doi.org/10.1080/14670100.2022.2136591

Wang, S., & Gathercole, S. E. (2015). Interference control in children with reading difficulties. *Child Neuropsychology, 21*(4), 418–431. https://doi.org/10.1080/09297049.2014.918594

Wang, Y., Hartman, M., Aziz, N. A. A., Arora, S., Shi, L., & Tunison, E. (2017). A systematic review of the use of LENA technology. *American Annals of the Deaf, 162*(3), 295–311. www.jstor.org/stable/26235350

Weber, M. (2007). DIALANG. *The Canadian Modern Language Review/La revue Canadienne des langues vivantes, 64*(1), 233–238. ISSN 1710-1131

Wen, Z., & Skehan, P. (2011). A new perspective on foreign language aptitude research: Building and supporting a case for "working memory as language aptitude." *Ilha do Desterro: A Journal of English Language, Literatures in English and Cultural Studies,* (60), 15–43. E-ISSN: 2175-8026

Wenger, E., Fandakova, Y., & Shing, Y. L. (2021). Episodic memory training. In *Cognitive training* (pp. 169–184). Springer, Cham. https://doi.org/10.1007/978-3-030-39292-5_12

Wiebe, S. A., Sheffield, T., Nelson, J. M., Clark, C. A., Chevalier, N., & Espy, K. A. (2011). The structure of executive function in 3-year-olds. *Journal of Experimental Child Psychology*, *108*(3), 436–452. https://doi.org/10.1016/j.jecp.2010.08.008

Wiersema, J. R., van der Meere, J. J., & Roeyers, H. (2007). Developmental changes in error monitoring: An event-related potential study. *Neuropsychologia*, *45*(8), 1649–1657. https://doi.org/10.1016/j.neuropsychologia.2007.01.004

Wijnen, F. (2000). Input, intake and sequence in syntactic development. In M. Beers, B. van de Bogaerde, G. Bol, J. de Jong, & C. Rooijmans (Eds.), *From sound to sentence – Studies on first language acquisition* (pp. 163–186). Centre for Language and Cognition.

Williams, B. R., Ponesse, J. S., Schachar, R. J., Logan, G. D., & Tannock, R. (1999). Development of inhibitory control across the life span. *Developmental Psychology*, *35*(1), 205–213. https://doi.org/10.1037/0012-1649.35.1.205

Windsor, J., & Hwang, M. (1999). Testing the generalized slowing hypothesis in specific language impairment. *Journal of Speech, Language, and Hearing Research*, *42*(5), 1205–1218. https://doi.org/10.1044/jslhr.4205.1205

Wiseheart, M., Viswanathan, M., & Bialystok, E. (2016). Flexibility in task switching by monolinguals and bilinguals. *Bilingualism: Language and Cognition*, *19*(1), 141–146. https://doi.org/10.1017/S1366728914000273

Wong, P., Skoe, E., Russo, N. M., Dees, T., & Kraus, N. (2007). Musical experience shapes human brainstem encoding of linguistic pitch patterns. *Nature Neuroscience*, *10*(4), 420–422. https://doi.org/10.1038/nn1872

Wong, W. (2001). Modality and attention to meaning and form in the input. *Studies in Second Language Acquisition*, *23*(3), 345–368. https://doi.org/10.1017/S0272263101003023

Wyer Jr, R. S., & Srull, T. K. (2014). *Memory and cognition in its social context.* Psychology Press.

Ye, Z., & Zhou, X. (2009). Executive control in language processing. *Neuroscience & Biobehavioral Reviews*, *33*(8), 1168–1177. https://doi.org/10.1016/j.neubiorev.2009.03.003

Yeung, N., Botvinick, M. M., & Cohen, J. D. (2004). The neural basis of error detection: Conflict monitoring and the error-related negativity. *Psychological Review*, *111*(4), 931–959. https://doi.org/10.1037/0033-295X.111.4.931

Yeung, M. K., Lee, T. L., & Chan, A. S. (2020). Neurocognitive development of flanker and Stroop interference control: A near-infrared spectroscopy study. *Brain and Cognition*, *143*, 105585. https://doi.org/10.1016/j.bandc.2020.105585

Young, A. R., Beitchman, J. H., Johnson, C., Douglas, L., Atkinson, L., Escobar, M., & Wilson, B. (2002). Young adult academic outcomes in a longitudinal sample of early identified language impaired and control children. *The Journal of Child Psychology and Psychiatry*, *43*(5), 635–645. https://doi.org/10.1111/14697610.00052

Yow, W. Q., & Markman, E. M. (2011). Young bilingual children's heightened sensitivity to referential cues. *Journal of Cognition and Development, 12*(1), 12–31. https://doi.org/10.1080/15248372.2011.539524

Yudes, C., Mazico, P., & Bajo, T. (2011). The influence of expertise in simultaneous interpreting on non-verbal executive processes. *Frontiers in Psychology, 2*(309), 1–9. https://doi.org/10.3389/fpsyg.2011.00309

Zelaznik, H. N., & Goffman, L. (2010). Generalized motor abilities and timing behavior in children with specific language impairment. *Journal of Speech, Language, and Hearing Research, 53*(2), 383–393. https://doi.org/10.1044/1092-4388(2009/08-0204)

Zelazo, P. D. (2006). The Dimensional Change Card Sort (DCCS): A method of assessing executive function in children. *Nature Protocols, 1*(1), 297–301. https://doi.org/10.1038/nprot.2006.46

Zelazo, P. D., Anderson, J. E., Richler, J., Wallner-Allen, K., Beaumont, J. L., & Weintraub, S. (2013). II. NIH Toolbox Cognition Battery (CB): Measuring executive function and attention. *Monographs of the Society for Research in Child Development, 78*(4), 16–33. https://doi.org/10.1111/mono.12032

Zelazo, P. D., & Müller, U. (2002). Executive function in typical and atypical development. *Blackwell Handbook of Childhood Cognitive Development,* 445–469. https://doi.org/10.1002/9780470996652

Zeromskaite, I. (2014). The potential role of music in second language learning: A review article. *Journal of European Psychology Students, 5*(3), 78–88. http://doi.org/10.5334/jeps.ci

Zimmerman, M. A., Stoddard, S. A., Eisman, A. B., Caldwell, C. H., Aiyer, S. M., & Miller, A. (2013). Adolescent resilience: Promotive factors that inform prevention. *Child Development Perspectives, 7*(4), 215–220. https://doi.org/10.1111/cdep.12042

Zubrick, S. R.; Taylor, C. L.; Rice, M. L.; & Slegers, D. W. (2007). Late language emergence at 24 months: An epidemiological study of prevalence, predictors, and covariates. *Journal of Speech, Language, and Hearing Research, 50,* 1562–1592. https://doi.org/10.1044/1092-4388(2007/106)

Web Pages

DIALANG. https://dialangweb.lancaster.ac.uk
English Language Learners. (2018, 2021). www.pewresearch.org
LENA. www.lena.org
WHO. (2021). www.who.int/news/item/17-06-2021-one-in-100-deaths-is-by-suicide

Index

accuracy, 11, 13, 21, 26, 30, 35, 49–50, 56, 62–63, 66–68, 76, 83, 85, 107, 119, 122, 126, 136, 140, 146, 154, 159

activation, 24, 26–28, 30, 37, 44, 47, 58, 60, 74, 83, 94, 102, 107–108, 147
  neural, 58–59, 64, 94, 152. *See also* approach

adaptive control. *See* theory, Adaptive Control Hypothesis

age, 3, 6, 9–10, 18–20, 35, 39, 41, 47, 49, 54–71, 76, 80–81, 84, 95, 98–99, 105, 107, 117, 120, 124, 126–127, 136–137, 145, 153
  matched, 11, 42, 80, 82–83
  related changes, 30, 33, 39, 61–66, 121–123, 126, 133

alertness, 61–62, 78, 102

anterior cingulate cortex, 29, 63
  dorsolateral, 29, 30

approach, 3, 8, 17, 23, 28, 40–42, 52–53, 56, 73, 80, 99, 134, 146, 150, 154–155, 160
  behavioral, 25
  individual differences, 4, 8, 40, 42, 53–54, 73, 155, 158–160
  neural, 3, 25–26, 32, 39, 83, 109, 116, 159–160. *See also* mechanisms, neural
  training, 143, 150

assessment, dynamic, 8, 135

assumptions, 24, 141
  no difference, 51
  representivity, 42

attention, 9, 24, 28, 46, 49, 55, 61, 74, 78–81, 86, 88, 92, 99–102, 105, 109–112, 114, 118–122, 125, 133, 138, 143, 148, 155, 157
  capacity, 50, 97
  control, 22–23, 33, 69–70, 77–78, 80–81, 91, 122, 126, 150
  joint, 100–101
  selective, 43, 84, 102, 110, 127, 138
  shifting, 80, 100, 114, 118, 120
  sustained, 34, 69, 80–81, 84, 95, 101, 135
  tasks, 62, 81–82, 97

behavior, 22–23, 46–47, 54–55, 64, 87, 93, 95–96, 101, 109–110, 112, 115, 122, 132, 135, 138, 140
  automatic, 25–31, 34, 44, 64, 83, 112, 118–119, 122. *See also* cognitive control, automaticity
  goal-directed, 22, 26–29, 39, 107–108, 156, 159
  post-error. *See* post-error adjustment

bilingualism, 1, 5, 16, 19–21, 40–43, 47, 51, 53–54, 59–60, 70, 73, 78, 84–85, 89, 92, 98, 102, 127–128, 131, 158–159. *See also* studies, bilingualism
  advantage, 43, 51, 69, 75, 79, 85, 98, 127–129
  bilingual experience, 5, 14–15, 18, 60, 69–70, 75, 127, 131

brain, 17, 33, 47, 60, 79, 92, 102, 118, 133–134, 144
  connectivity, 32–33, 47, 118, 160
  function, 92, 133, 138. *See also* cognitive control functions
  maturation, 3, 32, 35, 54–56, 58, 60, 66, 71
  networks, 32–33, 39, 73, 118, 160
  plasticity, 3, 133–134, 137, 140–141, 145
  regions (areas), 27, 32, 44, 60, 92, 118, 134, 144, 147
  structures, 79, 92, 94, 144
  training, 141

Brown-Peterson paradigm, 65

clitics, 12, 149

code. *See* switching

coding, 25, 28, 44, 78–79, 86, 102, 110, 122, 140, 143

cognition, 91, 109, 121, 139, 155, 159
  social, 9
  visual, 93

cognitive control, 154. *See also* performance; studies; theory
  automaticity, 27–28. *See also* behavior, automatic
  functions, 1–3, 9, 22, 33–35, 39–40, 44, 46–49, 66, 71, 77–78, 84, 90, 93, 102, 105, 107, 122–129, 132–133, 138, 143, 160

Index

215

processes, 1, 2, 22–25, 27–29, 31, 32–39, 43–46, 64, 71, 75, 85, 91–92, 99, 102, 105–107, 118, 123, 128, 138, 146–148, 150, 153, 155–156, 158, 160

skills, 25, 27–29, 32, 34–35, 37, 40, 49, 61, 63, 66–68, 76, 80, 91, 104, 109–110, 112, 114–116, 120, 122–123, 127, 134, 137–138, 140, 145, 150, 154, 156–157, 159. *See also* language, skills

system, 1, 9, 22–23, 25–31, 33, 44, 46, 91–92, 99, 102, 107, 111–113, 116, 119, 121, 128, 133, 146, 156

weaknesses, 9–10, 12, 27–28, 34, 37, 39, 44, 66, 79–82, 84–86, 95–98, 114–116, 118, 125–127, 131, 149, 156

cognitive routine framework, 141

collaboration, 52

complementarity, 53, 160

interprofessional, 4, 10, 160

Common European Framework of Reference for Languages (CEFR), 14

common factor, 123, 137

complexity, 9, 24, 53, 55–56, 117, 127, 144, 151–152

linguistic, 11, 61, 87, 91

task, 3, 16, 47–50, 62, 65–66, 120, 123, 129, 132

comprehension, 8–9, 12–13, 23, 25, 54–55, 57, 91, 142, 146–147, 150, 157

conflict, 29–31, 62–64, 69–70, 83, 92, 108, 115, 128, 152, 156–157

constraints. *See also* limitations

capacity, 23–25, 39, 121, 157

memory, 24, 96

numeric, 24

time, 24–25, 31

context, 22, 26–29, 33, 35–39, 49, 73–74, 101, 119, 121, 132, 135, 156, 159

binding, 35, 37, 50

communicative, 5, 105, 128

interference, 61

language, 18, 74, 98–99, 111–113

learning, 8, 78

obligatory, 11, 20

social, 1, 3, 13, 56, 105–116

continuum, 5, 25, 28, 56, 59, 72–74, 114, 125, 157–158

accuracy, 140

language ability, 7, 8, 43, 47, 73, 129, 153

language proficiency, 73, 157

control

allocation, 31, 119

attention. *See* attention, control

interference. *See* interference, control

motor. *See* motor, control

proactive, 26, 64–65, 107, 120

signal, 31, 140

top-down, 27, 119

conversation, 72, 74, 88–90, 95, 111, 114

costs, 20, 31, 37–39, 62, 76, 120, 136–137, 140

mixing, 37, 101

switching, 101, 112–113

decision-making, 31–32, 46, 86, 105, 117, 148

cognitive labor, 31

reward-based, 139–140

density, gray matter, 60

developmental language disorder (DLD), 2, 6–13, 15–16, 19–21, 43, 57, 59, 66–68, 73, 79–85, 95–98, 114–116, 125–127, 131–132, 148–151, 156–157, 159

diagnosis, 9–10, 20, 59, 66–68, 84

Diagnostic and Statistical Manual of Mental Disorders (DSM-5), 8

Diagnostic Language Assessment (DIALANG), 13–14

dichotomania, 25, 51, 56

disability, 9, 45. *See also* language, impairment

distractors. *See* interference

effects, 3, 16, 18–19, 25, 28, 39, 42, 44, 54, 64, 84, 88, 90, 109, 113–114, 116, 126, 129, 131–133, 159

reward expectancy, 32, 94, 139

Stroop, 44–45

training, 133, 138–139, 143, 145, 151

transfer, 133, 135, 141, 148

efficiency, 23, 25, 35–36, 91, 123, 141

processing, 35, 55, 114, 121

emotion, 21, 73, 93, 107–108, 110, 114, 116, 124, 138, 143, 156

engagement, 75, 87, 91, 107, 119, 138. *See also* theory, disengagement

English language learners (ELL), 6, 16, 155–156

error, 30–31, 49, 54, 136, 148

children's, 20, 66, 73, 77, 90, 107, 122, 129

monitoring. *See* monitoring, error

patterns. *See* patterns, error

post-error. *See* post-error adjustment

rate. *See* rates, error

error types, 11–13, 19–20, 49, 61, 154

agreement, 20

classification, 6

diagnostic, 7

grammatical, 19

interference. *See* interference, errors

omission, 20

substitution, 11–12

syntax, 12, 19

word order. *See* error types, syntax

error-related negativity (ERN), 30, 45, 63

executive functions, 22. *See also* cognitive control

Index

experiments. *See also* studies
  serial order in a box, 25
  time series, 136
  working memory training. *See* studies
exposure, 69
external validity, 42
eye-mind link hypothesis, 122

flexibility, 28–29, 31, 43, 75, 116, 118, 120, 140
  cognitive, 28, 32, 37, 66–68, 84, 93, 97–98,
    100–102, 105, 111–112, 144, 150–151
  scores, 144–145
fractionation, 46

games, 42, 89, 107, 134
generalizability, 42, 135
giftedness, 8, 78. *See also* language, talent

heterogeneity, 9, 17, 42, 154, 158

immersion, 59, 69, 102
impurity. *See* tasks, impurity
inflection, 10–11
information processing, 24, 28–29, 56, 64, 73,
  78–79, 82, 91, 97, 117–118, 121, 125, 143
inhibition, 32–35, 44, 46–49, 64–65, 92, 107,
  118–119, 126–127
  response, 44, 49, 64–65, 82–83, 85–86,
    101–102, 126, 131, 157
input
  parental, 7, 87, 89, 93–96, 98–101, 104
  rate. *See* rates, input
interference, 16, 22, 25–26, 31, 34–39, 44, 61,
  79–80, 91–92, 109, 111, 113, 119, 129–132,
  157–158
  control, 44, 54, 64, 69, 75, 77, 83–85, 92, 122,
    126–127, 131, 136, 147, 157–158
  distractor, 37, 47, 64, 69, 76, 82–84, 120, 131,
    157–158
  errors, 49, 61, 80, 122
  proactive, 82–83, 142, 157–158
issues. *See also* problems
  methodological, 2, 17, 33, 40, 43–45, 47,
    51–53, 59, 65, 72, 76, 133, 136, 154

language, 7–8, 72–73. *See also* studies,
  cross-linguistic
  ability, 1–3, 5–8, 15–16, 21, 42–43, 72–73, 76,
    79, 86, 92, 125, 129, 132, 153, 156. *See also*
    continuum
  acquisition, 3, 7–8, 11, 17–18, 20, 22, 28, 39,
    41, 54–61, 69–73, 78, 84, 87, 91–92, 97, 99,
    119, 124, 127, 133, 145–148, 153
  aptitude, 7, 73, 78–79, 100, 155
  context. *See* context

delay, 5, 29, 31, 57–59, 68, 71, 83, 88, 93–95
dominance, 14, 76, 112–113, 129
English, 10–12, 14–17, 19–20, 60, 68–69,
  73–76, 79, 89, 99, 113, 129, 147
exposure, 3, 5, 14–15, 54, 59, 69, 74–75, 87, 89,
  99, 155. *See also* theory, Grosjean's
French, 11–12, 19–20, 73, 89, 144
frequency of use, 5, 14–15, 18, 41, 69, 70,
  74–76, 127, 153
Frisian and Dutch, 20
German, 11–12, 14, 20, 78–79, 147
Hungarian, 11–12
impairment, 1, 9, 14–16, 19, 27, 40–43, 45, 47,
  51, 68, 85, 96, 113–114, 116, 125–127, 131, 149,
  153, 156, 158
Italian, 11–12, 20, 78–79, 147
Japanese, 12, 110–111
Ladin, 78–79
modality, 13, 24, 74, 80, 82, 117, 127, 132, 152
parental input. *See* input
problems. *See* problems, language
sign language, 8
skills, 1–4, 8, 20, 22, 42–43, 54–60, 68, 70–72,
  75–76, 79, 86–88, 93, 95–96, 101, 114, 116,
  124, 131, 133, 143, 145, 148–155, 158–159
socialization, 42, 110
Spanish, 11–12, 14, 16–17, 60, 69, 73, 75–76
strategy, 24, 46, 86, 90, 120
Swedish, 12, 89
talent, 2, 5, 27, 78–79, 153–154, 157
Turkish, 20, 87, 99
use, 5, 8–9, 13–15, 18, 72–77, 105, 111
Language Experience and Proficiency
  Questionnaire (LEAP-Q), 14, 17
learning, 17, 22, 26, 32, 39, 73, 87, 90, 94, 97,
  107, 133, 137, 140, 156, 159. *See also* context,
  learning
  implicit, 34, 49, 76, 78
  second language, 25, 61, 78–79, 124,
    146–148, 155
  statistical, 96
  styles, 54–57, 155
life experience, 41–42, 156, 158
limitations, 25. *See also* constraints

MacArthur Communicative Development
  Inventories (CDI), 54
measures, 89, 101
  electrophysiological, 46, 90
  experience-based, 15
  N-back, 35. *See also* tasks, N-back
  neuropsychological. *See* testing
  objective, 13, 72, 74–75, 89
  processing-dependent, 15
  reaction time, 49, 117, 136

Index 217

sensitivity, 45, 73, 139
specificity. *See* specificity
Sternberg, 35
Stroop, 44
subjective, 13, 72, 74–75
mechanisms, neural, 101–102, 118, 133, 144–145.
    See also activation, neural
mismatch. *See* problems, mismatch
modeling, structural equation, 97, 123
monitoring, 26, 29–31, 34, 49, 54, 63, 70, 79, 92,
    101–102, 107, 111–112, 115, 157
    behavior, 22
    error, 32–33
    performance, 63, 76–77, 119, 129
monolingualism, 159. *See also* speakers,
    monolingual
morphology, 9, 10–11, 99
motivation, 8, 21, 73, 78, 107–108, 137, 139–140,
    150, 156
motor
    activity, 119, 122, 143
    control, 26
    impairment, 124
    reaction. *See* motor response
    response, 117, 119
    tasks, 26
multilingualism, 7, 73. *See also* speakers,
    multilingual
music, 42–43
    training, 141, 143–146, 150–151

novelty, 63, 119, 141, 150

orienting. *See* theory, orienting

parent, 56, 87–90
    child relationship, 108–109
    SES, 93–95, 109, 116, 138, 140, 155
patterns, 1, 104, 107, 112, 129, 134, 142, 153, 155,
    157, 159
    behavioral, 95, 114
    developmental, 17–19, 54–55, 57–59, 84,
        126, 154
    error, 12, 45, 80, 159
    linguistic, 2–3, 11, 96, 99
    performance, 19–20, 61, 68, 70, 76, 85–86, 94,
        97–98, 101, 156
performance, 4, 49, 51, 124, 126, 131, 137, 159
    academic, 1, 3, 9, 41, 80, 92. *See also* problems,
        academic
    behavioral, 63
    children's, 16, 20–21, 33–35, 39, 44, 61, 65, 78,
        80–82, 84–85, 93–94, 96–99, 138–140
    cognitive control, 47, 75, 84–86, 109, 128,
        153, 157

gap, 19–21
goal-directed, 25–26
language, 3, 8, 14, 19, 59, 70, 75, 95, 116
memory, 11, 25, 60, 68, 78, 91, 94, 96, 108,
    122, 124, 136, 142, 145, 149–150, 156
monitoring. *See* monitoring
patterns. *See* patterns, performance
task, 16, 23–24, 27–30, 43–44, 46, 62, 66, 69,
    73, 80, 83, 109, 112, 118–120, 128, 131, 135,
    138, 140
perseverator, 35, 65–68, 120
phonology, 9, 66, 99
post-error adjustment, 26, 30, 46, 63, 119–120, 136
prefrontal cortex, 26–27, 29, 35, 45, 66, 92, 94,
    102, 107, 121, 138
proactive, interference, 64–65, 76
problems, 9, 28, 43–45, 72, 114, 119, 125, 141,
    153, 156
    academic, 7, 10, 15, 21, 58–59
    bias, 51, 159–161
    grammar, 10
    language, 6, 9–12, 21, 31, 57, 68, 71, 84, 96,
        98, 116, 125
    learning, 58
    memory, 37, 80–82, 114
    mental health, 10, 114–115
    mismatch, 2, 41, 47, 144, 152
    replicability, 43, 51
problem-solving, 23, 86, 138
processing speed, 3, 63, 65–66, 68, 72, 77, 96,
    114, 117–132. *See also* tasks, processing speed
proficiency, 1–3, 5–8, 13–17, 21–22, 41–42, 47, 51,
    60, 66, 69–70, 72–78, 86, 89, 127, 129, 146,
    148, 153–154, 157–158. *See also* continuum,
    proficiency

rates, 34, 47, 51, 144
    accuracy. *See* accuracy
    acquisition, 17, 54–55, 58, 119
    error, 25–26, 64, 83
    input, 80, 97
    transfer, 142
reading, 10, 13–14, 24, 29, 89, 91, 124, 142,
    146–148
reasoning, 87, 137–138
recall, 25, 35, 50, 68, 121, 138, 146
rehearsal, verbal, 24
relevance, 34, 53, 95, 124, 156
resources, 23–24, 49, 97, 99–100, 108, 119, 122,
    124. *See also* theory, resource
response
    automatic. *See* behavior, automatic
    inhibition. *See* inhibition, response
    time. *See* time, reaction
retrieval, 25, 37, 85, 120, 122

Index

rewards, 31–32, 139–140
  decision-making. *See* decision-making, reward-based
  expected. *See* effects, reward expectancy

scores, 17, 21, 50, 96, 115, 117, 144–145
  flexibility. *See* flexibility
  global, 34, 39, 43–44, 46
  vocabulary, 17, 57, 157
  Z-scores, 49
scoring, 40, 49–51. *See also* coding
selection, 2, 8, 15, 21, 23, 27, 39, 53, 58, 91, 113, 119, 128, 138, 156
  participants, 42, 51, 154, 158
  task, 47, 51, 141
shifting, 33–34, 37, 47, 62, 80, 100, 114, 118, 120
  attention. *See* attention, shifting
significancy, 51, 58
similarity, 25. *See also* interference
speakers
  bilingual, 15–16, 43, 51, 59–60, 69–71, 75, 111, 128–129
  early, 57–59
  emerging bilingual, 2, 8, 21, 69, 85, 154, 157, 159
  late, 54, 57–59, 66–68
  minority language, 2, 10, 19, 53, 99–100, 153–154, 161
  monolingual, 5, 15–21, 42–43, 51, 54, 60, 69–70, 75–76, 78, 84–86, 91, 99–102, 111, 125–129, 138, 157, 159
  multilingual, 2, 5, 73, 77–79
specific language impairment (SLI). *See* developmental language disorder (DLD); language, impairment
specificity, 16, 34, 39, 42, 44–45, 58, 135, 155
speech, spontaneous, 19–20
stability, 28, 31, 111
stigmatization, 159
stimulation, 93–94, 113, 149
stimulus, 29, 34, 37, 46, 60–64, 80–83, 92, 117, 119, 129, 135, 137, 159
strategy, 136–137, 140
Stroop, 64
  effect. *See* effects
  measures. *See* measures
  tasks. *See* tasks
  test. *See* tests
studies, 21, 23–26, 35, 40–42, 45–47, 51, 53–54, 57–60, 73, 75–76, 78–81, 83–85, 87–92, 98, 107, 114, 118–119, 124, 126–127, 129, 133–139, 141–143, 153–155
  behavioral, 33, 49, 75, 160
  bilingualism, 5, 13–15, 25, 98
  brain, 133

Brown-Peterson paradigm, 65
Cogmed, 142
cognitive control, 1
computational, 25, 31–32
cross-linguistic, 13
culture, 110–111
developmental, 32, 57, 61–63, 69, 126
electrophysiological, 30
eye-tracking, 46, 81, 90, 100, 109–110, 122. *See also* studies, eye-tracking
family-based training, 138
gating model, 26
N-back, 147. *See also* tasks, N-back
neurophysiological, 60, 63, 75, 92, 108, 142
neuropsychological, 45
training, 141
working memory, 24, 43, 80, 90, 94, 142–143, 146–147
switching, 15, 22–24, 34, 37–39, 65–68, 95, 99, 101–102
  code, 100, 102, 111–113
  costs. *See* costs, switching
  task, 28–29, 31, 34, 37, 44, 54, 65, 69, 76, 101–102, 110, 112, 120–121, 126–127, 136

talkers. *See* speakers
tasks
  adaptive, 141
  AX Continuous Performance, 34
  card sorting, 34, 37, 49, 66, 101, 110
  complexity. *See* complexity, task
  cue-based. *See* retrieval
  flanker, 44–45, 62–63
  impurity, 2, 34, 43–45, 47, 64, 66, 154–155
  marking, 10–12, 20–21, 55–56
  matching, 26, 46–47, 82
  N-back, 16, 85, 94, 131, 142. *See also* measures, N-back
  neuropsychological, 44
  nonverbal, 9, 16, 126, 155
  objective. *See* measures, objective
  performance. *See* performance, task
  processing speed, 49, 117–118, 128
  selection. *See* selection, task
  sentence completion, 74
  Simon, 44, 47, 64–65
  span, 24, 49–50, 61, 68, 79–80, 94, 121–122, 143
  stop signal (Go-NoGo), 64
  Stroop, 26, 29, 44–45, 64–65, 82
  switching. *See* switching, task
  working memory, 35, 50
testing, 68, 135, 141. *See also* assessment
  epoch, 80
  neuropsychological, 45
  online, 40

tests
  Expressive One Word Picture Vocabulary
    Test, 14
  flanker, 110. *See also* tasks, flanker
  neuropsychological, 33, 44–45
  standardized language, 5, 8, 13, 15, 21, 72–73,
    76, 125
  Stroop, 26, 44–45, 64
  vocabulary, 74–75
  Wisconsin Card Sorting, 34, 44, 49
theory, 134
  activation, 26. *See also* activation
  Adaptive Control Hypothesis, 92, 127
  binding, 35, 50, 83
  cognition, 121, 123
  cognitive control, 31
  conflict monitoring account. *See* monitoring
  decay, 24, 80
  disengagement, 119. *See also* engagement
  EVC, 31, 139. *See also* Expected Value of
    Control (EVC)
  Grosjean's, 74. *See also* language exposure
  mental speed, 121, 123
  mind development, 97
  orienting, 61–62, 78, 119–120
  resilience, 109
  resource, 2, 7, 23–24, 39, 80, 121–122, 124
  time-base resource-sharing, 24
  unity and diversity account, 34, 46–47, 158
time, 19, 24–26, 30, 32, 46, 54, 74, 77–78, 81, 94,
    98, 101, 124, 135–137, 142, 146, 149

constraints. *See* constraints, time
preparation, 30
reaction, 26, 30, 36–37, 49–50, 63, 68, 83, 85,
    97, 107, 112–113, 117–120, 122, 136. *See also*
    measures, reaction time
training
  approach. *See* approach
  brain. *See* brain
  effect. *See* effects
  music. *See* music
  studies. *See* studies
transfer, 3, 135–137, 140–144, 146–147, 149–152
  effect. *See* effects, transfer
  rate. *See* rates, transfer

updating, 26, 28, 33–36, 44, 47–49, 66, 80, 85,
    100, 102, 135, 142–143

vocabulary, 5, 9, 14, 17–18, 54–58, 60, 66, 91, 93,
    98–99, 124, 138, 142, 145–148, 157–158
  scores. *See* scores
  tests. *See* tests

weakness. *See* cognitive control weaknesses
working memory, 9, 11–12, 22–25, 28, 32–37,
    43–44, 49–50, 54, 60–61, 65–66, 68, 73, 78,
    80, 82–86, 90–92, 95–97, 107, 120–123
  capacity, 25, 56, 61, 91, 94–97, 118, 141, 149
  performance. *See* performance
  tasks. *See* tasks
  updating. *See* updating